Python GUI Programming Cookbook

Over 80 object-oriented recipes to help you create mind-blowing GUIs in Python

Burkhard A. Meier

[PACKT] PUBLISHING

BIRMINGHAM - MUMBAI

Python GUI Programming Cookbook

First published: November 2015

Production reference: 1261115

Published by Packt Publishing Ltd.
Livery Place
35 Livery Street
Birmingham B3 2PB, UK.

ISBN 978-1-78528-375-8

www.packtpub.com

Credits

Author
Burkhard A. Meier

Reviewers
Joy Bindroo

Peter Bouda

Joseph Rex

Commissioning Editor
Nadeem Bagban

Acquisition Editor
Vivek Anantharaman

Content Development Editor
Sumeet Sawant

Technical Editor
Pramod Kumavat

Copy Editor
Janbal Dharmaraj

Project Coordinator
Shweta H. Birwatkar

Proofreader
Safis Editing

Indexer
Priya Sane

Graphics
Kirk Dpenha

Production Coordinator
Komal Ramchandani

Cover Work
Komal Ramchandani

About the Author

Burkhard A. Meier has more than 15 years of professional experience working in the software industry as a software tester and developer, specializing in software test automation development, execution, and analysis. He has a very strong background in SQL relational database administration, the development of stored procedures, and debugging code.

While experienced in Visual Studio .NET C#, Visual Test, TestComplete, and other testing languages (such as C/C++), the main focus of the author over the past two years has been developing test automation written in Python 3 to test the leading edge of FLIR ONE infrared cameras for iPhone and Android smart phones as well as handheld tablets.

Being highly appreciative of art, beauty, and programming, the author developed GUIs in C# and Python to streamline everyday test automation tasks, enabling these automated tests to run unattended for weeks, collecting very useful data to be analyzed and automatically plotted into graphs and e-mailed to upper management upon completion of nightly automated test runs.

His previous jobs include working as a senior test automation engineer and designer for InfoGenesis (now Agilysys), QAD, InTouch Health, and presently, FLIR Systems.

You can get in touch with him through his LinkedIn account, `https://www.linkedin.com/pub/burkhard-meier/5/246/296`.

I would like to thank all truly great artists such as Leonardo Da Vinci, Charles Baudelaire, Edgar Poe, and so many more for bringing the presence of beauty into our human lives. This book is about creating very beautiful GUIs written in the Python programming language, and it was inspired by these truly great artists.

I would like to thank all of the great people that made this book possible. Without any of you, this book would only exist in my mind. I would like to especially thank all of my editors at Packt Publishing: Vivek, Arwa, Sumeet, Pramod, Nikhil and so many more. I would also like to thank all of the reviewers of the code of this book. Without them this book would be harder to read and apply to real-world problems. Last but not least, I like to thank my wife, our daughter, and our parents for the emotional support they provided so successfully during the writing of this book. I also like to give thanks to the creator of this very beautiful and powerful programming language that Python truly is. Thank you Guido.

About the Reviewers

Joy Bindroo holds a bachelor's degree in computer science and engineering. He is currently pursuing his post-graduate studies in the field of information management. He is a creative person and enjoys working on Linux platform and other open source technologies. He enjoys writing about Python and sharing his ideas and skills on his website, `http://www.joybindroo.com/`. He likes to sketch, write poems, listen to music, and have fun with his friends in his free time.

> I would like to thank my family, teachers, and friends for always encouraging and supporting me. I'm most thankful to Lord Shiva who enables me to achieve greater heights.

Peter Bouda works as a senior web developer for MAJ Digital and is a specialist in full stack JavaScript applications based on LoopBack and AngularJS. He develops Python GUIs for companies and research projects since 2003 and wrote a German book, *PyQt und PySide – GUI- und Anwendungsentwicklung mit Python und Qt*, on Python GUI development, which was published in 2012. Currently, he is getting crazy with embedded and open hardware platforms and is working on a modular game console based on open hardware.

Joseph Rex is a full stack developer with a background in computer security. He has worked on Python GUI products and some CLI programs to experiment with information security. He came out of security to web development and developed a passion for rails and JavaScript MVC frameworks after working on several projects using jQuery. He has been in the web industry for 3 years, building web applications and mobile apps. He has also written articles on security for InfoSec Institute and has written some scripts to back them up. He has to his credit several personal experimental projects written in Python.

www.PacktPub.com

Support files, eBooks, discount offers, and more

For support files and downloads related to your book, please visit www.PacktPub.com.

Did you know that Packt offers eBook versions of every book published, with PDF and ePub files available? You can upgrade to the eBook version at www.PacktPub.com and as a print book customer, you are entitled to a discount on the eBook copy. Get in touch with us at service@packtpub.com for more details.

At www.PacktPub.com, you can also read a collection of free technical articles, sign up for a range of free newsletters and receive exclusive discounts and offers on Packt books and eBooks.

https://www2.packtpub.com/books/subscription/packtlib

Do you need instant solutions to your IT questions? PacktLib is Packt's online digital book library. Here, you can search, access, and read Packt's entire library of books.

Why Subscribe?

 ▸ Fully searchable across every book published by Packt
 ▸ Copy and paste, print, and bookmark content
 ▸ On demand and accessible via a web browser

Free Access for Packt account holders

If you have an account with Packt at www.PacktPub.com, you can use this to access PacktLib today and view 9 entirely free books. Simply use your login credentials for immediate access.

Table of Contents

Preface

In this book, we will explore the beautiful world of graphical user interfaces (GUIs) using the Python programming language.

Along the way, we will talk to networks, queues, the OpenGL graphical library, and many more technologies.

This is a programming cookbook. Every chapter is self-contained and explains a certain programming solution.

We will start very simply, yet throughout this book we will build a working program written in Python 3.

We will also apply some design patterns and use best practices throughout this book.

The book assumes that the reader has some basic experience using the Python programming language, but that is not really required to use this book.

If you are an experienced programmer in any programming language, you will have a fun time extending your skills to programming GUIs using Python!

Are you ready?

Let's start on our journey...

What this book covers

Chapter 1, Creating the GUI Form and Adding Widgets, explains the steps to develop our first GUI in Python. We will start with the minimum code required to build a running GUI application. Each recipe then adds different widgets to the GUI form.

Chapter 2, Layout Management, explores how to arrange widgets to create our Python GUI. The grid layout manager is one of the most important layout tools built into tkinter that we will be using.

Chapter 3, Look and Feel Customization, shows several examples of how to create a good "look and feel" GUI. On a practical level, we will add functionality to the **Help | About** menu item we created in one of the recipes.

Chapter 4, Data and Classes, discusses saving the data our GUI displays. We will start using object-oriented programming (OOP) in order to extend Python's built-in functionality.

Chapter 5, Matplotlib Charts, explains how to create beautiful charts that visually represent data. Depending upon the format of the data source, we can plot one or several columns of data within the same chart.

Chapter 6, Threads and Networking, explains how to extend the functionality of our Python GUI using threads, queues, and network connections. This will show us that our GUI is not limited at all to the local scope of our PC.

Chapter 7, Storing Data in Our MySQL Database via Our GUI, shows us how to connect to a MySQL database server. The first recipe in this chapter will show how to install the free MySQL Server Community Edition, and in the following recipes we will create databases, tables, and then load data into those tables as well as modify these data. We will also read the data back out from the MySQL server into our GUI.

Chapter 8, Internationalization and Testing, shows how to internationalize our GUI by displaying text on labels, buttons, tabs, and other widgets in different languages. We will start simple and then explore how we can prepare our GUI for internationalization at the design level. We will also explore several ways to automatically test our GUI using Python's built-in unit testing framework.

Chapter 9, Extending Our GUI with the wxPython Library, introduces another Python GUI toolkit that currently does not ship with Python. It is called wxPython, and we will be using the Phoenix version of wxPython which was designed to work well with Python 3.

Chapter 10, Creating Amazing 3D GUIs with PyOpenGL and PyGLet, shows how to transform our GUI by giving it true three-dimensional capabilities. We will use two Python third-party packages. PyOpenGL is a Python binding to the OpenGL standard, which is a graphics library that comes built-in with all major operating systems. This gives the resulting widgets a native look and feel. PyGLet is one such binding that we will explore in this chapter.

Chapter 11, Best Practices, explores different best practices that can help us to build our GUI in an efficient way and keep it both maintainable and extendible. Best practices are applicable to any good code and our GUI is no exception to designing and implementing good software practices.

What you need for this book

All required software for this book is available online and is free of charge. This starts with Python 3 itself, and then extends to Python's add-on modules. In order to download any required software, you will need a working Internet connection.

Who this book is for

This book is for programmers who wish to create a graphical user interface (GUI). You might be surprised by what we can achieve by creating beautiful, functional, and powerful GUIs using the Python programming language. Python is a wonderful, intuitive programming language, and is very easy to learn.

I like to invite you to start on this journey now. It will be a lot of fun!

Conventions

In this book, you will find a number of styles of text that distinguish between different kinds of information. Here are some examples of these styles, and an explanation of their meaning.

Code words in text, database table names, folder names, filenames, file extensions, pathnames, and user input are shown as follows: "Using Python, we can create our own classes using the `class` keyword instead of the `def` keyword."

A block of code is set as follows:

```
import tkinter as tk       # 1
win = tk.Tk()              # 2
win.title("Python GUI")    # 3
win.mainloop()             # 4
```

Any command-line input or output is written as follows:

```
pip install numpy-1.9.2+mkl-cp34-none-win_amd64.whl
```

New terms and **important words** are shown in bold. Words that you see on the screen, in menus or dialog boxes for example, appear in the text like this: "Next, we will add functionality to the menu items, for example, closing the main window when clicking the **Exit** menu item and displaying a **Help | About** dialog."

Warnings or important notes appear in a box like this.

Tips and tricks appear like this.

Reader feedback

Feedback from our readers is always welcome. Let us know what you think about this book—what you liked or disliked. Reader feedback is important for us as it helps us develop titles that you will really get the most out of.

To send us general feedback, simply e-mail feedback@packtpub.com, and mention the book's title in the subject of your message.

If there is a topic that you have expertise in and you are interested in either writing or contributing to a book, see our author guide at www.packtpub.com/authors.

Customer support

Now that you are the proud owner of a Packt book, we have a number of things to help you to get the most from your purchase.

Downloading the example code

You can download the example code files from your account at http://www.packtpub.com for all the Packt Publishing books you have purchased. If you purchased this book elsewhere, you can visit http://www.packtpub.com/support and register to have the files e-mailed directly to you.

Errata

Although we have taken every care to ensure the accuracy of our content, mistakes do happen. If you find a mistake in one of our books—maybe a mistake in the text or the code—we would be grateful if you could report this to us. By doing so, you can save other readers from frustration and help us improve subsequent versions of this book. If you find any errata, please report them by visiting http://www.packtpub.com/submit-errata, selecting your book, clicking on the **Errata Submission Form** link, and entering the details of your errata. Once your errata are verified, your submission will be accepted and the errata will be uploaded to our website or added to any list of existing errata under the Errata section of that title.

To view the previously submitted errata, go to https://www.packtpub.com/books/content/support and enter the name of the book in the search field. The required information will appear under the **Errata** section.

Piracy

Piracy of copyrighted material on the Internet is an ongoing problem across all media. At Packt, we take the protection of our copyright and licenses very seriously. If you come across any illegal copies of our works in any form on the Internet, please provide us with the location address or website name immediately so that we can pursue a remedy.

Please contact us at copyright@packtpub.com with a link to the suspected pirated material.

We appreciate your help in protecting our authors and our ability to bring you valuable content.

Questions

If you have a problem with any aspect of this book, you can contact us at questions@packtpub.com, and we will do our best to address the problem.

1

Creating the GUI Form and Adding Widgets

In this chapter, we start creating amazing GUIs using Python 3:

- ▶ Creating our first Python GUI
- ▶ Preventing the GUI from being resized
- ▶ Adding a label to the GUI form
- ▶ Creating buttons and changing their text property
- ▶ Text box widgets
- ▶ Setting the focus to a widget and disabling widgets
- ▶ Combo box widgets
- ▶ Creating a check button with different initial states
- ▶ Using radio button widgets
- ▶ Using scrolled text widgets
- ▶ Adding several widgets in a loop

Introduction

In this chapter, we will develop our first GUI in Python. We start with the minimum code required to build a running GUI application. Each recipe then adds different widgets to the GUI form.

In the first two recipes, we show the entire code, consisting of only a few lines of code. In the following recipes we only show the code to be added to the previous recipes.

By the end of this chapter, we will have created a working GUI application that consists of labels, buttons, text boxes, combo boxes, and check buttons in various states, as well as radio buttons that change the background color of the GUI.

Creating our first Python GUI

Python is a very powerful programming language. It ships with the built-in tkinter module. In only a few lines of code (four, to be precise) we can build our first Python GUI.

Getting ready

To follow this recipe, a working Python development environment is a prerequisite. The IDLE GUI that ships with Python is enough to start. IDLE was built using tkinter!

All the recipes in this book were developed using Python 3.4 on a Windows 7 64-bit OS. They have not been tested on any other configuration. As Python is a cross-platform language, the code from each recipe is expected to run everywhere.

If you are using a Mac, it does come built-in with Python, yet it might be missing some modules such as tkinter, which we will use throughout this book.

We are using Python 3 and the creator of Python intentionally chose not to make it backwards compatible with Python 2.

If you are using a Mac or Python 2, you might have to install Python 3 from www.python.org in order to successfully run the recipes in this book.

How to do it...

Here are the four lines of Python code required to create the resulting GUI:

```
import tkinter as tk        # 1
win = tk.Tk()               # 2
win.title("Python GUI")     # 3
win.mainloop()              # 4
```

Execute this code and admire the result:

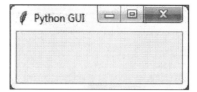

How it works...

In line 1, we import the built-in `tkinter` module and alias it as `tk` to simplify our Python code. In line 2, we create an instance of the `Tk` class by calling its constructor (the parentheses appended to `Tk` turn the class into an instance). We are using the alias `tk` so we don't have to use the longer word `tkinter`. We are assigning the class instance to a variable named `win` (short for a window). As Python is a dynamically typed language, we did not have to declare this variable before assigning to it and we did not have to give it a specific type. *Python infers the type from the assignment of this statement.* Python is a strongly typed language, so every variable always has a type. We just don't have to specify its type beforehand like in other languages. This makes Python a very powerful and productive language to program in.

A little note about classes and types:

In Python every variable always has a type. We cannot create a variable without assigning it a type. Yet, in Python, we do not have to declare the type beforehand, as we have to do in the C programming language.

Python is smart enough to infer the type. At the time of writing, C# also has this capability.

Using Python, we can create our own classes using the `class` keyword instead of the `def` keyword.

In order to assign the class to a variable, we first have to create an instance of our class. We create the instance and assign this instance to our variable.

```
class AClass(object):
    print('Hello from AClass')


classInstance = AClass()
```

Now the variable `classInstance` is of the type `AClass`.

If this sounds confusing, do not worry. We will cover OOP in the coming chapters.

In line 3, we use the instance variable of the class (`win`) to give our window a title via the `title` property. In line 4, we start the window's event loop by calling the `mainloop` method on the class instance `win`. Up to this point in our code, we created an instance and set one property *but the GUI will not be displayed until we start the main event loop.*

An event loop is a mechanism that makes our GUI work. We can think of it as an endless loop where our GUI is waiting for events to be sent to it. A button click creates an event within our GUI or our GUI being resized also creates an event.

We can write all of our GUI code in advance and nothing will be displayed on the user's screen until we call this endless loop (`win.mainloop()` in the code shown above).

The event loop ends when the user clicks the red **X** button or a widget that we have programmed to end our GUI. When the event loop ends, our GUI also ends.

There's more...

This recipe used a minimum amount of Python code to create our first GUI program. However, throughout this book, we will use OOP when it makes sense.

Preventing the GUI from being resized

Getting ready

This recipe extends the previous one. Therefore, it is necessary to have typed Recipe 1 yourself into a project of your own or downloaded the code from `https://www.packtpub.com/support`.

How to do it...

We are preventing the GUI from being resized.

```
import tkinter as tk          # 1 imports

win = tk.Tk()                 # 2 Create instance
win.title("Python GUI")       # 3 Add a title

win.resizable(0, 0)           # 4 Disable resizing the GUI

win.mainloop()                # 5 Start GUI
```

Running the code creates this GUI:

How it works...

Line 4 prevents the Python GUI from being resized.

Running this code will result in a GUI similar to the one we created in Recipe 1. However, the user can no longer resize it. Also, notice how the maximize button in the toolbar of the window is grayed out.

Why is this important? Because, once we add widgets to our form, resizing can make our GUI look not as good as we want it to be. We will add widgets to our GUI in the next recipes.

`Resizable()` is a method of the `Tk()` class and, by passing in `(0, 0)`, we prevent the GUI from being resized. If we pass in other values, we hard-code the x and y start up size of the GUI, *but that won't make it nonresizable*.

We also added comments to our code in preparation for the recipes contained in this book.

 In visual programming IDEs such as Visual Studio .NET, C# programmers often do not think of preventing the user from resizing the GUI they developed in this language. That creates inferior GUIs. Adding this one line of Python code can make our users appreciate our GUI.

Adding a label to the GUI form

Getting ready

We are extending the first recipe. We will leave the GUI resizable, so don't use the code from the second recipe (or comment the `win.resizable` line 4 out).

How to do it...

In order to add a `Label` widget to our GUI, we are importing the `ttk` module from `tkinter`. Please note the two import statements.

```
# imports                    # 1
import tkinter as tk         # 2
from tkinter import ttk      # 3
```

Add the following code just above `win.mainloop()` located at the bottom of recipes 1 and 2.

```
# Adding a Label             # 4
ttk.Label(win, text="A Label").grid(column=0, row=0) # 5
```

Running the code adds a label to our GUI:

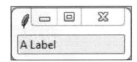

How it works...

In line 3 of the above code, we are importing a separate module from `tkinter`. The `ttk` module has some advanced widgets that make our GUI look great. In a sense, `ttk` is an extension within `tkinter`.

We still need to import `tkinter` itself, but we have to specify that we now want to also use `ttk` from `tkinter`.

 `ttk` stands for 'themed tk". It improves our GUI look and feel.

Line 5 above adds the label to the GUI, just before we call `mainloop` (not shown here to preserve space. See recipes 1 or 2).

We are passing our window instance into the `ttk.Label` constructor and setting the text property. This becomes the text our `Label` will display.

We are also making use of the *grid layout manager*, which we'll explore in much more depth in *Chapter 2, Layout Management*.

Note how our GUI suddenly got much smaller than in previous recipes.

The reason why it became so small is that we added a widget to our form. Without a widget, `tkinter` uses a default size. Adding a widget causes optimization, which generally means using as little space as necessary to display the widget(s).

If we make the text of the label longer, the GUI will expand automatically. We will cover this automatic form size adjustment in a later recipe in *Chapter 2, Layout Management*.

There's more...

Try resizing and maximizing this GUI with a label and watch what happens.

Creating buttons and changing their text property

Getting ready

This recipe extends the previous one. You can download the entire code from the Packt Publishing website.

How to do it...

We are adding a button that, when clicked, performs an action. In this recipe, we will update the label we added in the previous recipe, as well as updating the text property of the button.

```
# Modify adding a Label                              # 1
aLabel = ttk.Label(win, text="A Label")              # 2
aLabel.grid(column=0, row=0)                          # 3


# Button Click Event Callback Function               # 4
```

```
def clickMe():                                                      # 5
    action.configure(text="** I have been Clicked! **")
    aLabel.configure(foreground='red')

# Adding a Button                                                   # 6
action = ttk.Button(win, text="Click Me!", command=clickMe)        # 7
action.grid(column=1, row=0)                                        # 8
```

Before clicking the button:

After clicking the button, the color of the label has been changed, and so has the text of the button. Action!

How it works...

In line 2 we are now assigning the label to a variable and in line 3 we use this variable to position the label within the form. We will need this variable to change its properties in the `clickMe()` function. By default, this is a module-level variable so we can access it inside the function as long as we declare the variable above the function that calls it.

Line 5 is the event handler that is being invoked once the button gets clicked.

In line 7, we create the button and bind the command to the `clickMe()` function.

> GUIs are event-driven. Clicking the button creates an event. We bind what happens when this event occurs in the callback function using the command property of the `ttk.Button` widget. Notice how we do not use parentheses; only the name `clickMe`.

We also change the text of the label to include `red` as in the printed book, this might otherwise not be obvious. When you run the code you can see that the color did indeed change.

Lines 3 and 8 both use the grid layout manager, which will be discussed in the following chapter. This aligns both the label and the button.

There's more...

There's more...

We will continue to add more and more widgets to our GUI and we will make use of many built-in properties in other recipes in the book.

Text box widgets

In `tkinter`, the typical textbox widget is called `Entry`. In this recipe, we will add such an `Entry` to our GUI. We will make our label more useful by describing what the `Entry` is doing for the user.

Getting ready

This recipe builds upon the *Creating buttons and changing their text property* recipe.

How to do it...

```
# Modified Button Click Function    # 1
def clickMe():                      # 2
    action.configure(text='Hello ' + name.get())

# Position Button in second row, second column (zero-based)
action.grid(column=1, row=1)

# Changing our Label                # 3
ttk.Label(win, text="Enter a name:").grid(column=0, row=0) # 4

# Adding a Textbox Entry widget     # 5
name = tk.StringVar()               # 6
nameEntered = ttk.Entry(win, width=12, textvariable=name) # 7
nameEntered.grid(column=0, row=1)   # 8
```

Now our GUI looks like this:

After entering some text and clicking the button, there is the following change in the GUI:

How it works...

In line 2 we are getting the value of the Entry widget. We are not using OOP yet, so how come we can access the value of a variable that was not even declared yet?

Without using OOP classes, in Python procedural coding we have to physically place a name above a statement that tries to use that name. So how come this works (it does)?

The answer is that the button click event is a callback function, and by the time the button is clicked by a user, the variables referenced in this function are known and do exist.

Life is good.

Line 4 gives our label a more meaningful name, because now it describes the textbox below it. We moved the button down next to the label to visually associate the two. We are still using the grid layout manager, to be explained in more detail in *Chapter 2, Layout Management*.

Line 6 creates a variable name. This variable is bound to the Entry and, in our clickMe() function, we are able to retrieve the value of the Entry box by calling get() on this variable. This works like a charm.

Now we see that while the button displays the entire text we entered (and more), the textbox Entry widget did not expand. The reason for this is that we had hard-coded it to a width of 12 in line 7.

Python is a dynamically-typed language and infers the type from the assignment. What this means is if we assign a string to the variable name, the variable will be of the type string, and if we assign an integer to name, this variable's type will be integer.

Using tkinter, we have to declare the variable name as the type tk.StringVar() before we can use it successfully. The reason is this that Tkinter is not Python. We can use it from Python but it is not the same language.

Setting the focus to a widget and disabling widgets

While our GUI is nicely improving, it would be more convenient and useful to have the cursor appear in the `Entry` widget as soon as the GUI appears. Here we learn how to do this.

Getting ready

This recipe extends the previous recipe.

How to do it...

Python is truly great. All we have to do to set the focus to a specific control when the GUI appears is call the `focus()` method on an instance of a `tkinter` widget we previously created. In our current GUI example, we assigned the `ttk.Entry` class instance to a variable we named `nameEntered`. Now we can give it the focus.

Place the following code just above the bottom of the module that starts the main windows event loop, just like in previous recipes. If you get some errors, make sure you are placing calls to variables below the code where they are declared. We are not using OOP as of yet, so this is still necessary. Later, it will no longer be necessary to do this.

```
nameEntered.focus()              # Place cursor into name Entry
```

On a Mac, you might have to set the focus to the GUI window first before being able to set the focus to the `Entry` widget in this window.

Adding this one line of Python code places the cursor into our text `Entry` box, giving the text `Entry` box the focus. As soon as the GUI appears, we can type into this text box without having to click it first.

[Note how the cursor now defaults to residing inside the text `Entry` box.]

We can also disable widgets. To do that, we set a property on the widget. We can make the button disabled by adding this one line of Python code:

```
action.configure(state='disabled')     # Disable the Button Widget
```

After adding the above line of Python code, clicking the button no longer creates any action!

How it works...

This code is self-explanatory. We set the focus to one control and disable another widget. Good naming in programming languages helps to eliminate lengthy explanations. Later in this book, there will be some advanced tips on how to do this while programming at work or practicing our programming skills at home.

There's more...

Yes. This is only the first chapter. There is much more to come.

Combo box widgets

In this recipe, we will improve our GUI by adding drop-down combo boxes that can have initial default values. While we can restrict the user to only certain choices, at the same time, we can allow the user to type in whatever they wish.

Getting ready

This recipe extends the previous recipes.

How to do it...

We are inserting another column between the `Entry` widget and the `Button` using the grid layout manager. Here is the Python code.

```
ttk.Label(win, text="Choose a number:").grid(column=1, row=0)  # 1
number = tk.StringVar()                                        # 2
numberChosen = ttk.Combobox(win, width=12, textvariable=number) #3
```

```
numberChosen['values'] = (1, 2, 4, 42, 100)      # 4
numberChosen.grid(column=1, row=1)               # 5
numberChosen.current(0)                          # 6
```

This code, when added to previous recipes, creates the following GUI. Note how, in line 4 in the preceding code, we assign a tuple with default values to the combo box. These values then appear in the drop-down box. We can also change them if we like (by typing in different values when the application is running).

How it works...

Line 1 adds a second label to match the newly created combo box (created in line 3). Line 2 assigns the value of the box to a variable of a special `tkinter` type (`StringVar`), as we did in a previous recipe.

Line 5 aligns the two new controls (label and combo box) within our previous GUI layout, and line 6 assigns a default value to be displayed when the GUI first becomes visible. This is the first value of the `numberChosen['values']` tuple, the string `"1"`. We did not place quotes around our tuple of integers in line 4, but they got casted into strings because, in line 2, we declared the values to be of type `tk.StringVar`.

The screenshot shows the selection made by the user (**42**). This value gets assigned to the `number` variable.

There's more...

If we want to restrict the user to only be able to select the values we have programmed into the `Combobox`, we can do that by passing the *state property* into the constructor. Modify line 3 in the previous code to:

```
numberChosen = ttk.Combobox(win, width=12, textvariable=number,
state='readonly')
```

Now users can no longer type values into the Combobox. We can display the value chosen by the user by adding the following line of code to our Button Click Event Callback function:

```
# Modified Button Click Callback Function

def clickMe():
    action.configure(text='Hello ' + name.get()+ ' ' +
        numberChosen.get())
```

After choosing a number, entering a name, and then clicking the button, we get the following GUI result, which now also displays the number selected:

Creating a check button with different initial states

In this recipe, we will add three Checkbutton widgets, each with a different initial state.

Getting ready

This recipe extends the previous recipes.

How to do it...

We are creating three Checkbutton widgets that differ in their states. The first is disabled and has a checkmark in it. The user cannot remove this checkmark as the widget is disabled.

The second Checkbutton is enabled and, by default, has no checkmark in it, but the user can click it to add a checkmark.

The third Checkbutton is both enabled and checked by default. The users can uncheck and recheck the widget as often as they like.

```
# Creating three checkbuttons     # 1
chVarDis = tk.IntVar()            # 2
check1 = tk.Checkbutton(win, text="Disabled", variable=chVarDis, state
='disabled')                      # 3
check1.select()                   # 4
```

```
check1.grid(column=0, row=4, sticky=tk.W) # 5

chVarUn = tk.IntVar()                # 6
check2 = tk.Checkbutton(win, text="UnChecked", variable=chVarUn)
check2.deselect()                    # 8
check2.grid(column=1, row=4, sticky=tk.W) # 9

chVarEn = tk.IntVar()                # 10
check3 = tk.Checkbutton(win, text="Enabled", variable=chVarEn)
check3.select()                      # 12
check3.grid(column=2, row=4, sticky=tk.W) # 13
```

Running the new code results in the following GUI:

<h2>How it works...</h2>

In lines 2, 6, and 10, we create three variables of type `IntVar`. In the following line, for each of these variables we create a `Checkbutton`, passing in these variables. They will hold the state of the `Checkbutton` (unchecked or checked). By default, that is either 0 (unchecked) or 1 (checked) so the type of the variable is a `tkinter` integer.

We place these `Checkbutton` widgets in our main window so the first argument passed into the constructor is the parent of the widget; in our case `win`. We give each `Checkbutton` a different label via its `text` property.

Setting the sticky property of the grid to `tk.W` means that the widget will be aligned to the west of the grid. This is very similar to Java syntax and it means that it will be aligned to the left. When we resize our GUI, the widget will remain on the left side and not be moved towards the center of the GUI.

Lines 4 and 12 place a checkmark into the `Checkbutton` widget by calling the `select()` method on these two `Checkbutton` class instances.

We continue to arrange our widgets using the grid layout manager, which will be explained in more detail in *Chapter 2, Layout Management*.

Using radio button widgets

In this recipe, we will create three `tkinter Radiobutton` widgets. We will also add some code that changes the color of the main form depending upon which `Radiobutton` is selected.

Getting ready

This recipe extends the previous recipes.

How to do it...

We are adding the following code to the previous recipe:

```
# Radiobutton Globals      # 1
COLOR1 = "Blue"            # 2
COLOR2 = "Gold"            # 3
COLOR3 = "Red"             # 4


# Radiobutton Callback   # 5
def radCall():            # 6
    radSel=radVar.get()
    if    radSel == 1: win.configure(background=COLOR1)
    elif radSel == 2: win.configure(background=COLOR2)
    elif radSel == 3: win.configure(background=COLOR3)


# create three Radiobuttons      # 7
radVar = tk.IntVar()             # 8
rad1 = tk.Radiobutton(win, text=COLOR1, variable=radVar, value=1,
command=radCall)                 # 9
rad1.grid(column=0, row=5, sticky=tk.W)  # 10

rad2 = tk.Radiobutton(win, text=COLOR2, variable=radVar, value=2, comm
and=radCall)                     # 11
rad2.grid(column=1, row=5, sticky=tk.W)  # 12

rad3 = tk.Radiobutton(win, text=COLOR3, variable=radVar, value=3, comm
and=radCall)                     # 13
rad3.grid(column=2, row=5, sticky=tk.W)  # 14
```

Running this code and selecting the `Radiobutton` named **Gold** creates the following window:

How it works...

In lines 2-4 we create some module-level global variables, which we will use in the creation of each radio button as well as in the callback function that creates the action of changing the background color of the main form (using the instance variable `win`).

We are using global variables to make it easier to change the code. By assigning the name of the color to a variable and using this variable in several places, we can easily experiment with different colors. Instead of doing a global search-and-replace of a hard-coded string (which is prone to errors), we just need to change one line of code and everything else will work. This is known as the **DRY principle**, which stands for **Don't Repeat Yourself**. This is an OOP concept that we will use in later recipes of the book.

 The names of the colors we are assigning to the variables (COLOR1, COLOR2 ...) are `tkinter` keywords (technically, they are *symbolic names*). If we use names that are not `tkinter` color keywords, then the code will not work.

Line 6 is the *callback function* that changes the background of our main form (`win`) depending upon the user's selection.

In line 8 we are creating a `tk.IntVar` variable. What is important about this is that we are creating only one variable to be used by all three radio buttons. As can be seen from the above screenshot, no matter which `Radiobutton` we select, all the others will automatically be unselected for us.

Lines 9 to 14 create the three radio buttons, assign them to the main form, and pass in the variable to be used in the callback function that creates the action of changing the background of our main window.

 While this is the first recipe that changes the color of a widget, quite honestly, it looks a bit ugly. A large portion of the following recipes in this book explain how to make our GUI look truly amazing.

There's more...

Here is a small sample of the available symbolic color names that you can look up at the official tcl manual page:

`http://www.tcl.tk/man/tcl8.5/TkCmd/colors.htm`

Name	Red	Green	Blue
alice blue	240	248	255
AliceBlue	240	248	255
Blue	0	0	255
Gold	255	215	0
Red	255	0	0

Some of the names create the same color, so `alice blue` creates the same color as `AliceBlue`. In this recipe we used the symbolic names `Blue`, `Gold`, and `Red`.

Using scrolled text widgets

`ScrolledText` widgets are much larger than simple `Entry` widgets and span multiple lines. They are widgets like Notepad and wrap lines, automatically enabling vertical scrollbars when the text gets larger than the height of the `ScrolledText` widget.

Getting ready

This recipe extends the previous recipes. You can download the code for each chapter of this book from the Packt Publishing website.

How to do it...

By adding the following lines of code, we create a `ScrolledText` widget:

```
# Add this import to the top of the Python Module    # 1
from tkinter import scrolledtext       # 2

# Using a scrolled Text control       # 3
scrolW  = 30       # 4
scrolH  =  3       # 5
```

```
scr = scrolledtext.ScrolledText(win, width=scrolW, height=scrolH,
wrap=tk.WORD)                            # 6
scr.grid(column=0, columnspan=3)         # 7
```

We can actually type into our widget, and if we type enough words, the lines will automatically wrap around!

Once we type in more words than the height of the widget can display, the vertical scrollbar becomes enabled. This all works out-of-the-box without us needing to write any more code to achieve this.

How it works...

In line 2 we are importing the module that contains the `ScrolledText` widget class. Add that to the top of the module, just below the other two `import` statements.

Lines 4 and 5 define the width and height of the `ScrolledText` widget we are about to create. These are hard-coded values we are passing into the `ScrolledText` widget constructor in line 6.

These values are *magic numbers* found by experimentation to work well. You might experiment by changing `srcolW` from 30 to 50 and observe the effect!

In line 6 we are setting a property on the widget by passing in `wrap=tk.WORD`.

By setting the `wrap` property to `tk.WORD` we are telling the `ScrolledText` widget to break lines by words, so that we do not wrap around within a word. The default option is `tk.CHAR`, which wraps any character regardless of whether we are in the middle of a word.

The second screenshot shows that the vertical scrollbar moved down because we are reading a longer text that does not entirely fit into the x, y dimensions of the `SrolledText` control we created.

Setting the `columnspan` property of the grid widget to 3 for the `SrolledText` widget makes this widget span all three columns. If we did not set this property, our `SrolledText` widget would only reside in column one, which is not what we want.

Adding several widgets in a loop

So far we have created several widgets of the same type (for example. `Radiobutton`) by basically copying and pasting the same code and then modifying the variations (for example, the column number). In this recipe, we start refactoring our code to make it less redundant.

Getting ready

We are refactoring some parts of the previous recipe's code, so you need that code to apply to this recipe to.

How to do it...

```
# First, we change our Radiobutton global variables into a list.
colors = ["Blue", "Gold", "Red"]                # 1

# create three Radiobuttons using one variable
radVar = tk.IntVar()

Next we are selecting a non-existing index value for radVar.
radVar.set(99)                                  # 2

Now we are creating all three Radiobutton widgets within one loop.

for col in range(3):                            # 3
    curRad = 'rad' + str(col)
    curRad = tk.Radiobutton(win, text=colors[col],
        variable=radVar,      value=col, command=radCall)
```

```
        curRad.grid(column=col, row=5, sticky=tk.W)
```

We have also changed the callback function to be zero-based, using the list instead of module-level global variables.

```
# Radiobutton callback function                    # 4
def radCall():
    radSel=radVar.get()
    if    radSel == 0: win.configure(background=colors[0])
    elif radSel == 1: win.configure(background=colors[1])
    elif radSel == 2: win.configure(background=colors[2])
```

Running this code will create the same window as before, but our code is much cleaner and easier to maintain. This will help us when we expand our GUI in the following recipes.

How it works...

In line 1, we have turned our global variables into a list.

In line 2, we are setting a default value to the tk.IntVar variable we named radVar. This is important because, while in the previous recipe we had set the value for Radiobutton widgets starting at 1, in our new loop it is much more convenient to use Python's zero-based indexing. If we did not set the default value to a value outside the range of our Radiobutton widgets, one of the radio buttons would be selected when the GUI appears. While this in itself might not be so bad, *it would not trigger the callback* and we would end up with a radio button selected that does not do its job (that is, change the color of the main win form).

In line 3 we are replacing the three previously hard-coded creations of the Radiobutton widgets with a loop, which does the same. It is just more concise (fewer lines of code) and much more maintainable. For example, if we want to create 100 instead of just 3 Radiobutton widgets, all we have to change is the number inside Python's range operator. We would not have to type or copy and paste 97 sections of duplicate code, just one number.

Line 4 shows the modified callback, which physically lives above the previous lines. We placed it below to give emphasis to the more important parts of this recipe.

There's more...

This recipe concludes the first chapter of this book. All the following recipes in all of the next chapters will build upon the GUI we have constructed so far, greatly enhancing it.

2
Layout Management

In this chapter we will lay out our GUI using Python 3:

- ▸ Arranging several labels within a label frame widget
- ▸ Using padding to add space around widgets
- ▸ How widgets dynamically expand the GUI
- ▸ Aligning the GUI widgets by embedding frames within frames
- ▸ Creating menu bars
- ▸ Creating tabbed widgets
- ▸ Using the grid layout manager

Introduction

In this chapter, we will explore how to arrange widgets within widgets to create our Python GUI. Learning the fundamentals of GUI layout design will enable us to create great looking GUIs. There are certain techniques that will help us to achieve this layout design.

The grid layout manager is one of the most important layout tools built into tkinter that we will be using.

We can very easily create menu bars, tabbed controls (aka Notebooks), and many more widgets using tk.

One widget that is missing out of the box from tk is a status bar.

In this chapter, we will not bother to hand-craft this widget, but it can be done.

Arranging several labels within a label frame widget

The LabelFrame widget allows us to design our GUI in an organized fashion. We are still using the grid layout manager as our main layout design tool, yet by using LabelFrame widgets we get much more control over our GUI design.

Getting ready

We are starting to add more and more widgets to our GUI, and we will make the GUI fully functional in the coming recipes. Here, we are starting to use the LabelFrame widget. We will reuse the GUI from the last recipe of the previous chapter.

How to do it...

Add the following code just above the main event loop towards the bottom of the Python module:

```
# Create a container to hold labels
labelsFrame = ttk.LabelFrame(win, text=' Labels in a Frame ') # 1
labelsFrame.grid(column=0, row=7)

# Place labels into the container element # 2
ttk.Label(labelsFrame, text="Label1").grid(column=0, row=0)
ttk.Label(labelsFrame, text="Label2").grid(column=1, row=0)
ttk.Label(labelsFrame, text="Label3").grid(column=2, row=0)

# Place cursor into name Entry
nameEntered.focus()
```

We can easily align the labels vertically by changing our code, as shown next. Note that the only change we had to make was in the column and row numberings.

```
# Place labels into the container element - vertically # 3
ttk.Label(labelsFrame, text="Label1").grid(column=0, row=0)
ttk.Label(labelsFrame, text="Label2").grid(column=0, row=1)
ttk.Label(labelsFrame, text="Label3").grid(column=0, row=2)
```

How it works...

Comment # 1: Here, we will create our first ttk LabelFrame widget and give the frame a name. The parent container is `win`, our main window.

The three lines following comment # 2 create label names and place them in the LabelFrame. We are using the important grid layout tool to arrange the labels within the LabelFrame. The column and row properties of this layout manager give us the power to control our GUI layout.

 The parent of our labels is the LabelFrame, not the `win` instance variable of the main window. We can see the beginning of a layout hierarchy here.

The highlighted comment # 3 shows how easy it is to change our layout via the column and row properties. Note how we change the column to 0, and how we layer our labels vertically by numbering the row values sequentially.

 The name ttk stands for "themed tk". The tk-themed widget set was introduced in Tk 8.5.

There's more...

In a recipe later in this chapter, we will embed LabelFrame(s) within LabelFrame(s), nesting them to control our GUI layout.

Using padding to add space around widgets

Our GUI is being created nicely. Next, we will improve the visual aspects of our widgets by adding a little space around them, so they can breathe...

Getting ready

While tkinter might have had a reputation for creating ugly GUIs, this has dramatically changed since version 8.5, which ships with Python 3.4.x. You just have to know how to use the tools and techniques that are available. That's what we will do next.

How to do it...

The procedural way of adding spacing around widgets is shown first, and then we will use a loop to achieve the same thing in a much better way.

Our LabelFrame looks a bit tight as it blends into the main window towards the bottom. Let's fix this now.

Modify the following line of code by adding `padx` and `pady`:

```
labelsFrame.grid(column=0, row=7, padx=20, pady=40)
```

And now our LabelFrame got some breathing space:

How it works...

In tkinter, adding space horizontally and vertically is done by using the built-in properties named `padx` and `pady`. These can be used to add space around many widgets, improving horizontal and vertical alignments, respectively. We hard-coded 20 pixels of space to the left and right of the LabelFrame, and we added 40 pixels to the top and bottom of the frame. Now our LabelFrame stands out more than it did before.

 The screenshot above only shows the relevant change.

We can use a loop to add space around the labels contained within the LabelFrame:

```
for child in labelsFrame.winfo_children():
    child.grid_configure(padx=8, pady=4)
```

Now the labels within the LabelFrame widget have some space around them too:

The `grid_configure()` function enables us to modify the UI elements before the main loop displays them. So, instead of hard-coding values when we first create a widget, we can work on our layout and then arrange spacing towards the end of our file, just before the GUI is being created. This is a neat technique to know.

The `winfo_children()` function returns a list of all the children belonging to the `labelsFrame` variable. This enables us to loop through them and assign the padding to each label.

 One thing to notice is that the spacing to the right of the labels is not really visible. This is because the title of the LabelFrame is longer than the names of the labels. We can experiment with this by making the names of the labels longer.

```
ttk.Label(labelsFrame, text="Label1 -- sooooo much loooonger...").
grid(column=0, row=0)
```

Now our GUI looks like the following. Note how there is now some space added to the right of the long label next to the dots. The last dot does not touch the LabelFrame, which it would without the added space.

We can also remove the name of the LabelFrame to see the effect `padx` has on positioning our labels.

How widgets dynamically expand the GUI

You probably noticed in previous screenshots and by running the code that widgets have a capability to extend themselves to the space they need to visually display their text.

Java introduced the concept of dynamic GUI layout management. In comparison, visual development IDEs like VS.NET lay out the GUI in a visual manner, and are basically hard-coding the x and y coordinates of UI elements.

Using `tkinter`, this dynamic capability creates both an advantage and a little bit of a challenge, because sometimes our GUI dynamically expands when we would prefer it rather not to be so dynamic! Well, we are dynamic Python programmers, so we can figure out how to make the best use of this fantastic behavior!

Getting ready

At the beginning of the previous recipe we added a label frame widget. This moved some of our controls to the center of column 0. We might not wish this modification to our GUI layout. Next, we will explore some ways to fix this.

How to do it...

Let us first become aware of the subtle details that are going on in our GUI layout, in order to understand it better.

We are using the grid layout manager widget and it lays out our widgets in a zero-based grid.

Row 0; Col 0	Row 0; Col 1	Row 0; Col 2
Row 1; Col 0	Row 1; Col 1	Row 1; Col 2

Using the grid layout manager, what is happening is that the width of any given column is determined by the longest name or widget in that column. This affects all rows.

By adding our LabelFrame widget and giving it a title that is longer than some hard-coded size widget like the top-left label and the text entry below it, we dynamically move those widgets to the center of column 0, adding space to the left and right sides of those widgets.

Incidentally, because we used the sticky property for the Checkbutton and ScrolledText widgets, those remain attached to the left side of the frame.

Let's look in more detail at the screenshot from the first recipe of this chapter:

We added the following code to create the LabelFrame and then placed labels into this frame:

```
# Create a container to hold labels
labelsFrame = ttk.LabelFrame(win, text=' Labels in a Frame ')
labelsFrame.grid(column=0, row=7)
```

Since the text property of the LabelFrame, which is displayed as the title of the LabelFrame, is longer than both our **Enter a name:** label and the textbox entry below it, those two widgets are dynamically centered with the new width of column 0.

The Checkbutton and Radiobutton widgets in column 0 did not get centered because we used the `sticky=tk.W` property when we created those widgets.

For the ScrolledText widget we used `sticky=tk.WE`, which binds the widget to both the west (aka left) and east (aka right) side of the frame.

Let's remove the sticky property from the ScrolledText widget and observe the effect this change has.

```
scr = scrolledtext.ScrolledText(win, width=scrolW, height=scrolH,
wrap=tk.WORD)
#### scr.grid(column=0, sticky='WE', columnspan=3)
scr.grid(column=0, columnspan=3)
```

Now our GUI has new space around the ScrolledText widget both on the left and right sides. Because we used the `columnspan=3` property, our ScrolledText widget still spans all three columns.

If we remove `columnspan=3`, we get the following GUI, which is not what we want. Now our ScrolledText only occupies column 0, and, because of its size, it stretches the layout.

One way to get our layout back to where we were before adding the LabelFrame is to adjust the grid column position. Change the column value from 0 to 1.

```
labelsFrame.grid(column=1, row=7, padx=20, pady=40)
```

Now our GUI looks like this:

How it works...

Because we are still using individual widgets, our layout can get messed up. By moving the column value of the LabelFrame from 0 to 1, we were able to get the controls back to where they used to be and where we prefer them to be. At least the left-most label, text, checkbox, scrolledtext, and radio button widgets are now located where we intended them to be. The second label and text `Entry` located in column 1 have aligned themselves to the center of the length of the **Labels in a Frame** widget, so we basically moved our alignment challenge one column to the right. It is not so visible because the size of the **Choose a number:** label is almost the same as the size of the **Labels in a Frame** title, and so the column width was already close to the new width generated by the LabelFrame.

There's more...

In the next recipe, we will embed frames within frames to avoid the accidental misalignment of widgets we just experienced in this recipe.

Aligning the GUI widgets by embedding frames within frames

We have much better control of our GUI layout if we embed frames within frames. This is what we will do in this recipe.

Getting ready

The dynamic behavior of Python and its GUI modules can create a little bit of a challenge to really get our GUI looking the way we want. Here we will embed frames within frames to get more control of our layout. This will establish a stronger hierarchy among the different UI elements, making the visual appearance easier to achieve.

We will continue to use the GUI we created in the previous recipe.

How to do it...

Here, we will create a top-level frame that will contain other frames and widgets. This will help us to get our GUI layout just the way we want.

In order to do so, we will have to embed our current controls within a central ttk.LabelFrame. This ttk.LabelFrame is a child of the main parent window and all controls will be children of this ttk.LabelFrame.

Up to this point in our recipes, we have assigned all widgets to our main GUI frame directly. Now we will only assign our LabelFrame to our main window, and after that, we will make this LabelFrame the parent container for all the widgets.

This creates the following hierarchy in our GUI layout:

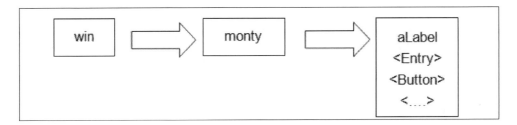

In this diagram, **win** is the variable that references our main GUI tkinter window frame; **monty** is the variable that references our LabelFrame and is a child of the main window frame (**win**); and **aLabel** and all other widgets are now placed into the LabelFrame container (**monty**).

Add the following code towards the top of our Python module (see comment # 1):

```
# Create instance
win = tk.Tk()

# Add a title
win.title("Python GUI")

# We are creating a container frame to hold all other widgets # 1
monty = ttk.LabelFrame(win, text=' Monty Python ')
monty.grid(column=0, row=0)
```

Next, we will modify all the following controls to use `monty` as the parent, replacing `win`. Here is an example of how to do this:

```
# Modify adding a Label
aLabel = ttk.Label(monty, text="A Label")
```

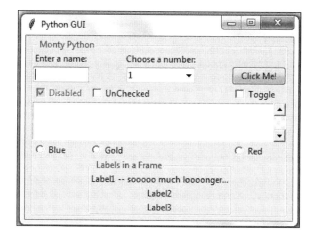

Note how all the widgets are now contained in the **Monty Python** LabelFrame, which surrounds all of them with a barely visible thin line. Next, we can reset the **Labels in a Frame** widget to the left without messing up our GUI layout:

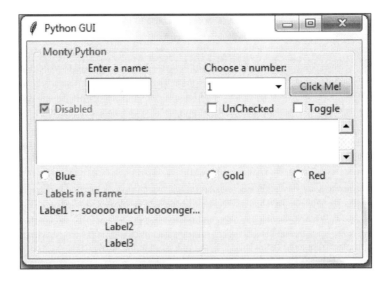

Oops - maybe not. While our frame within another frame aligned nicely to the left, it again pushed our top widgets into the center (a default).

In order to align them to the left, we have to force our GUI layout by using the `sticky` property. By assigning it "W" (West), we can control the widget to be left-aligned.

```
# Changing our Label
ttk.Label(monty, text="Enter a name:").grid(column=0, row=0,
sticky='W')
```

How it works...

Note how we aligned the label, but not the text box below it. We have to use the `sticky` property for all the controls we want to left-align. We can do that in a loop, using the `winfo_children()` and `grid_configure(sticky='W')` properties, as we did before in recipe 2 of this chapter.

The `winfo_children()` function returns a list of all the children belonging to the parent. This enables us to loop through all of the widgets and change their properties.

Using tkinter to force left, right, top, bottom the naming is very similar to Java: west, east, north and south, abbreviated to: "W" and so on. We can also use the following syntax: tk.W instead of "W".

In a previous recipe, we combined both "W" and "E" to make our ScrolledText widget attach itself both to the left and right sides of its container using "WE". We can add more combinations: "NSE" will stretch our widget to the top, bottom and right side. If we have only one widget in our form, for example a button, we can make it fill in the entire frame by using all options: "NSWE". We can also use tuple syntax: `sticky=(tk.N, tk.S, tk.W, tk.E)`.

Let's change the very long label back and align the entry in column 0 to the left.

```
ttk.Label(monty, text="Enter a name:").grid(column=0, row=0,
sticky='W')

name = tk.StringVar()
nameEntered = ttk.Entry(monty, width=12, textvariable=name)
nameEntered.grid(column=0, row=1, sticky=tk.W)
```

In order to separate the influence that the length of our **Labels in a Frame** LabelFrame has on the rest of our GUI layout, we must not place this LabelFrame into the same LabelFrame as the other widgets. Instead we assign it directly to the main GUI form (`win`).

We will do this in later chapters.

Creating menu bars

In this recipe, we will add a menu bar to our main window, add menus to the menu bar, and then add menu items to the menus.

Getting ready

We will start by learning the techniques of how to add a menu bar, several menus and a few menu items to show the principle of how to do it. Clicking on a menu item will have no effect. Next, we will add functionality to the menu items, for example, closing the main window when clicking the **Exit** menu item and displaying a **Help | About** dialog.

We are continuing to extend the GUI we created in the current and previous chapter.

How to do it...

First, we have to import the `Menu` class from `tkinter`. Add the following line of code to the top of the Python module, where the import statements live:

```
from tkinter import Menu
```

Next, we will create the menu bar. Add the following code towards the bottom of the module, just above where we create the main event loop:

```
menuBar = Menu(win)                          # 1
win.config(menu=menuBar)
```

Now we add a menu to the bar and also assign a menu item to the menu.

```
fileMenu = Menu(menuBar)                     # 2
fileMenu.add_command(label="New")
menuBar.add_cascade(label="File", menu=fileMenu)
```

Running this code adds a menu bar, with a menu, which has a menu item.

Next, we add a second menu item to the first menu we added to the menu bar.

```
fileMenu.add_command(label="New")
fileMenu.add_command(label="Exit")          # 3
menuBar.add_cascade(label="File", menu=fileMenu)
```

We can add a separator line between the MenuItems by adding the following line of code (# 4) in between the existing MenuItems.

```
fileMenu.add_command(label="New")
fileMenu.add_separator()                    # 4
fileMenu.add_command(label="Exit")
```

By passing in the property `tearoff` to the constructor of the menu, we can remove the first dashed line that, by default, appears above the first MenuItem in a menu.

```
# Add menu items
fileMenu = Menu(menuBar, tearoff=0)          # 5
```

We will add a second menu, which will be horizontally placed to the right of the first menu. We will give it one MenuItem, which we name `About`, and, in order for this to work, we have to add this second menu to the MenuBar.

File and **Help** | **About** are very common Windows GUI layouts that we are all familiar with, and we can create those same menus using Python and tkinter.

The order of creation and the naming of menu, menu item, and menu bar might at first be a little bit confusing, but, once we get used to how tkinter requires us to code it, this actually becomes fun.

```
helpMenu = Menu(menuBar, tearoff=0)                    # 6
helpMenu.add_command(label="About")
menuBar.add_cascade(label="Help", menu=helpMenu)
```

At this point, our GUI has a MenuBar and two menus that contain some MenuItems. Clicking on them does not do much, until we add some commands. That's what we will do next. Add the following code above the creation of the MenuBar:

```
def _quit():          # 7
    win.quit()
    win.destroy()
    exit()
```

Next, we bind the **File | Exit** MenuItem to this function by adding the following command to the MenuItem:

```
fileMenu.add_command(label="Exit", command=_quit)     # 8
```

Now, when we click the `Exit` MenuItem, our application will indeed exit.

How it works...

In comment # 1, we are calling the `tkinter` constructor of the menu and assigning the menu to our main GUI window. We save a reference in the instance variable named `menuBar` and, in the following line of code, we use this instance to configure our GUI to use `menuBar` as our menu.

Comment # 2 shows how we first add a MenuItem and then create a menu. This seems to be unintuitive, but this is how tkinter works. The `add_cascade()` method aligns the MenuItems one below the other, in a vertical layout.

Comment # 3 shows how to add a second MenuItem to the menu.

In comment # 4, we are adding a separator line between the two MenuItems. This is usually used to group related MenuItems and separate them from less related items (hence the name).

Comment # 5 disables the tearoff dashed line to make our menu look much better.

Without disabling this default feature, the user can "tear off" the menu from the main window. I find this capability to be of little value. Feel free to play around with it by double-clicking the dashed line (before disabling this feature).

If you are using a Mac, this feature might not be enabled, so you do not have to worry about it at all.

Comment # 6 shows you how to add a second menu to the MenuBar. We can keep on adding menus by using this technique.

Comment # 7 creates a function to quit our GUI application cleanly. This is the recommended Pythonic way to end the main event loop.

In # 8 we bind the function we created in # 7 to the MenuItem, using the `tkinter` command property. Whenever we want our MenuItems to actually do something, we have to bind each of them to a function.

 We are using a recommended Python naming convention by preceding our quit function with one single underscore, to indicate that this is a private function not to be called by clients of our code.

There's more...

We will add the **Help | About** functionality in the next chapter, which introduces message boxes and much more.

Creating tabbed widgets

In this recipe, we will create tabbed widgets to further organize our expanding GUI written in tkinter.

Getting ready

In order to improve our Python GUI using tabs, we will start at the beginning, using the minimum amount of code necessary. In the following recipes, we will add widgets from previous recipes and place them into this new tabbed layout.

How to do it...

Create a new Python module and place the following code into this module:

```python
import tkinter as tk                          # imports
from tkinter import ttk
win = tk.Tk()                                 # Create instance
win.title("Python GUI")                       # Add a title
tabControl = ttk.Notebook(win)                # Create Tab Control
tab1 = ttk.Frame(tabControl)                  # Create a tab
tabControl.add(tab1, text='Tab 1')            # Add the tab
tabControl.pack(expand=1, fill="both")        # Pack to make visible
win.mainloop()                                # Start GUI
```

This creates the following GUI:

While not amazingly impressive as of yet, this widget adds another very powerful tool to our GUI design toolkit. It comes with its own limitations in the minimalist example above (for example, we cannot reposition the GUI nor does it show the entire GUI title).

While in previous recipes, we used the grid layout manager for simpler GUIs, we can use a simpler layout manager and "pack" is one of them.

In the preceding code, we "pack" tabControl ttk.Notebook into the main GUI form expanding the notebook tabbed control to fill in all sides.

```
tabControl.pack(fill="both")   # Pack to make visible
win.mainloop()                 # Start GUI
```

We can add a second tab to our control and click between them.

```
tab2 = ttk.Frame(tabControl)        # Add a second tab
tabControl.add(tab2, text='Tab 2')  # Make second tab visible
win.mainloop()                      # Start GUI
```

Now we have two tabs. Click on **Tab 2** to give it the focus.

We would really like to see our windows title. So, to do this, we have to add a widget to one of our tabs. The widget has to be wide enough to expand our GUI dynamically to display our window title. We are adding Ole Monty back, together with his children.

```
monty = ttk.LabelFrame(tab1, text=' Monty Python ')
monty.grid(column=0, row=0, padx=8, pady=4)
ttk.Label(monty, text="Enter a name:").grid(column=0, row=0,
sticky='W')
```

Now we got our **Monty Python** inside **Tab1**.

We can keep placing all the widgets we have created so far into our newly created tab controls.

Now all the widgets reside inside **Tab1**. Let's move some to **Tab2**. First, we create a second LabelFrame to be the container of our widgets relocating to **Tab2**:

```
monty2 = ttk.LabelFrame(tab2, text=' The Snake ')
monty2.grid(column=0, row=0, padx=8, pady=4)
```

Next, we move the check and radio buttons to **Tab2**, by specifying the new parent container, which is a new variable we name `monty2`. Here is an example which we apply to all controls that relocate to **Tab2**:

```
chVarDis = tk.IntVar()
check1 = tk.Checkbutton(monty2, text="Disabled", variable=chVarDis,
state='disabled')
```

When we run the code, our GUI now looks different. **Tab1** has less widgets than it had before when it contained all of our previously created widgets.

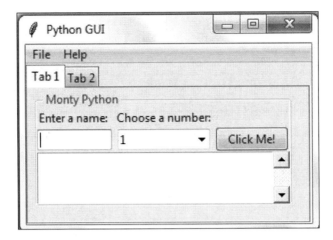

We can now click **Tab 2** and see our relocated widgets.

Clicking the relocated Radiobutton(s) no longer has any effect, so we will change their actions to rename the text property, which is the title of the LabelFrame widget, to the name the Radiobuttons display. When we click the **Gold** Radiobutton, we no longer set the background of the frame to the color gold but here replace the LabelFrame text title instead. Python "The Snake" now becomes "Gold".

```
# Radiobutton callback function
def radCall():
    radSel=radVar.get()
    if   radSel == 0: monty2.configure(text='Blue')
    elif radSel == 1: monty2.configure(text='Gold')
    elif radSel == 2: monty2.configure(text='Red')
```

Now, selecting any of the RadioButton widgets results in changing the name of the LabelFrame.

How it works...

After creating a second tab, we moved some of the widgets that originally resided in **Tab1** to **Tab2**. Adding tabs is another excellent way to organize our ever-increasing GUI. This is one very nice way to handle complexity in our GUI design. We can arrange widgets in groups where they naturally belong, and free our users from clutter by using tabs.

In tkinter, creating tabs is done via the Notebook widget, which is the tool that allows us to add tabbed controls. The tkinter notebook widget, like so many other widgets, comes with additional properties that we can use and configure. An excellent place to start exploring additional capabilities of the tkinter widgets at our disposal is the official website:
https://docs.python.org/3.1/library/tkinter.ttk.html#notebook

Using the grid layout manager

The grid layout manager is one of the most useful layout tools at our disposal. We have already used it in many recipes because it is just so powerful.

Getting ready...

In this recipe, we will review some of the techniques of the grid layout manager. We have used them already and here we will explore them further.

How to do it...

In this chapter, we have created rows and columns, which truly is a database approach to GUI design (MS Excel does the same). We hard-coded the first four rows but then we forgot to give the next row a specification of where we wish it to reside.

Tkinter did fill this in for us without us even noticing.

Here is what we did in our code:

```
check3.grid(column=2, row=4, sticky=tk.W, columnspan=3)
scr.grid(column=0, sticky='WE', columnspan=3)                    # 1
curRad.grid(column=col, row=6, sticky=tk.W, columnspan=3)
labelsFrame.grid(column=0, row=7)
```

Tkinter automatically adds the missing row (emphasized in comment # 1) where we did not specify any particular row. We might not realize this.

We laid out the checkbuttons on row 4 then we "forgot" to specify the row for our ScrolledText widget, which we reference via the scr variable and then we added the Radiobutton widgets to be laid out in row 6.

This works nicely because tkinter automatically incremented the row position for our ScrolledText widget to use the next highest row number, which was row 5.

Looking at our code and not realizing that we "forgot" to explicitly position our ScrolledText widget to row 5, we might think nothing resides there.

So, we might try the following.

If we set the variable `curRad` to use row 5, we might get an unpleasant surprise:

How it works...

Note how our row of RadioButton(s) suddenly ended up in the middle of our ScrolledText widget! This is definitely not what we intended our GUI to look like!

 If we forget to explicitly specify the row number, by default, `tkinter` will use the next available row.

We also used the `columnspan` property to make sure our widgets did not get limited to just one column. Here is how we made sure that our ScrolledText widget spans all the columns of our GUI:

```
# Using a scrolled Text control
scrolW = 30; scrolH = 3
scr = ScrolledText(monty, width=scrolW, height=scrolH, wrap=tk.WORD)
scr.grid(column=0, sticky='WE', columnspan=3)
```

3

Look and Feel Customization

In this chapter, we will customize our GUI using Python 3:

- ▸ Creating message boxes – information, warning, and error
- ▸ How to create independent message boxes
- ▸ How to create the title of a tkinter window form
- ▸ Changing the icon of the main root window
- ▸ Using a spin box control
- ▸ Relief, sunken, and raised appearance of widgets
- ▸ Creating tooltips using Python
- ▸ How to use the canvas widget

Introduction

In this chapter, we will customize some of the widgets in our GUI by changing some of their properties. We are also introducing a few new widgets tkinter offers us.

The *Creating tooltips using Python* recipe will create a ToolTip OOP-style class, which will be a part of the one single Python module we have been using up to now.

Creating message boxes – information, warning, and error

A message box is a pop-up window that gives feedback to the user. It can be informational, hinting at potential problems, and even catastrophic errors.

Using Python to create message boxes is very easy.

Getting ready

We will add functionality to the **Help | About** menu item we created in the previous recipe. The typical feedback to the user when clicking the **Help | About** menu in most applications is informational. We start with this information and then vary the design pattern to show warnings and errors.

How to do it...

Add the following line of code to the top of the module where the import statements live:

```
from tkinter import messagebox as mBox
```

Next, we will create a callback function that will display a message box. We have to locate the code of the callback above the code where we attach the callback to the menu item, because this is still procedural and not OOP code.

Add this code just above the lines where we create the help menu:

```
# Display a Message Box
# Callback function
def _msgBox():
    mBox.showinfo('Python Message Info Box', 'A Python GUI created
using tkinter:\nThe year is 2015.')

# Add another Menu to the Menu Bar and an item
helpMenu = Menu(menuBar, tearoff=0)
helpMenu.add_command(label="About", command=_msgBox)
```

Clicking **Help** | **About** now causes the following pop-up window to appear:

Let's transform this code into a warning message box pop-up window instead. Comment out the previous line and add the following code:

```
# Display a Message Box
def _msgBox():
#    mBox.showinfo('Python Message Info Box', 'A Python GUI
#       created using tkinter:\nThe year is 2015.')
    mBox.showwarning('Python Message Warning Box', 'A Python GUI
created using tkinter:\nWarning: There might be a bug in this code.')
```

Running the above code will now result in the following slightly modified message box:

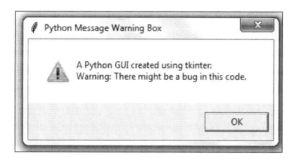

Displaying an error message box is simple and usually warns the user of a serious problem. As above, so below. Comment out and add this code, as we have done here:

```
# Display a Message Box
def _msgBox():
#    mBox.showinfo('Python Message Info Box', 'A Python GUI
#       created using tkinter:\nThe year is 2015.')
```

```
#    mBox.showwarning('Python Message Warning Box', 'A Python GUI
#       created using tkinter:\nWarning: There might be a bug in
#       this code.')
    mBox.showerror('Python Message Error Box', 'A Python GUI created
using tkinter:\nError: Houston ~ we DO have a serious PROBLEM!')
```

How it works...

We have added another callback function and attached it as a delegate to handle the click event. Now, when we click the **Help | About** menu, an action takes place. We are creating and displaying the most common pop-up message box dialogs. They are modal, so the user can't use the GUI until they click the **OK** button.

In the first example we display an information box, as can be seen by the icon to the left of it. Next, we create warning and error message boxes that automatically change the icon associated with the pop-up. All we have to do is specify which mBox we want to display.

There are different message boxes that display more than one **OK** button and we can program our responses according to the user's selection.

The following is a simple example that illustrates this technique:

```
# Display a Message Box
def _msgBox():
    answer = mBox.askyesno("Python Message Dual Choice Box", "Are you
sure you really wish to do this?")
    print(answer)
```

Running this GUI code results in a pop-up whose user response can be used to branch on the answer of this event-driven GUI loop by saving it in the answer variable.

The console output using Eclipse shows that clicking the **Yes** button results in the Boolean value of `True` being assigned to the `answer` variable.

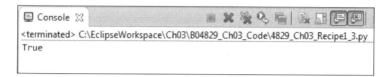

For example, we could use the following code:

```
If answer == True:
    <do something>
```

How to create independent message boxes

In this recipe, we will create our tkinter message boxes as stand-alone top-level GUI windows.

We will first notice that, by doing so, we end up with an extra window so we will explore ways to hide this window.

In the previous recipe, we invoked tkinter message boxes via our **Help | About** menu from our main GUI form.

So why would we wish to create an independent message box?

One reason is that we might customize our message boxes and reuse them in several of our GUIs. Instead of having to copy and paste the same code into every Python GUI we design, we can factor it out of our main GUI code. This can create a small reusable component, which we can then import into different Python GUIs.

Getting ready

We have already created the title of a message box in the previous recipe. We will not reuse the code from the previous recipe, but instead we will build a new GUI in very few lines of Python code.

How to do it...

We can create a simple message box like this:

```
from tkinter import messagebox as mBox
mBox.showinfo('A Python GUI created using tkinter:\nThe year is 2015')
```

This will result in these two windows:

This does not look like what we had in mind. Now we have two windows, one undesired and the second having its text displayed as its title.

Oops.

Let's fix this now. We can change the Python code by adding a single or double quote, followed by a comma.

```
mBox.showinfo('', 'A Python GUI created using tkinter:\nThe year is
2015')
```

The first parameter is the title and the second is the text displayed in the pop-up message box. By adding an empty pair of single or double quotes followed by a comma, we can move our text from the title into the pop-up message box.

We still need a title and we definitely want to get rid of this unnecessary second window.

 In languages like C#, the same phenomenon of a second window appears. It is basically a DOS-style debug window. Many programmers seem not to mind having this extra window floating around. I personally find it distasteful from a GUI programming perspective. We will remove it next.

The second window is caused by a Windows event loop. We can get rid of it by suppressing it.

Add the following code:

```
from tkinter import messagebox as mBox
from tkinter import Tk
root = Tk()
root.withdraw()
mBox.showinfo('', 'A Python GUI created using tkinter:\nThe year is
2015')
```

Now we have only one window. The `withdraw()` function removes the debug window we are not interested in having floating around.

In order to add a title, all we have to do is place some string into our empty first argument.

For example:

```
from tkinter import messagebox as mBox
from tkinter import Tk
root = Tk()
root.withdraw()
mBox.showinfo('This is a Title', 'A Python GUI created using tkinter:\
nThe year is 2015')
```

Now our dialog has a title:

How it works...

We are passing more arguments into the tkinter constructor of the message box to add a title to the window form and display the text in the message box, instead of displaying it as its title. This happens due to the position of the arguments we are passing. If we leave out an empty quote or double quote, then the message box widget takes the first position of the arguments as the title, not the text to be displayed within the message box. By passing an empty quote followed by a comma, we change where the message box displays the text we are passing into the function.

We suppress the second pop-op window that automatically gets created by the tkinter message box widget by calling the `withdraw()` method on our main root window.

How to create the title of a tkinter window form

The principle of changing the title of a tkinter main root window is the same as was discussed in the previous recipe. We just pass in a string as the first argument to the constructor of the widget.

Getting ready

Instead of a pop-up dialog window, we create the main root window and give it a title.

The GUI displayed in this recipe is the code from the previous chapter. It does not build upon the previous recipe in this chapter.

How to do it...

The following code creates the main window and adds a title to it. We have already done this in previous recipes. Here, we just focus on this aspect of our GUI.

```
import tkinter as tk
win = tk.Tk()                  # Create instance
win.title("Python GUI")        # Add a title
```

How it works...

This gives a title to the main root window by using the built-in tkinter `title` property. After we create a `Tk()` instance we can use all of the built-in tkinter properties to customize our GUI.

Changing the icon of the main root window

One way to customize our GUI is to give it a different icon than the default icon that ships out of the box with tkinter. Here is how we do this.

Getting ready

We are improving our GUI from the previous recipe. We will use an icon that ships with Python but you can use any icon you find useful. Make sure you have the full path to where the icon lives in your code, or you might get errors.

 While it might seem a little bit confusing which recipe of the last chapter this recipe refers to, the best approach is to just download the code for this book and then step through the code to understand it.

How to do it...

Place the following code somewhere above the main event loop. The example uses the path where I installed Python 3.4. You might have to adjust it to match your installation directory.

Notice how the "feather" default icon in the top-left corner of the GUI changed.

```
# Change the main windows icon
win.iconbitmap(r'C:\Python34\DLLs\pyc.ico')
```

How it works...

This is another property that ships with tkinter, which ships with Python 3.x. `iconbitmap`, is the property we are using to change the icon of our main root window form by passing in the absolute (hard-coded) path to an icon. This overrides tkinter's default icon, replacing it with our icon of choice.

 Using "r" in the string of the absolute path in the code above escapes the backslashes, so instead of writing C:\\ we can use the "raw" string, which lets us write the more natural single backslash C:\. This is a neat trick Python has created for us.

Using a spin box control

In this recipe, we will use a `Spinbox` widget and we will also bind the *Enter* key on the keyboard to one of our widgets.

Getting ready

We are using our tabbed GUI and will add a `Spinbox` widget above the `ScrolledText` control. This simply requires us to increment the `ScrolledText` row value by one and to insert our new `Spinbox` control in the row above the `Entry` widget.

How to do it...

First, we add the `Spinbox` control. Place the following code above the `ScrolledText` widget:

```
# Adding a Spinbox widget
spin = Spinbox(monty, from_=0, to=10)
spin.grid(column=0, row=2)
```

This will modify our GUI, as shown:

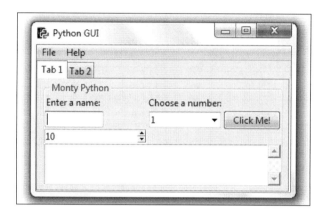

Next, we will reduce the size of the `Spinbox` widget.

```
spin = Spinbox(monty, from_=0, to=10, width=5)
```

Next, we add another property to customize our widget further, bd is a short-hand notation for the `borderwidth` property.

```
spin = Spinbox(monty, from_=0, to=10, width=5 , bd=8)
```

Here, we add functionality to the widget by creating a callback and linking it to the control.

This will print the selection of the Spinbox into `ScrolledText` as well as onto stdout. The variable named `scr` is our reference to the `ScrolledText` widget.

```
# Spinbox callback
def _spin():
    value = spin.get()
    print(value)
    scr.insert(tk.INSERT, value + '\n')


spin = Spinbox(monty, from_=0, to=10, width=5, bd=8, command=_spin)
```

Instead of using a range, we can also specify a set of values.

```
# Adding a Spinbox widget using a set of values
spin = Spinbox(monty, values=(1, 2, 4, 42, 100), width=5, bd=8,
command=_spin)
spin.grid(column=0, row=2)
```

This will create the following GUI output:

How it works...

Notice how, in the first screenshot, our new `Spinbox` control defaulted to a width of 20, pushing out the column width of all controls in this column. This is not what we want. We gave the widget a range from 0 to 10 and it defaults to show the `to=10` value, which is the highest value. If we try to reverse the `from_`/`to` range from 10 to 0, tkinter does not like it. Do try this out for yourself.

In the second screenshot, we reduced the width of the `Spinbox` control, which aligned it in the center of the column.

In the third screenshot, we added the `borderwidth` property of the Spinbox, which automatically made the entire `Spinbox` appear no longer flat but three-dimensional.

In the fourth screenshot, we added a callback function to display the number chosen in the `ScrolledText` widget and print it to the standard out-stream. We added "\n" to print on new lines. Notice how the default value does not get printed. It is only when we click the control that the callback function gets called. By clicking the up arrow with the default of 10, we can print the "10" value.

Lastly, we restrict the values available to a hard-coded set. This could also be read in from a data source (for example, a text or XML file).

Relief, sunken, and raised appearance of widgets

We can control the appearance of our `Spinbox` widgets by a property that makes them look either in relief, sunken, or in a raised format.

Getting ready

We will add one more `Spinbox` control to demonstrate the available appearances of widgets using the relief property of the `Spinbox` control.

How to do it...

First, let's increase the `borderwidth` to distinguish our second `Spinbox` from the first `Spinbox`.

```
# Adding a second Spinbox widget
spin = Spinbox(monty, values=(0, 50, 100), width=5, bd=20, command=_
spin)
spin.grid(column=1, row=2)
```

Both of our Spinbox widgets above have the same relief style. The only difference is that our new widget to the right of the first Spinbox has a much larger border width.

In our code, we did not specify which relief property to use, so the relief defaulted to tk.SUNKEN.

Here are the available relief property options that can be set:

tk.SUNKEN	tk.RAISED	tk.FLAT	tk.GROOVE	tk.RIDGE

By assigning the different available options to the `relief` property, we can create different appearances for this widget.

Assigning the tk.RIDGE relief and reducing the border width to the same value as our first Spinbox widget results in the following GUI:

How it works...

First, we created a second `Spinbox` aligned in the second column (index == 1). It defaults to SUNKEN, so it looks similar to our first `Spinbox`. We distinguished the two widgets by increasing the border width of the second control (the one to the right).

Next, we implicitly set the relief property of the Spinbox widget. We made the border width the same as our first Spinbox because, by giving it a different relief, the differences became visible without having to change any other properties.

Creating tooltips using Python

This recipe will show us how to create ToolTips. When the user hovers the mouse over a widget, additional information will be available in the form of a ToolTip.

We will code this additional information into our GUI.

Getting ready

We are adding more useful functionality to our GUI. Surprisingly, adding a ToolTip to our controls should be simple, but it is not as simple as we wish it to be.

In order to achieve this desired functionality, we will place our ToolTip code into its own OOP class.

How to do it...

Add this class just below the import statements:

```python
class ToolTip(object):
    def __init__(self, widget):
        self.widget = widget
        self.tipwindow = None
        self.id = None
        self.x = self.y = 0

    def showtip(self, text):
        "Display text in tooltip window"
        self.text = text
        if self.tipwindow or not self.text:
            return
        x, y, _cx, cy = self.widget.bbox("insert")
        x = x + self.widget.winfo_rootx() + 27
        y = y + cy + self.widget.winfo_rooty() +27
        self.tipwindow = tw = tk.Toplevel(self.widget)
        tw.wm_overrideredirect(1)
        tw.wm_geometry("+%d+%d" % (x, y))

        label = tk.Label(tw, text=self.text, justify=tk.LEFT,
    background="#ffffe0", relief=tk.SOLID, borderwidth=1,
                    font=("tahoma", "8", "normal"))

        label.pack(ipadx=1)

    def hidetip(self):
        tw = self.tipwindow
        self.tipwindow = None
        if tw:
            tw.destroy()

#================================================================
def createToolTip( widget, text):
    toolTip = ToolTip(widget)
    def enter(event):
        toolTip.showtip(text)
    def leave(event):
        toolTip.hidetip()
    widget.bind('<Enter>', enter)
    widget.bind('<Leave>', leave)
```

In an **object-oriented programming** (**OOP**) approach we create a new class in our Python module. Python allows us to place more than one class into the same Python module and it also enables us to "mix-and-match" classes and regular functions in the same module.

The code above is doing exactly this.

The `ToolTip` class is a Python class and in order to use it, we have to instantiate it.

If you are not familiar with OOP programming, "instantiating an object to create an instance of the class" may sound rather boring.

The principle is quite simple and very similar to creating a Python function via a `def` statement and then later in the code actually calling this function.

In a very similar manner, we first create a blueprint of a class and simply assign it to a variable by adding parentheses to the name of the class as follows:

```
class AClass():
    pass
instanceOfAClass = AClass()
print(instanceOfAClass)
```

The above code prints out a memory address and also shows that our variable now has a reference to this class instance.

The cool thing about OOP is that we can create many instances of the same class.

In our preceding code, we declare a Python class and explicitly make it inherit from the object that is the foundation of all Python classes. We can also leave it out as we have done in the `AClass` code example because it is the default for all Python classes.

After all of the necessary tooltip creation code that occurs within the `ToolTip` class, we next switch over to non-OOP Python programming by creating a function just below it.

We define the function `createToolTip()` and it expects one of our GUI widgets to be passed in as an argument so we can display a ToolTip when we hover our mouse over this control.

The `createToolTip()` function actually creates a new instance of our `ToolTip` class for every widget we call it for.

We can add a tooltip for our Spinbox widget, like this:

```
# Add a Tooltip
createToolTip(spin, 'This is a Spin control.')
```

As well as for all of our other GUI widgets in the very same manner. We just have to pass in the parent of the widget we wish to have a tooltip displaying some extra information. For our ScrolledText widget we made the variable `scr` point to it so this is what we pass into the constructor of our ToolTip creation function.

```
# Using a scrolled Text control
scrolW  = 30; scrolH  =  3
scr = scrolledtext.ScrolledText(monty, width=scrolW, height=scrolH,
wrap=tk.WORD)
scr.grid(column=0, row=3, sticky='WE', columnspan=3)

# Add a Tooltip to the ScrolledText widget
createToolTip(scr, 'This is a ScrolledText widget.')
```

How it works...

This is the beginning of OOP programming in this book. This might appear a little bit advanced, but do not worry, we will explain everything and it actually does work!

Well, running this code actually does NOT work or make any difference as of yet.

Add the following code just below the creation of the spinner:

```
# Add a Tooltip
createToolTip(spin, 'This is a Spin control.')
```

Now, when we hover the mouse over the spinner widget, we get a tooltip, providing additional information to the user.

We are calling the function that creates the tooltip, and then we pass in a reference to the widget and the text we wish to display when we hover the mouse over the widget.

The rest of the recipes in this book will use OOP when it makes sense. Here, we show the simplest OOP example possible. As a default, every Python class we create inherits from the `object` base class. Python, being the pragmatic programming language that it truly is, simplifies the class creation process.

We can write this syntax:

```
class ToolTip(object):
    pass
```

We can also simplify it by leaving the default base class out:

```
class ToolTip():
    pass
```

In this same pattern, we can inherit and expand any tkinter class.

How to use the canvas widget

This recipe shows how to add dramatic color effects to our GUI by using the tkinter canvas widget.

Getting ready

We will improve our previous code and the look of our GUI by adding some more colors to it.

How to do it...

First, we will create a third tab in our GUI in order to isolate our new code.

Here is the code to create the new third tab:

```
# Tab Control introduced here --------------------------------
tabControl = ttk.Notebook(win)            # Create Tab Control

tab1 = ttk.Frame(tabControl)              # Create a tab
tabControl.add(tab1, text='Tab 1')        # Add the tab

tab2 = ttk.Frame(tabControl)              # Add a second tab
tabControl.add(tab2, text='Tab 2')        # Make second tab visible

tab3 = ttk.Frame(tabControl)              # Add a third tab
tabControl.add(tab3, text='Tab 3')        # Make second tab visible

tabControl.pack(expand=1, fill="both")    # Pack to make visible
```

```
# ~ Tab Control introduced here --------------------------------
```

Next, we use another built-in widget of tkinter, the canvas. A lot of people like this widget because it has powerful capabilities.

```
# Tab Control 3 -------------------------------
tab3 = tk.Frame(tab3, bg='blue')
tab3.pack()
for orangeColor in range(2):
    canvas = tk.Canvas(tab3, width=150, height=80,
highlightthickness=0, bg='orange')
    canvas.grid(row=orangeColor, column=orangeColor)
```

How it works...

The following screenshot shows the result created by running the preceding code and clicking on the new **Tab 3**. It really is orange and blue when you run the code. In this non-colored book, this might not be so visually obvious, but those colors are true; you can trust me on this.

You can check out the graphing and drawing capabilities by searching online. I will not go deeper into this widget in this book (but it is very cool).

4
Data and Classes

In this chapter, we will use data and OOP classes using Python 3:

- ▸ How to use StringVar()
- ▸ How to get data from a widget
- ▸ Using module-level global variables
- ▸ How coding in classes can improve the GUI
- ▸ Writing callback functions
- ▸ Creating reusable GUI components

Introduction

In this chapter, we will save our GUI data into tkinter variables.

We will also start using **object-oriented programming** (**OOP**) to extend the existing tkinter classes in order to extend tkinter's built-in functionality. This will lead us into creating reusable OOP components.

How to use StringVar()

There are built-in programming types in tkinter that differ slightly from the Python types we are used to programming with. StringVar() is one of those tkinter types.

This recipe will show you how to use the StringVar() type.

Getting ready

We are learning how to save data from the tkinter GUI into variables so we can use that data. We can set and get their values, very similar to the Java getter/setter methods.

Here are some of the available types of coding in tkinter:

`strVar = StringVar()`	# Holds a string; the default value is an empty string ""
`intVar = IntVar()`	# Holds an integer; the default value is 0
`dbVar = DoubleVar()`	# Holds a float; the default value is 0.0
`blVar = BooleanVar()`	# Holds a Boolean, it returns 0 for false and 1 for true

 Different languages call numbers with decimal points, floats, or doubles. Tkinter calls a DoubleVar for what in Python is called a float datatype. Depending on the level of precision, floats and double data can be different. Here, we are translating the tkinter DoubleVar into what Python turns into a Python float type.

How to do it...

We are creating a new Python module and the following screenshot shows both the code and the resulting output:

```python
import tkinter as tk

# Create instance of tkinter
win = tk.Tk()

# Assign tkinter Variable to strData variable
strData = tk.StringVar()

# Set strData variable
strData.set('Hello StringVar')

# Get value of strData variable
varData = strData.get()

# Print out current value of strData
print(varData)
```

```
Console ⊠
<terminated> C:\EclipseWorkspace\Ch04\B04829_Ch04_Code\B04829_Ch04_Recipe1.py
Hello StringVar
```

First, we import the tkinter module and alias it to the name `tk`.

Next, we use this alias to create an instance of the `Tk` class by appending parentheses to `Tk`, which calls the constructor of the class. This is the same mechanism as calling a function, only here we are creating an instance of a class.

Usually we use this instance assigned to the variable `win` to start the main event loop later in the code. But here, we are not displaying a GUI but demonstrating how to use the tkinter StringVar type.

> We still have to create an instance of `Tk()`. If we comment out this line, we will get an error from tkinter, so this call is necessary.

Then we create an instance of the tkinter StringVar type and assign it to our Python `strData` variable.

After that, we use our variable to call the `set()` method on StringVar and, after having it set to a value, we then get the value and save it in a new variable named `varData` and then print out its value.

In the Eclipse PyDev console, towards the bottom of the screenshot, we can see the output printed to the console, which is **Hello StringVar**.

Next, we will print the default values of tkinter's IntVar, DoubleVar, and BooleanVar types.

```
# Print out current value of strData
print(varData)

# Print out the default tkinter variable values
print(tk.IntVar())
print(tk.DoubleVar())
print(tk.BooleanVar())
```

```
Console ✕
<terminated> C:\EclipseWorkspace\Ch04\B04829_Ch04_Code\B04829_Ch04_Recipe1_1.py
Hello StringVar
PY_VAR1
PY_VAR2
PY_VAR3
```

How it works...

As can be seen in the preceding screenshot, the default values do not get printed as we would have expected.

The online literature mentions default values, but we won't see those values until we call the `get` method on them. Otherwise, we just get a variable name that automatically increments (for example PY_VAR3, as can be seen in the preceding screenshot).

Assigning the tkinter type to a Python variable does not change the outcome. We still do not get the default value.

Here, we are focusing on the simplest code (which creates PY_VAR0):

The value is PY_VAR0, not the expected 0, until we call the `get` method. Now we can see the default value. We did not call `set`, so we see the default value automatically assigned to each tkinter type once we call the `get` method on each type.

Notice how the default value of 0 gets printed to the console for the `IntVar` instance we saved in the `intData` variable. We can also see the values in the Eclipse PyDev debugger window at the top of the screenshot.

How to get data from a widget

When the user enters data, we want to do something with it in our code. This recipe shows how to capture data in a variable. In the previous recipe, we created several tkinter class variables. They were standalone. Now we are connecting them to our GUI, using the data we get from the GUI and storing it in Python variables.

Getting ready

We are continuing to use the Python GUI we were building in the previous chapter.

How to do it...

We are assigning a value from our GUI to a Python variable.

Add the following code towards the bottom of our module, just above the main event loop:

```
strData = spin.get()
print("Spinbox value: " + strData)

# Place cursor into name Entry
nameEntered.focus()
#=======================
# Start GUI
#=======================
win.mainloop()
```

Running the code gives us the following result:

We are retrieving the current value of the Spinbox control.

 We placed our code above the GUI main event loop and so the printing happens before the GUI becomes visible. We would have to place the code in a callback function if we wanted to print out the current value after displaying the GUI and changing the value of the Spinbox control.

We created our Spinbox widget using the following code, hard-coding the available values into it:

```
# Adding a Spinbox widget using a set of values
spin = Spinbox(monty, values=(1, 2, 4, 42, 100), width=5, bd=8,
command=_spin)
spin.grid(column=0, row=2)
```

We can also move the hard-coding of the data out of the creation of the Spinbox class instance and set it later.

```
# Adding a Spinbox widget assigning values after creation
spin = Spinbox(monty, width=5, bd=8, command=_spin)
spin['values'] = (1, 2, 4, 42, 100)
spin.grid(column=0, row=2)
```

It does not matter how we create our widget and insert data into it because we can access this data by using the `get()` method on the instance of the widget.

How it works...

In order to get values out of our GUI written using tkinter, we use the tkinter `get()` method on an instance of the widget we wish to get the value from.

In the above example we used the Spinbox control, but the principle is the same for all widgets that have a `get()` method.

Once we have gotten the data, we are in a pure Python world and tkinter did serve us to build our GUI. Now that we know how to get the data out of our GUI, we can use this data.

Using module-level global variables

Encapsulation is a major strength in any programming language that enables us to program using OOP. Python is both OOP and procedural. We can create global variables that are localized to the module they reside in. They are global only to this module, which is one form of encapsulation. Why do we want this? Because, as we add more and more functionality to our GUI, we want to avoid naming conflicts, which could result in bugs in our code.

We do not want naming clashes creating bugs in our code!
Namespaces are one way to avoid these bugs, and in Python, we can do this by using Python modules (which are unofficial namespaces).

Getting ready

We can declare module-level globals in any module just above and outside of functions.

We then have to use the `global` Python keyword to refer to them. If we forget to use `global` in functions, we will accidentally create new local variables. This would be a bug and something we really do not want to do.

Python is a dynamic, strongly typed language. We will only notice bugs like this (forgetting to scope variables with the global keyword) at runtime.

How to do it...

Add the code shown on line 15 to the GUI we used in the previous recipe and the last chapter, which creates a module-level global variable. We use the C-style all uppercase convention, which is not truly "Pythonic" but I think this does emphasize the principle we are addressing in this recipe.

```
 6 #=========================
 7 # imports
 8 #=========================
 9 import tkinter as tk
10 from tkinter import ttk
11 from tkinter import scrolledtext
12 from tkinter import Menu
13 from tkinter import Spinbox
14
15 GLOBAL_CONST = 42
```

Running the code results in a printout of the global. Notice **42** being printed to the Eclipse console.

```
228 # Printing the Global works
229 print(GLOBAL_CONST)
230
231 # Place cursor into name Entry
232 nameEntered.focus()
233 #=========================
234 # Start GUI
235 #=========================
236 win.mainloop()
```

Console ⌗

<terminated> C:\EclipseWorkspace\Ch04\B04829_Ch04_Code\4829_Ch04_Recipe3.py

42

How it works...

We define a global variable at the top of our module and, later, towards the bottom of our module, we print out its value.

That works.

Add this function towards the bottom of our module:

```
231  def usingGlobal():
232      print(GLOBAL_CONST)
233
234  # call function
235  usingGlobal()
```

Console

<terminated> C:\EclipseWorkspace\Ch04\B04829_Ch04_Code\4829_Ch04_Recipe3_2.py

42

Above, we are using the module-level global. It is easy to make a mistake by shadowing the global, as demonstrated in the following screenshot:

```
231  def usingGlobal():
232      GLOBAL_CONST = 777
233      print(GLOBAL_CONST)
234
```

Console

C:\EclipseWorkspace\Ch04\B04829_Ch04_Code\4829_Ch04_Recipe3_3.py

777

Note how 42 became 777, even though we are using the same variable name.

There is no compiler in Python that warns us if we overwrite global variables in a local function. This can lead to difficulties in debugging at runtime.

Using the global qualifier (line 234) prints out the value we originally assigned it (42) towards the top of our module, as can be seen in the following screenshot:

```
228⊖ # Printing the Global works
229  # print(GLOBAL_CONST)
230
231⊖ def usingGlobal():
232⊖ #     GLOBAL_CONST = 777
233  #     print(GLOBAL_CONST)
234      global GLOBAL_CONST
235      print(GLOBAL_CONST)
236
237  # call function
238  usingGlobal()
239
```

🖵 Console ⊠

\<terminated\> C:\EclipseWorkspace\Ch04\B0482
42

But, be careful. When we uncomment the local global, we print out the value of the local, not the global:

```
231⊖ def usingGlobal():
232      GLOBAL_CONST = 777
233  #     print(GLOBAL_CONST)
234      global GLOBAL_CONST
235      print(GLOBAL_CONST)
236
237  # call function
238  usingGlobal()
```

🖵 Console ⊠

C:\EclipseWorkspace\Ch04\B04829_Ch04_Code\B04829_Ch04_Recipe3_4.py
C:\EclipseWorkspace\Ch04\B04829_Ch04_Code\B04829_Ch04_Recipe3_4.py:234:
  global GLOBAL_CONST
777

Even though we are using the `global` qualifier, the local variable seems to override it. We are getting a warning from the Eclipse PyDev plug-in that our GLOBAL_CONST = 777 is not being used, yet running the code still prints 777 instead of the expected 42.

This might not be the behavior we expect. Using the `global` qualifier we might expect that we are pointing to the global variable created earlier.

Instead, it seems that Python creates a new global variable in a local function and overwrites the one we created earlier.

Global variables can be very useful when programming small applications. They can help to make data available across methods and functions within the same Python module and sometimes the overhead of OOP is not justified.

As our programs grow in complexity, the benefit we gained from using globals can quickly diminish.

 It is best to avoid globals and accidentally shadowing variables by using the same name in different scopes. We can use OOP instead of using globals.

We played around with global variables within procedural code and learned how that can lead to hard-to-debug bugs. In the next chapter, we will move on to OOP, which can eliminate these kinds of bugs.

How coding in classes can improve the GUI

So far, we have been coding in a procedural style. This is a quick scripting method from Python. Once our code gets larger and larger, we need to advance to coding in OOP.

Why?

Because, among many other benefits, OOP allows us to move code around by using methods. Once we use classes, we no longer have to physically place code above the code that calls it. This gives us great flexibility in organizing our code.

We can write related code next to other code and no longer have to worry that the code will not run because the code does not sit above the code that calls it.

We can take that to some rather fancy extremes by coding up modules that refer to methods that are not being created within that module. They rely on the runtime state having created those methods during the time the code runs.

 If the methods we call have not been created by that time, we get a runtime error.

Getting ready

We will turn our entire procedural code into OOP very simply. We just turn it into a class, indent all the existing code, and prepend `self` to all variables.

It is very easy.

While at first it might feel a little bit annoying having to prepend everything with the `self` keyword, making our code more verbose (hey, we are wasting so much paper...); in the end, it will be worth it.

How to do it...

In the beginning, all hell breaks loose, but we will very soon fix this apparent mess.

Note that, in Eclipse, the PyDev editor hints at coding problems by highlighting them in red on the right-side portion of the code editor.

Maybe we should not code in OOP after all, but this is what we do, and for very good reasons.

```
  4829_Ch04_Recipe4

57  #===========================================================
58  class OOP():
59      # Create instance
60      win = tk.Tk()
61
62      # Add a title
63      win.title("Python GUI")
64
65      # Tab Control introduced here ------------------------------
66      tabControl = ttk.Notebook(win)              # Create Tab Control
67
68      tab1 = ttk.Frame(tabControl)                # Create a tab
69      tabControl.add(tab1, text='Tab 1')          # Add the tab
70
71      tab2 = ttk.Frame(tabControl)                # Add a second tab
72      tabControl.add(tab2, text='Tab 2')          # Make second tab visible
73
74      tabControl.pack(expand=1, fill="both")      # Pack to make visible
75      # ~ Tab Control introduced here ------------------------------
76
77      # We are creating a container frame to hold all other widgets
78      monty = ttk.LabelFrame(tab1, text=' Monty Python ')
79      monty.grid(column=0, row=0, padx=8, pady=4)
80
81      # Modified Button Click Function
82      def clickMe():
83          action.configure(text='Hello ' + name.get())
84
85      # Changing our Label
86      ttk.Label(monty, text="Enter a name:").grid(column=0, row=0, sticky=
87
88      # Adding a Textbox Entry widget
```

Writable   Insert   58 : 1

We just have to prepend all variables with the `self` keyword and also bind the functions to the class by using `self`, which officially and technically turns the functions into methods.

> There is a difference between functions and methods. Python makes this very clear. Methods are bound to a class while functions are not. We can even mix the two within the same Python module.

Let's prefix everything with `self` to get rid of the red, so we can run our code again.

```
80
81      # Modified Button Click Function
82      def clickMe(self):
83          self.action.configure(text='Hello ' + self.name.get())
84
```

Once we do this for all of the errors highlighted in red, we can run our Python code again.

The `clickMe` function is now bound to the class and has officially become a method.

Unfortunately, starting in a procedural way and then translating it into OOP is not as simple as I stated above. The code became a huge mess. This is a very good reason to start programming in Python using the OOP paradigm.

> Python is good at doing things the easy way. The easy code often becomes more complex (because it was easy to begin with). Once we get too complex, refactoring our procedural code into what truly could be OOP code becomes harder with every single line of code.

We are translating our procedural code into object-oriented code. Looking at all the troubles we got ourselves into, translating only 200+ lines of Python code into OOP could suggest that we might as well start coding in OOP from the beginning.

We actually did break some of our previously working functionality. Using Tab 2 and clicking the radio buttons no longer works. We have to refactor more.

The procedural code was easy in the sense that it was simply top to bottom coding. Now that we have placed our code into a class, we have to move all callback functions into methods. This works, but does take some work to translate our original code.

Our procedural code looked like this:

```
# Button Click Function
def clickMe():
```

```
        action.configure(text='Hello ' + name.get())

# Changing our Label
ttk.Label(monty, text="Enter a name:").grid(column=0, row=0,
sticky='W')

# Adding a Textbox Entry widget
name = tk.StringVar()
nameEntered = ttk.Entry(monty, width=12, textvariable=name)
nameEntered.grid(column=0, row=1, sticky='W')

# Adding a Button
action = ttk.Button(monty, text="Click Me!", command=clickMe)
action.grid(column=2, row=1)
```

The new OOP code looks like this:

```
class OOP():
    def __init__(self):
        # Create instance
        self.win = tk.Tk()

        # Add a title
        self.win.title("Python GUI")
        self.createWidgets()

    # Button callback
    def clickMe(self):
        self.action.configure(text='Hello ' + self.name.get())

    # ... more callback methods

    def createWidgets(self):
        # Tab Control introduced here ----------------------
        tabControl = ttk.Notebook(self.win)      # Create Tab Control

        tab1 = ttk.Frame(tabControl)             # Create a tab
        tabControl.add(tab1, text='Tab 1')       # Add the tab

        tab2 = ttk.Frame(tabControl)             # Create second tab
        tabControl.add(tab2, text='Tab 2')       # Add second tab
```

```
            tabControl.pack(expand=1, fill="both")   # Pack make visible
    #======================
    # Start GUI
    #======================
    oop = OOP()
    oop.win.mainloop()
```

We moved the callback methods to the top of the module, inside the new OOP class. We moved all the widget creation code into one rather long method, which we call in the initializer of the class.

Technically, deep underneath the hood of low-level code, Python does have a constructor, yet Python frees us from any worries about this. It is taken care of for us.

Instead, in addition to a "real" constructor, Python provides us with an initializer.

We are strongly encouraged to use this initializer. We can use it to pass in parameters to our class, initializing variables we wish to use inside of our class instance.

 In Python, several classes can exist within the same Python module.

Unlike Java, which has a very rigid naming convention (without which it does not work), Python is much more flexible.

 We can create multiple classes within the same Python module. Unlike Java, we do not depend on a file name that has to match each class name.

Python truly rocks!

Once our Python GUI gets large, we will break some classes out into their own modules but, unlike Java, we do not have to. In this book and project, we will keep some classes in the same module, while at the same time, we will break out some other classes into their own modules, importing them into what can be considered as a main() function (this is not C, but we can think C-like because Python is very flexible).

What we have achieved so far is to add the ToolTip class to our Python module and refactor our procedural Python code into OOP Python code.

Here, in this recipe, we can see that more than one class can live in the same Python module.

Cool stuff, indeed!

```
P  4829_Ch04_Recipe5  ⋉
16
17⊖ class ToolTip(object):
18⊖     def __init__(self, widget):
19          self.widget = widget
20          self.tipwindow = None
21          self.id = None
22          self.x = self.y = 0
23
24⊖     def showtip(self, text):
25          "Display text in tooltip window"
26          self.text = text
```

Both the `ToolTip` class and the `OOP` class reside within the same Python module.

```
P  B04829_Ch04_RecipeLast_OOP  ⋉
18  #=================================================================
19⊖ class OOP():
20⊖     def __init__(self):
21          # Create instance
22          self.win = tk.Tk()
23
24          tt.createToolTip(self.win, 'Hello GUI.')
25
26          # Add a title
27          self.win.title("Python GUI")
28          self.createWidgets()
29
30      # Button callback
31⊖     def clickMe(self):
32          self.action.configure(text='Hello ' + self.name.get())
33
```

How it works...

In this recipe, we advanced our procedural code into object-oriented-programming (OOP) code.

Python enables us to write code in both a practical, procedural style like the C-programming language.

At the same time, we have the option to code in an OOP style, like Java, C#, and C++.

Writing callback functions

At first, callback functions can seem to be a little bit intimidating. You call the function, passing it some arguments, and now the function tells you that it is really very busy and it will call you back!

You wonder: "Will this function *ever* call me back?"
"And how long do I have to *wait*?"

In Python, even callback functions are easy and, yes, they usually do call you back.

They just have to complete their assigned task first (hey, it was you who coded them in the first place...).

Let us understand a little bit more about what happens when we code callbacks into our GUI.

Our GUI is event-driven. After it has been created and displayed onscreen, it typically sits there waiting for an event to happen. It is basically waiting for an event to be sent to it. We can send an event to our GUI by clicking one of its action buttons.

This creates an event and, in a sense, we "called" our GUI by sending it a message.

Now, what is supposed to happen after we send a message to our GUI?

What happens after clicking the button depends on whether we created an event handler and associated it with this button. If we did not create an event handler, clicking the button will have no effect.

The event handler is a callback function (or method, if we use classes).

The callback method is also sitting there passively, like our GUI, waiting to be invoked.

Once our GUI gets its button clicked, it will invoke the callback.

The callback often does some processing and, when done, it returns the result to our GUI.

[In a sense, we can see that our callback function is calling back to our GUI.]

Getting ready

The Python interpreter runs through all the code in a project once, finding any syntax errors and pointing them out. You cannot run your Python code if you do not have the syntax right. This includes indentation (if not resulting in a syntax error, wrong indentation usually results in a bug).

On the next parsing round, the interpreter interprets our code and runs it.

At runtime, many GUI events can be generated and it is usually callback functions that add functionality to GUI widgets.

How to do it...

Here is the callback for the Spinbox widget:

```
# Spinbox callback
def _spin(self):
    value = self.spin.get()
    print(value)
    self.scr.insert(tk.INSERT, value + '\n')


# Adding a Spinbox widget using a set of values
self.spin = Spinbox(self.monty, values=(1, 2, 4, 42, 100), width=5, bd=8, command=self._spin)
self.spin.grid(column=0, row=2)
```

How it works...

We created a callback method in the OOP class, which gets called when we select a value from the Spinbox widget because we bound the method to the widget via the command argument (command=self._spin). We use a leading underscore to hint at the fact that this method should be respected like a private Java method.

Python intentionally avoids language restrictions such as private, public, friend, and so on.

In Python, we use naming conventions instead. Leading and trailing double underscores surrounding a keyword are expected to be restricted to the Python language, and we should not use them in our own Python code.

However, we can use a leading underscore prefix to a variable name or function to provide a hint that this name should be respected as a private helper.

At the same time, we can postfix a single underscore if we wish to use what otherwise would be Python built-in names. For example, if we wished to abbreviate the length of a list, we could do the following:

```
len_ = len(aList)
```

Often, the underscore is hard to read and easy to oversee, so this might not be the best idea in practice.

Creating reusable GUI components

We are creating reusable GUI components using Python.

In this recipe, we will keep it simple by moving our ToolTip class into its own module. Next, we will import and use it for displaying tooltips over several widgets of our GUI.

Getting ready

We are building on our previous code.

How to do it...

We will start by breaking out our ToolTip class into a separate Python module. We will slightly enhance it to pass in the control widget and the tooltip text we wish to display when we hover the mouse over the control.

We create a new Python module and place the ToolTip class code into it and then import this module into our primary module.

We then reuse the imported ToolTip class by creating several tooltips, which can be seen when hovering the mouse over several of our GUI widgets.

Refactoring our common ToolTip class code out into its own module helps us to reuse this code from other modules. Instead of copy/paste/modify we use the DRY principle and our common code is located in only one place, so when we modify the code, all modules that import it will automatically get the latest version of our module.

> DRY stands for Don't Repeat Yourself and we will look at it again in a later chapter.
>
> We can do similar things by turning our Tab3 image into a reusable component.
>
> To keep this recipe's code simple, we removed Tab 3, but you can experiment with the code from the previous chapter.

```
# Add a Tooltip to the Spinbox
tt.createToolTip(self.spin, 'This is a Spin control.')

# Add Tooltips to more widgets
tt.createToolTip(nameEntered, 'This is an Entry control.')
tt.createToolTip(self.action, 'This is a Button control.')
tt.createToolTip(self.scr, 'This is a ScrolledText control.')
```

This also works on the second tab.

The new code structure looks like this now:

```
▲ 📁 Ch04
    ▲ 🔲 B04829_Ch04_Code
        📄 _init_.py
    ▷ 📄 4829_Ch04_RecipeLast_OOP.py
    ▷ 📄 4829_Ch04_Recipes.py
    ▷ 📄 B04829_Ch04_RecipeLastOPP_ToolTip.py
▷ 🐍 Python 3.4.3 (C:\Python34\python.exe)
```

The import statement looks like this:

```
📄 4829_Ch04_RecipeLast_OOP  ☒    📄 B04829_Ch04_RecipeLastOPP_ToolTip

11   from tkinter import scrolledtext
12   from tkinter import Menu
13   from tkinter import Spinbox
14   import B04829_Ch04_RecipeLastOPP_ToolTip as tt
15
16   GLOBAL_CONST = 42
17
18   #==============================================================
19 ⊖ class OOP():
20 ⊖     def __init__(self):
21           # Create instance
```

And the broken out (aka refactored) code in a separate module looks like this:

```
P 4829_Ch04_RecipeLast_OOP        P B04829_Ch04_RecipeLastOPP_ToolTip ⊠
  9  import tkinter as tk
 10
 11⊝ class ToolTip(object):
 12⊝     def __init__(self, widget):
 13             self.widget = widget
 14             self.tipwindow = None
 15             self.id = None
 16             self.x = self.y = 0
 17
 18⊝     def showtip(self, text):
 19             "Display text in tooltip window"
 20             self.text = text
```

How it works...

In the preceding screenshots, we can see several tooltip messages being displayed. The one for the main window might appear a little bit annoying, so it is better not to display a tooltip for the main window because we really wish to highlight the functionality of the individual widgets. The main window form has a title that explains its purpose; no need for a tooltip.

5

Matplotlib Charts

In this chapter, we will create beautiful charts using Python 3 with the Matplotlib module.

- ▶ Creating beautiful charts using Matplotlib
- ▶ Matplotlib – downloading modules using pip
- ▶ Matplotlib – downloading modules with whl extensions
- ▶ Creating our first chart
- ▶ Placing labels on charts
- ▶ How to give the chart a legend
- ▶ Scaling charts
- ▶ Adjusting the scale of charts dynamically

Introduction

In this chapter, we will create beautiful charts that visually represent data. Depending on the format of the data source, we can plot one or several columns of data in the same chart.

We will be using the Python Matplotlib module to create our charts.

In order to create these graphical charts, we need to download additional Python modules and there are several ways to install them.

This chapter will explain how to download the Matplotlib Python module, all other required Python modules, and the ways to do this.

After we have the required modules installed, we will then create our own Pythonic charts.

Creating beautiful charts using Matplotlib

This recipe introduces us to the Matplotlib Python module, which enables us to create visual charts using Python 3.

The following URL is a great place to start exploring the world of Matplotlib and will teach you how to create many charts that are not presented in this chapter:

```
http://matplotlib.org/users/screenshots.html
```

Getting ready

In order to use the Matplotlib Python module, we first have to install this module, as well as several other related Python modules such as numpy.

If you are running a version of Python less than 3.4.3, I would encourage you to upgrade your version of Python as we will be using the Python pip module throughout this chapter to install the required Python modules, and pip is installed with 3.4.3 and above.

 It is possible to install pip with earlier versions of Python 3 but the process is not very intuitive, so it is definitely better to upgrade to 3.4.3 or above.

How to do it...

The following picture is an example of what incredible graphical charts can be created using Python with the Matplotlib module.

I have copied the following code from the `http://matplotlib.org/` website, which creates this incredible chart. There are many examples available on this site and I encourage you to try them out until you find the kind of charts you like to create.

Here is the code to create the chart, in less than 25 lines of Python code, including whitespaces.

```python
from mpl_toolkits.mplot3d import Axes3D
from matplotlib import cm
from matplotlib.ticker import LinearLocator, FormatStrFormatter
import matplotlib.pyplot as plt
import numpy as np

fig = plt.figure()
ax = fig.gca(projection='3d')
X = np.arange(-5, 5, 0.25)
Y = np.arange(-5, 5, 0.25)
```

```
X, Y = np.meshgrid(X, Y)
R = np.sqrt(X**2 + Y**2)
Z = np.sin(R)
surf = ax.plot_surface(X, Y, Z, rstride=1, cstride=1, cmap=cm.
coolwarm, linewidth=0, antialiased=False)

ax.set_zlim(-1.01, 1.01)

ax.zaxis.set_major_locator(LinearLocator(10))
ax.zaxis.set_major_formatter(FormatStrFormatter('%.02f'))

fig.colorbar(surf, shrink=0.5, aspect=5)

plt.show()
```

Running the code creates the chart pictured as follows:

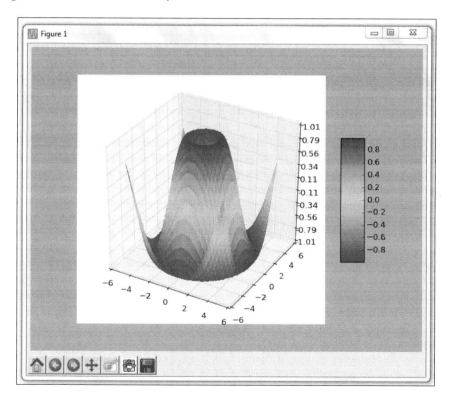

Running the code using Python 3.4 or above with the Eclipse PyDev plugin might show some unresolved import errors. This seems to be a bug in PyDev or Java.

Just ignore those errors if you are developing using Eclipse, as the code will run successfully.

How it works...

In order to create beautiful graphs as shown in the preceding screenshot, we need to download several other Python modules.

The following recipes will guide us through how to successfully download all the required modules, which enables us to create our own beautiful charts.

Matplotlib – downloading modules using pip

The usual way to download additional Python modules is by using pip. The pip module comes pre-installed with the latest version of Python (3.4 and above).

 If you are using an older version of Python, you might have to download both pip and setuptools yourself.

In addition to using the Python installer, there are several other precompiled Windows executables that make it easy for us to install Python modules such as Matplotlib.

This recipe will show how to successfully install Matplotlib via a Windows executable, as well as using pip in order to install the additional modules that the Matplotlib library requires.

Getting ready

All we need to do to download the required Python modules to use the Matplotlib module is to have a Python release of 3.4 (or later) installed on our PC.

How to do it...

We can install Matplotlib via a Windows executable from the official Matplotlib website.

Make sure you install the Matplotlib version that matches the Python version you are using. For example, download and install `Matplotlib-1.4.3.win-amd64-py3.4.exe` if you have Python 3.4 installed on a 64-bit OS such as Microsoft Windows 7.

 The "amd64" in the middle of the executable name means you are installing the 64-bit version. If you are using a 32-bit x86 system then installing amd64 will not work. Similar problems can occur if you have installed a 32-bit version of Python and download 64-bit Python modules.

Running the executable will get us started and looks like this:

We can verify that we have successfully installed Matplotlib by looking at our Python installation directory.

After a successful installation, the Matplotlib folder is added to site-packages. Using a default installation, the full path to the site-packages folder on Windows is:

```
C:\Python34\Lib\site-packages\matplotlib\
```

The simplest plotting example on the official Matplotlib website requires the use of the Python numpy module, so let's download and install this module next.

> Numpy is a mathematical module that enables the graphing of the Matplotlib charts but goes well beyond Matplotlib. If the software you are developing requires a lot of mathematical computations, you definitely want to check out numpy.

There is one excellent website that gives us quick links to pretty much all the Python modules out there. It serves as a great time saver by pointing out which other Python modules are necessary to use Matplotlib successfully and gives us hyperlinks to download these modules, which enables us to install them quickly and easily.

Here is the link:

http://www.lfd.uci.edu/~gohlke/pythonlibs/

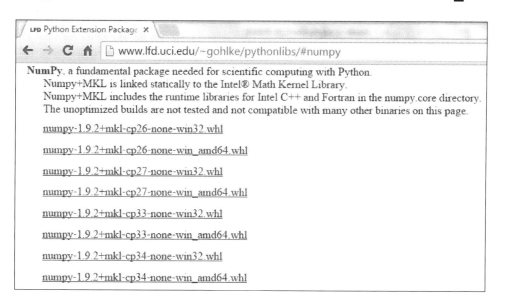

NumPy, a fundamental package needed for scientific computing with Python.
Numpy+MKL is linked statically to the Intel® Math Kernel Library.
Numpy+MKL includes the runtime libraries for Intel C++ and Fortran in the numpy.core directory.
The unoptimized builds are not tested and not compatible with many other binaries on this page.

numpy-1.9.2+mkl-cp26-none-win32.whl

numpy-1.9.2+mkl-cp26-none-win_amd64.whl

numpy-1.9.2+mkl-cp27-none-win32.whl

numpy-1.9.2+mkl-cp27-none-win_amd64.whl

numpy-1.9.2+mkl-cp33-none-win32.whl

numpy-1.9.2+mkl-cp33-none-win_amd64.whl

numpy-1.9.2+mkl-cp34-none-win32.whl

numpy-1.9.2+mkl-cp34-none-win_amd64.whl

Notice how the file extensions of the installer packages all end in whl. In order to use them, we have to install the Python wheel module, and we do this using pip.

 Wheels are the new standard of Python distribution and are intended to replace eggs.

You can find more details at the following website:

http://pythonwheels.com/

It is best to run the Windows command processor as an administrator to avoid potential installation errors.

```
Microsoft Windows [Version 6.1.7601]
Copyright (c) 2009 Microsoft Corporation.  All rights reserved.

C:\Windows\system32>pip install wheel
Collecting wheel
  Using cached wheel-0.24.0-py2.py3-none-any.whl
Installing collected packages: wheel
Successfully installed wheel-0.24.0

C:\Windows\system32>
```

How it works...

The common way to download Python modules is by using pip, as shown above. In order to install all the modules that Matplotlib requires, the download format of the main website where we can download them has changed to using a whl format.

The next recipe will explain how to install Python modules using wheel.

Matplotlib – downloading modules with whl extensions

We will use several additional Python modules that Matplotlib requires and, in this recipe, we will download them using Python's new module distribution standard, called wheel.

 You can find the Python Enhancement Proposal (PEP) for the new wheel standard at the following URL: `https://www.python.org/dev/peps/pep-0427/`

Getting ready

In order to download Python modules with a whl extension, the Python wheel module has to be installed first, which was explained in the previous recipe.

How to do it...

Let's download `numpy-1.9.2+mkl-cp34-none-win_amd64.whl` from the web. After installing the wheel module, we can use pip to install packages with whl file extensions.

 Pip ships with Python 3.4.3 and above. If you are using an older version of Python, I would recommend installing pip because it makes installing all other additional Python modules so much easier.

An even better suggestion might be to upgrade your Python version to the latest stable release. By the time you read this book, that most likely will be Python 3.5.0 or above.

Python is free software. It does not cost us anything to upgrade.

Browse to the folder where the package to be installed is located, and install it using the following command:

```
pip install numpy-1.9.2+mkl-cp34-none-win_amd64.whl
```

Now we can create our first Matplotlib chart, using the simplest example application from the official website. After that, we will be creating our own charts.

```
 7  import numpy as np
 8  import matplotlib.pyplot as plt
 9
10  x = np.arange(0, 5, 0.1);
11  y = np.sin(x)
12  plt.plot(x, y)
13
```

```
Console 
<terminated> C:\EclipseWorkspace\Ch05\B04829_Ch05_Code\B04829_Ch05_FirstChart.py
Traceback (most recent call last):
  File "C:\EclipseWorkspace\Ch05\B04829_Ch05_Code\B04829_Ch05_FirstChart.py", line 8, in <module>
    import matplotlib.pyplot as plt
  File "C:\Python34\lib\site-packages\matplotlib\__init__.py", line 105, in <module>
    import six
ImportError: No module named 'six'
```

The fact that we are not quite ready to run the preceding code shows that we need to download more modules. While at first having to download more modules might seem to be a little bit annoying, it really is a form of code reuse.

So let's download and install the six and all the other required modules (dateutil, pyparsing, and so on) using pip with wheel until our code works and creates a nice chart from only a few lines of Python code.

We can download all the required modules from the same website we just used to install numpy. This website even lists all of the other modules the module we are installing depends on and has hyperlinks to jump to the installation software located in this very same website.

As mentioned previously, the URL for installing Python modules is:
`http://www.lfd.uci.edu/~gohlke/pythonlibs/`

How it works...

The website that enables us to download many Python modules from one convenient place also provides other Python modules. Not all dependencies shown are required. It depends on what you are developing. You might have to download and install additional modules as your journey into using the Matplotlib library advances.

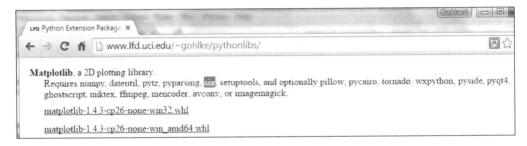

Creating our first chart

Now that we have all of the required Python modules installed, we can create our own charts using Matplotlib.

We can create charts from only a few lines of Python code.

Getting ready

Using the code from the previous recipe, we can now create a chart that looks similar to the one shown next.

How to do it...

Using the minimum amount of code as presented on the official website, we can create our first chart. Well, almost. The sample code shown on the website does not work until we import the `show` method and then call it.

```
import numpy as np
import matplotlib.pyplot as plt
from pylab import show

x = np.arange(0, 5, 0.1);
y = np.sin(x)
plt.plot(x, y)

show()
```

We can simplify the code and even improve it by using another of many examples provided on the official Matplotlib website.

```
from pylab import show, arange, sin, plot, pi

t = arange(0.0, 2.0, 0.01)
s = sin(2*pi*t)
plot(t, s)

show()
```

How it works...

The Python Matplotlib module, combined with add-ons such as numpy, create a very rich programming environment that enables us to do mathematical computations and plot them in visual charts very easily.

The Python numpy method `arange` does not intend to arrange anything. It means to create "a range", which in Python is used for the built-in "range" operator. The `linspace` method can create similar confusion. Who is "lin" and in what "space"?

As it turns out, the name means "linear spaced vector".

The pyglet function `show` displays the graph we created. Calling `show()` has some side-effects when you try to plot another graph after successfully creating the first one.

Placing labels on charts

So far, we have used the default Matplotlib GUI. Now we will create some tkinter GUIs using Matplotlib.

This will require a few more lines of Python code and importing some more libraries, and it is well worth the effort, because we are gaining control of our paintings using canvases.

We will position labels onto both the horizontal as well as the vertical axes, aka x and y.

We will do this by creating a Matplotlib figure upon which we will draw.

We will also learn how to use sub plots, which will enable us to draw more than one graph in the same window.

Getting ready

With the necessary Python modules installed and knowing where to find the official online documentation and tutorials, we can now carry on with our creation of Matplotlib charts.

How to do it...

While `plot` is the easiest way to create a Matplotlib chart, using `Figure` in combination with `Canvas` creates a more custom-made graph, which looks much better and also enables us to add buttons and other widgets to it.

```
from matplotlib.figure import Figure
from matplotlib.backends.backend_tkagg import FigureCanvasTkAgg
import tkinter as tk
#-----------------------------------------------------------
fig = Figure(figsize=(12, 8), facecolor='white')
#-----------------------------------------------------------
# axis = fig.add_subplot(111)    # 1 row,  1 column, only graph
axis = fig.add_subplot(211)      # 2 rows, 1 column, Top graph
#-----------------------------------------------------------
xValues = [1,2,3,4]
yValues = [5,7,6,8]
axis.plot(xValues, yValues)

axis.set_xlabel('Horizontal Label')
axis.set_ylabel('Vertical Label')

# axis.grid()                    # default line style
```

```
axis.grid(linestyle='-')          # solid grid lines
#------------------------------------------------------------
def _destroyWindow():
    root.quit()
    root.destroy()
#------------------------------------------------------------
root = tk.Tk()
root.withdraw()
root.protocol('WM_DELETE_WINDOW', _destroyWindow)
#------------------------------------------------------------
canvas = FigureCanvasTkAgg(fig, master=root)
canvas._tkcanvas.pack(side=tk.TOP, fill=tk.BOTH, expand=1)
#------------------------------------------------------------
root.update()
root.deiconify()
root.mainloop()
```

Running the preceding code results in the following chart:

In the first line of code after the import statements, we create an instance of a `Figure` object. Next, we add sub plots to this figure by calling `add_subplot(211)`. The first number in `211` tells the figure how many plots to add, the second number determines the number of columns and the third tells the figure in which order to display the plots.

We also add a grid and change its default line style.

Even though we only display one plot in the chart, by choosing 2 for the number of sub plots, we are moving the plot up, which results in extra whitespace at the bottom of the chart. This first plot now only occupies 50% of the screen, which affects how large the grid lines of this plot are when being displayed.

Experiment with the code by uncommenting the code for `axis =` and `axis.grid()` to see the different effects.

We can add more sub plots by assigning them to the second position using `add_subplot(212)`.

```python
from matplotlib.figure import Figure
from matplotlib.backends.backend_tkagg import FigureCanvasTkAgg
import tkinter as tk
#-------------------------------------------------------------
fig = Figure(figsize=(12, 8), facecolor='white')
#-------------------------------------------------------------
axis = fig.add_subplot(211)      # 2 rows, 1 column, Top graph
#-------------------------------------------------------------
xValues = [1,2,3,4]
yValues = [5,7,6,8]
axis.plot(xValues, yValues)

axis.set_xlabel('Horizontal Label')
axis.set_ylabel('Vertical Label')

axis.grid(linestyle='-')          # solid grid lines
#-------------------------------------------------------------
axis1 = fig.add_subplot(212)     # 2 rows, 1 column, Bottom graph
#-------------------------------------------------------------
xValues1 = [1,2,3,4]
yValues1 = [7,5,8,6]
axis1.plot(xValues1, yValues1)
axis1.grid()                      # default line style
#-------------------------------------------------------------
def _destroyWindow():
    root.quit()
    root.destroy()
#-------------------------------------------------------------
root = tk.Tk()
root.withdraw()
root.protocol('WM_DELETE_WINDOW', _destroyWindow)
#-------------------------------------------------------------
canvas = FigureCanvasTkAgg(fig, master=root)
```

```
canvas._tkcanvas.pack(side=tk.TOP, fill=tk.BOTH, expand=1)
#---------------------------------------------------------------
root.update()
root.deiconify()
root.mainloop()
```

Running the slightly modified code now adds axis1 to the chart. For the grid of the bottom plot, we left the line style at its default.

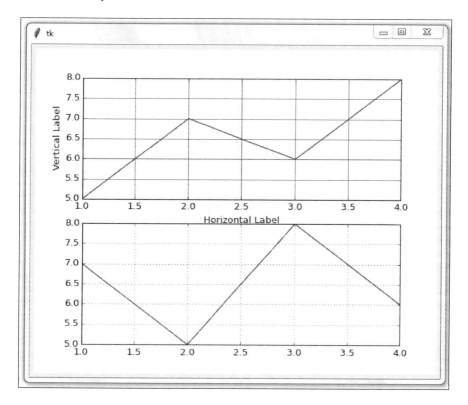

How it works...

We imported the necessary Matplotlib modules to create a figure and a canvas onto which to draw the chart. We gave it some values for the x and y axes and set a few of very many configuration options.

We created our own tkinter window in which to display the chart and customized the positioning of the plots.

As we have seen in previous chapters, in order to create a tkinter GUI, we first have to import the tkinter module and then create an instance of the `Tk` class. We assign this class instance to a variable we named `root`, which is a name that is often used in examples.

Our tkinter GUI will not become visible until we start the main event loop and, to do that, we use `root.mainloop()`.

One important reason to avoid the Matplotlib default GUI here and instead create our own GUI using tkinter is that we wanted to improve the not very pretty appearance of the default Matplotlib GUI and we can very easily do this using tkinter.

We no longer have those out-of-date looking buttons appearing at the bottom of the Matplotlib GUI if we build our GUI with tkinter.

At the same time, the Matplotlib GUI has a feature our tkinter GUI does not have and that is that we can actually see the x and y coordinates in the Matplotlib GUI when we move our mouse around within the chart. The x and y coordinate positions are displayed in the bottom right corner.

How to give the chart a legend

Once we start plotting more than one line of data points, things might become a little bit unclear. By adding a legend to our graphs, we can tell which data is what, and what it actually means.

We do not have to choose different colors to represent the different data. Matplotlib automatically assigns a different color to each line of data points.

All we have to do is create the chart and add a legend to it.

Getting ready

In this recipe, we will enhance the chart from the previous recipe. We will only plot one chart.

How to do it...

First, we will plot more lines of data in the same chart and then we will add a legend to the chart.

We do this by modifying the code from the previous recipe.

```python
from matplotlib.figure import Figure
from matplotlib.backends.backend_tkagg import FigureCanvasTkAgg
import tkinter as tk
#-------------------------------------------------------------
fig = Figure(figsize=(12, 5), facecolor='white')
#-------------------------------------------------------------
axis  = fig.add_subplot(111)                    # 1 row, 1 column

xValues  = [1,2,3,4]

yValues0 = [6,7.5,8,7.5]
yValues1 = [5.5,6.5,8,6]
yValues2 = [6.5,7,8,7]

t0, = axis.plot(xValues, yValues0)
t1, = axis.plot(xValues, yValues1)
t2, = axis.plot(xValues, yValues2)

axis.set_ylabel('Vertical Label')
axis.set_xlabel('Horizontal Label')

axis.grid()

fig.legend((t0, t1, t2), ('First line', 'Second line', 'Third line'),
'upper right')

#-------------------------------------------------------------
def _destroyWindow():
    root.quit()
    root.destroy()
#-------------------------------------------------------------
root = tk.Tk()
root.withdraw()
root.protocol('WM_DELETE_WINDOW', _destroyWindow)
#-------------------------------------------------------------
canvas = FigureCanvasTkAgg(fig, master=root)
canvas._tkcanvas.pack(side=tk.TOP, fill=tk.BOTH, expand=1)
#-------------------------------------------------------------
root.update()
root.deiconify()
root.mainloop()
```

Running the modified code creates the following chart, which has a legend in the upper right corner:

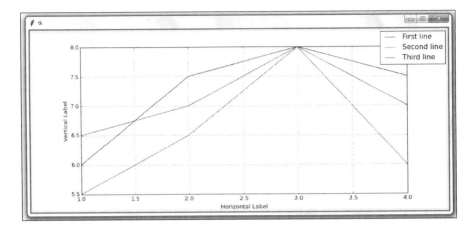

We are only plotting one graph in this recipe and we do this by changing `fig.add_subplot(111)`. We also slightly modify the size of the figure via the `figsize` property.

Next, we create three Python lists that contain the values to be plotted. When we plot the data, we save the references to the plots in local variables.

We create the legend by passing in a tuple with the references to the three plots, another tuple that contains the strings that are then displayed in the legend, and in the third argument we position the legend within the chart.

The default settings of Matplotlib assign a color scheme to the lines being plotted.

We can easily change this default setting of colors to the colors we prefer by setting a property when we plot each axis.

We do this by using the color property and assigning it an available color value.

```
t0, = axis.plot(xValues, yValues0, color = 'purple')

t1, = axis.plot(xValues, yValues1, color = 'red')

t2, = axis.plot(xValues, yValues2, color = 'blue')
```

Note how the comma after the variable assignments of t0, t1, and t2 is not a mistake but is required in order to create the legend.

The comma after each variable turns a list into a tuple. If we leave this out, our legend will not be displayed.

The code will still run, just without the intended legend.

When we remove the comma after the t0 = assignment, we get an error and the first line no longer appears in the figure. The chart and legend still get created, but without the first line appearing in the legend.

```
t0 = axis.plot(xValues, yValues0)
t1, = axis.plot(xValues, yValues1)
t2, = axis.plot(xValues, yValues2)
```

```
Console ⊠
C:\EclipseWorkspace\Ch05new\B04829_Ch05_ChartsWithLegend.py
C:\Python34\lib\site-packages\matplotlib\legend.py:611: UserWarning: Legend does not suppor
A proxy artist may be used instead.
See: http://matplotlib.org/users/legend_guide.html#using-proxy-artist
  "#using-proxy-artist".format(orig_handle))
```

How it works...

We enhanced our chart by plotting three lines of data in the same chart and giving it a legend in order to distinguish the data that those three lines plot.

Scaling charts

In the previous recipes, while creating our first charts and enhancing them, we hard-coded the scaling of how those values are visually represented.

While this served us well for the values we were using, we often plot charts from very large databases.

Depending on the range of that data, our hard-coded values for the vertical y-dimension might not always be the best solution, which may make it hard to see the lines in our charts.

Getting ready

We will improve our code from the previous recipe. If you have not typed in all of the code from all of the previous recipes, just download the code for this chapter and it will get you started (and then you can have a lot of fun creating GUIs, charts, and so on, using Python).

How to do it...

Modify the `yValues1` line of code from the previous recipe to use 50 as the third value.

```
axis   = fig.add_subplot(111)        # 1 row, 1 column

xValues  = [1,2,3,4]

yValues0 = [6,7.5,8,7.5]
yValues1 = [5.5,6.5,50,6]            # one very high value
yValues2 = [6.5,7,8,7]
```

The only difference to the code that created the chart in the previous recipe is one data value.

By changing one value that is not close to the average range of all the other values for all plotted lines, the visual representation of data has dramatically changed and we lost a lot of details about the overall data and now mainly see one high spike.

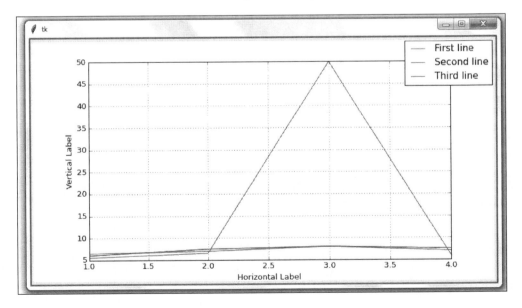

So far, our charts have adjusted themselves according to the data they visually represent.

While this is a practical feature of Matplotlib, this is not always what we want. We can restrict the scale of the chart being represented by limiting the vertical y-dimension.

```
yValues0 = [6,7.5,8,7.5]
yValues1 = [5.5,6.5,50,6]          # one very high value (50)
yValues2 = [6.5,7,8,7]

axis.set_ylim(5, 8)               # limit the vertical display
```

The `axis.set_ylim(5, 8)` line of code now limits the beginning value to 5 and the ending value of the vertical display to 8.

Now, when we create our chart, the high value peak no longer has the impact it had before.

How it works...

We increased one value in the data, which resulted in a dramatic effect. By setting limits to the vertical and horizontal displays of the chart, we can see the data we are most interested in.

Spikes such as the ones just shown, can be of great interest too. It all depends on what we are looking for. The visual representation of data is of great value.

[A picture is worth a thousand words.]

Adjusting the scale of charts dynamically

In the previous recipe, we learned how we can limit the scaling of our charts. In this recipe, we will go one step further by dynamically adjusting the scaling by setting both a limit and analyzing our data before we represent it.

Getting ready

We will enhance the code from the previous recipe by reading in the data we are plotting dynamically, averaging it, and then adjusting our chart.

While we would typically read in the data from an external source, in this recipe, we create the data we are plotting using Python lists, as can be seen in the following code.

How to do it...

We are creating our own data in our Python module by assigning lists with data to the xvalues and yvalues variables.

In many graphs, the beginning of the x and y coordinate system starts at (0, 0). This is usually a good idea, so let's adjust our chart coordinate code accordingly.

Let's modify the code to set limits on both the x and y dimensions:

```
xValues  = [1,2,3,4]

yValues0 = [6,7.5,8,7.5]
yValues1 = [5.5,6.5,50,6]          # one very high value (50)
yValues2 = [6.5,7,8,7]

axis.set_ylim(0, 8)                # lower limit (0)
axis.set_xlim(0, 8)                # use same limits for x
```

Now that we have set the same limits for x and y, our chart might look more balanced. When we run the modified code, we get the following result:

Maybe starting at (0, 0) was not such a great idea after all...

What we really want to do is to adjust our chart dynamically according to the range of the data, while at the same time, restricting values that are too high or too low.

We can do this by parsing all the data to be represented in the chart while at the same time, setting some explicit limits.

Modify the code, as shown here:

```
xValues  = [1,2,3,4]

yValues0 = [6,7.5,8,7.5]
yValues1 = [5.5,6.5,50,6]                 # one very high value (50)
yValues2 = [6.5,7,8,7]
yAll = [yValues0, yValues1, yValues2]  # list of lists

# flatten list of lists retrieving minimum value
minY = min([y for yValues in yAll for y in yValues])

yUpperLimit = 20
# flatten list of lists retrieving max value within defined limit
```

```
maxY = max([y for yValues in yAll for y in yValues if y <
yUpperLimit])

# dynamic limits
axis.set_ylim(minY, maxY)
axis.set_xlim(min(xValues), max(xValues))

t0, = axis.plot(xValues, yValues0)
t1, = axis.plot(xValues, yValues1)
t2, = axis.plot(xValues, yValues2)
```

Running the code results in the following chart. We adjusted both its x and y dimensions dynamically. Note how the y-dimension now starts at 5.5 instead of 5.0, as it did before. The chart also no longer starts at (0, 0), giving us more valuable information about our data.

We are creating a list of lists for the y-dimension data and then using a list comprehension wrapped into a call to Python's `min()` and `max()` functions.

If list comprehensions seem to be a little bit advanced, what they basically are is a very compressed loop.

They are also designed to be faster than a regular programming loop.

In the Python code that creates the preceding chart, we created three lists that hold the y-dimensional data to be plotted. We then created another list that holds those three lists, which created a list of lists.

Like this:

```
yValues0 = [6,7.5,8,7.5]
yValues1 = [5.5,6.5,50,6]                  # one very high value (50)
yValues2 = [6.5,7,8,7]
yAll = [yValues0, yValues1, yValues2]   # list of lists
```

We are interested in getting both the minimum value of all of the y-dimensional data, as well as the maximum value contained within these three lists.

We can do this via a Python list comprehension.

```
# flatten list of lists retrieving minimum value
minY = min([y for yValues in yAll for y in yValues])
```

After running the list comprehension, `minY` is: 5.5.

The one line of code above is the list comprehension that runs through all the values of all the data contained within the three lists and finds the minimum value using the Python `min` keyword.

In the very same pattern, we find the maximum value contained in the data we wish to plot. This time, we also set a limit within our list comprehension that ignores all values that are above the limit we specified, like this:

```
yUpperLimit = 20
# flatten list of lists retrieving max value within defined limit
maxY = max([y for yValues in yAll for y in yValues if y <
yUpperLimit])
```

After running the preceding code with our chosen restriction, `maxY` has the value of 8 (not 50).

We applied a restriction for the max value, according to a predefined condition choosing 20 as the maximum value to be displayed in the chart.

For the x-dimension, we simply called `min()` and `max()` in the Matplotlib method to scale the limits of the chart dynamically.

How it works...

In this recipe, we created several Matplotlib charts and adjusted some of the many available properties. We also used core Python to control the scaling of the charts dynamically.

6
Threads and Networking

In this chapter, we will create threads, queues, and TCP/IP sockets using Python 3.

- ▸ How to create multiple threads
- ▸ Starting a thread
- ▸ Stopping a thread
- ▸ How to use queues
- ▸ Passing queues among different modules
- ▸ Using dialog widgets to copy files to your network
- ▸ Using TCP/IP to communicate via networks
- ▸ Using URLOpen to read data from websites

Introduction

In this chapter, we will extend the functionality of our Python GUI using threads, queues, and network connections.

 A tkinter GUI is single-threaded. Every function that involves sleep or wait time has to be called in a separate thread, otherwise the tkinter GUI freezes.

When we run our Python GUI in Windows Task Manager, we can see that a new `python.exe` process has been launched.

When we give our Python GUI a `.pyw` extension, then the process created will be `python.pyw`, as can be seen in Task Manager.

When a process is created, the process automatically creates a main thread to run our application. This is called a single-threaded application.

For our Python GUI, a single-threaded application will lead to our GUI becoming frozen as soon as we call a longer-running task such as clicking a button that has a sleep of a few seconds.

In order to keep our GUI responsive we have to use multi-threading, and this is what we will study in this chapter.

We can also create multiple processes by creating multiple instances of our Python GUI, as can be seen in Task Manager.

Processes are isolated by design from each other and do not share common data. In order to communicate between separate processes we would have to use **Inter-Process-Communication (IPC)**, which is an advanced technique.

Threads, on the other hand, do share common data, code, and files, which makes communication between threads within the same process much easier than when using IPC.

A great explanation of threads can be found at:
`https://www.cs.uic.edu/~jbell/CourseNotes/`
`OperatingSystems/4_Threads.html`

In this chapter, we will learn how to keep our Python GUI responsive and not to freeze.

How to create multiple threads

We will create multiple threads using Python. This is necessary in order to keep our GUI responsive.

A thread is like weaving a fabric made out of yarn and is nothing to be afraid of.

Getting ready

Multiple threads run within the same computer process memory space. There is no need for Inter-Process-Communication (aka IPC), which would complicate our code. In this recipe, we will avoid IPC by using threads.

How to do it...

First we will increase the size of our `ScrolledText` widget, making it larger. Let's increase `scrolW` to 40 and `scrolH` to 10.

```
# Using a scrolled Text control
scrolW  = 40; scrolH  =  10
self.scr = scrolledtext.ScrolledText(self.monty, width=scrolW,
height=scrolH, wrap=tk.WORD)
self.scr.grid(column=0, row=3, sticky='WE', columnspan=3)
```

When we now run the resulting GUI, the `Spinbox` widget is center-aligned in relation to the `Entry` widget above it, which does not look good. We'll change this by left-aligning the widget.

Add `sticky='W'` to the `grid` control to left-align the `Spinbox` widget.

```
# Adding a Spinbox widget using a set of values
self.spin = Spinbox(self.monty, values=(1, 2, 4, 42, 100), width=5,
bd=8, command=self._spin)
self.spin.grid(column=0, row=2, sticky='W')
```

The GUI could still look better, so next, we will increase the size of the `Entry` widget to get a more balanced GUI layout.

Increase the width to 24, as shown in the following:

```
# Adding a Textbox Entry widget
self.name = tk.StringVar()
nameEntered = ttk.Entry(self.monty, width=24, textvariable=self.name)
nameEntered.grid(column=0, row=1, sticky='W')
```

Let us also slightly increase the width of the `Combobox` to 14.

```
ttk.Label(self.monty, text="Choose a number:").grid(column=1, row=0)
number = tk.StringVar()
numberChosen = ttk.Combobox(self.monty, width=14, textvariable=number)
numberChosen['values'] = (1, 2, 4, 42, 100)
numberChosen.grid(column=1, row=1)
numberChosen.current(0)
```

Running the modified and improved code results in a larger GUI, which we will use for this and the following recipes.

In order to create and use threads in Python, we have to import the `Thread` class from the threading module.

```
#=======================
#  imports
#=======================
import tkinter as tk
from tkinter import ttk
from tkinter import scrolledtext
from tkinter import Menu
from tkinter import Spinbox
import B04829_Ch06_ToolTip as tt

from threading import Thread

GLOBAL_CONST = 42
```

Let's add a method to be created in a thread to our OOP class.

```
class OOP():
    def methodInAThread(self):
        print('Hi, how are you?')
```

We can now call our threaded method in the code, saving the instance in a variable.

```
#=======================
# Start GUI
#=======================
oop = OOP()

# Running methods in Threads
runT = Thread(target=oop.methodInAThread)
oop.win.mainloop())
```

Now we have a method that is threaded, but when we run the code, nothing gets printed to the console!

We have to start the Thread first before it can run and the next recipe will show us how to do this.

However, setting a breakpoint after the GUI main event loop proves that we did indeed create a Thread object, as can been seen in the Eclipse IDE Debugger.

How it works...

In this recipe, we prepared our GUI to use threads by first increasing the GUI size, so we could better see the results printed to the ScrolledText widget.

We then imported the Thread class from the Python threading module.

After that, we created a method that we call in a thread from within our GUI.

Starting a thread

This recipe will show us how to start a thread. It will also demonstrate why threads are necessary to keep our GUI responsive during long-running tasks.

Getting ready

Let's first see what happens when we call a function or method of our GUI that has some sleep associated with it without using threads.

We are using a sleep here to simulate a real-world application that might have to wait for a web server or database to respond or a large file transfer or complex computation to complete its task.

The sleep is a very realistic place-holder and shows the principle involved.

Adding a loop into our button callback method with some sleep time results in our GUI becoming unresponsive and, when we try to close the GUI, things get even worse.

```python
# Button callback
def clickMe(self):
    self.action.configure(text='Hello ' + self.name.get())
    # Non-threaded code with sleep freezes the GUI
    for idx in range(10):
        sleep(5)
        self.scr.insert(tk.INSERT, str(idx) + '\n')
```

If we wait long enough, the method will eventually complete but during this time none of our GUI widgets respond to click events. We solve this problem by using threads.

 In the previous recipe, we created a method to be run in a thread, but so far, the thread has not run!

Unlike regular Python functions and methods, we have to `start` a method that is going to be run in its own thread!

This is what we will do next.

How to do it...

First, let's move the creation of the thread into its own method and then call this method from the button callback method.

```
# Running methods in Threads
def createThread(self):
    runT = Thread(target=self.methodInAThread)
    runT.start()
# Button callback
def clickMe(self):
    self.action.configure(text='Hello ' + self.name.get())
    self.createThread()
```

Clicking the button now results in the `createThread` method being called which, in turn, calls the `methodInAThread` method.

First, we create a thread and target it at a method. Next, we start the thread that will run the targeted method in a new thread.

 The GUI itself runs in its own thread, which is the main thread of the application.

We can print out the instance of the thread.

```
# Running methods in Threads
def createThread(self):
    runT = Thread(target=self.methodInAThread)
    runT.start()
    print(runT)
```

Clicking the button now creates the following printout:

```
Console ☒
C:\EclipseWorkspace\Ch06\B04829_Ch06_Code\B04829_Ch06_GUI.py
Hi, how are you?
<Thread(Thread-1, started 412)>
```

When we click the button several times, we can see that each thread gets assigned a unique name and ID.

```
Console ☒
C:\EclipseWorkspace\Ch06\B04829_Ch06_Code\B04829_Ch06_GUI.py
Hi, how are you?
<Thread(Thread-1, started 412)>
Hi, how are you?
<Thread(Thread-2, started 8180)>
Hi, how are you?
<Thread(Thread-3, started 6736)>
```

Let's now move our code with the `sleep` in a loop into the `methodInAThread` method to verify that threads really do solve our problem.

```
def methodInAThread(self):
    print('Hi, how are you?')
    for idx in range(10):
        sleep(5)
        self.scr.insert(tk.INSERT, str(idx) + '\n')
```

When clicking the button, while the numbers are being printed into the `ScrolledText` widget with a five second delay, we can click around anywhere in our GUI, switch tabs, and so on. Our GUI has become responsive again because we are using threads!

How it works...

In this recipe, we called methods of our GUI class in their own threads and learned that we have to start the threads. Otherwise, the thread gets created but just sits there waiting for us to run its target method.

We noticed that each thread gets assigned a unique name and ID.

We simulated long-running tasks by inserting a `sleep` statement into our code, which showed us that threads can indeed solve our problem.

Stopping a thread

We have to start a thread to actually make it do something by calling the `start()` method, so, intuitively, we would expect there to be a matching `stop()` method, but there is no such thing. In this recipe, we will learn how to run a thread as a background task, which is called a daemon. When closing the main thread, which is our GUI, all daemons will automatically be stopped as well.

Getting ready

When we call methods in a thread, we can also pass arguments and keyword arguments to the method. We start this recipe by doing exactly that.

How to do it...

By adding `args=[8]` to the thread constructor and modifying the targeted method to expect arguments, we can pass arguments to threaded methods. The parameter to `args` has to be a sequence, so we will wrap our number in a Python list.

```python
def methodInAThread(self, numOfLoops=10):
    for idx in range(numOfLoops):
        sleep(1)
        self.scr.insert(tk.INSERT, str(idx) + '\n')
```

In the following code, `runT` is a local variable which we only access within the scope of the method inside of which we created `runT`.

```python
# Running methods in Threads
def createThread(self):
    runT = Thread(target=self.methodInAThread, args=[8])
    runT.start()
```

By turning the local variable into a member, we can then check if the thread is still running by calling `isAlive` on it from another method.

```python
# Running methods in Threads
def createThread(self):
    self.runT = Thread(target=self.methodInAThread, args=[8])
    self.runT.start()
    print(self.runT)
    print('createThread():', self.runT.isAlive())
```

In the preceding code, we have elevated our local `runT` variable to a member of our class. What this does is enable us to assess the `self.runT` variable from any method in our class.

This is achieved like this:

```python
def methodInAThread(self, numOfLoops=10):
    for idx in range(numOfLoops):
        sleep(1)
        self.scr.insert(tk.INSERT, str(idx) + '\n')
    sleep(1)
    print('methodInAThread():', self.runT.isAlive())
```

When we click the button and then exit the GUI, we can see that the print statement in the `createThread` method was printed, but we do not see the second print statement from `methodInAThread`.

Instead, we get a RuntimeError.

```
    def methodInAThread(self, numOfLoops=10):
        for idx in range(numOfLoops):
            sleep(1)
            self.scr.insert(tk.INSERT, str(idx) + '\n')
        sleep(1)
        print('methodInAThread():', self.runT.isAlive())

    # Running methods in Threads
    def createThread(self):
        self.runT = Thread(target=self.methodInAThread, args=[8])
        self.runT.start()
        print(self.runT)
        print('createThread():', self.runT.isAlive())
```

```
Console ⌗
<terminated> C:\EclipseWorkspace\Ch06\B04829_Ch06_Code\B04829_Ch06_GUI.py
<Thread(Thread-1, started 7124)>
createThread(): True
Exception in thread Thread-1:
Traceback (most recent call last):
  File "C:\Python34\lib\threading.py", line 920, in _bootstrap_inner
    self.run()
  File "C:\Python34\lib\threading.py", line 868, in run
    self._target(*self._args, **self._kwargs)
  File "C:\EclipseWorkspace\Ch06\B04829_Ch06_Code\B04829_Ch06_GUI.py", line 83, in methodInAThread
    self.scr.insert(tk.INSERT, str(idx) + '\n')
  File "C:\Python34\lib\tkinter\__init__.py", line 3140, in insert
    self.tk.call((self._w, 'insert', index, chars) + args)
RuntimeError: main thread is not in main loop
```

Threads are expected to finish their assigned task so when we close the GUI while the thread has not completed, Python tells us that the thread we started is not in the main event loop.

We can solve this by turning the thread into a daemon, which will then execute as a background task.

What this gives us is that, as soon as we close our GUI, which is our main thread starting other threads, the daemon threads will cleanly exit.

We can do this by calling the `setDaemon(True)` method on the thread before we start the thread.

```
# Running methods in Threads
def createThread(self):
    runT = Thread(target=self.methodInAThread)
    runT.setDaemon(True)
    runT.start()
    print(runT)
```

When we now click the button and exit our GUI while the thread has not yet completed its assigned task, we no longer get any errors.

```
# Running methods in Threads
def createThread(self):
    self.runT = Thread(target=self.methodInAThread, args=[8])
    self.runT.setDaemon(True)
    self.runT.start()
    print(self.runT)
    print('createThread():', self.runT.isAlive())
```

Console ☒

`<terminated>` C:\EclipseWorkspace\Ch06\B04829_Ch06_Code\B04829_Ch06_GUI.py

```
<Thread(Thread-1, started daemon 356)>
createThread(): True
```

How it works...

While there is a start method to make threads run, surprisingly there is not really an equivalent stop method.

In this recipe, we are running a method in a thread, which prints numbers to our `ScrolledText` widget.

When we exit our GUI, we are no longer interested in the thread that used to print to our widget, so, by turning the thread into a background daemon, we can exit our GUI cleanly.

How to use queues

A Python queue is a data structure that implements the first-in-first-out paradigm, basically working like a pipe. You shovel something into the pipe on one side and it falls out on the other side of the pipe.

The main difference between this queue shoveling, and shoveling mud into physical pipes is that, in Python queues, things do not get mixed up. You put one unit in, and that unit comes back out on the other side. Next, you place another unit in (say, for example, an instance of a class), and this entire unit will come back out on the other end as one integral piece.

It comes back out at the other end in the exact order we inserted code into the queue.

 A queue is not a stack where we push and pop data. A stack is a last-in-first-out (LIFO) data structure.

Queues are containers that hold data being fed into the queue from potentially different data sources. We can have different clients providing data to the queue whenever those clients have data available. Whichever client is ready to send data to our queue sends it, and we can then display this data in a widget or send it forward to other modules.

Using multiple threads to complete assigned tasks in a queue is very useful when receiving the final results of the processing and displaying them. The data is inserted at one end of the queue and then comes out of the other end in an ordered fashion, First-In-First-Out (FIFO).

Our GUI might have five different button widgets that each kick off different tasks that we want to display in our GUI in a widget (for example, a ScrolledText widget).

These five different tasks take a different amount of time to complete.

Whenever a task has completed, we immediately need to know this and display this information in our GUI.

By creating a shared Python queue and having the five tasks write their results to this queue, we can display the result of whatever task has been completed immediately using a FIFO approach.

Getting ready

As our GUI is ever increasing in its functionality and usefulness, it starts to talk to networks, processes, and websites, and will eventually have to wait for data to be made available for the GUI to represent.

Creating queues in Python solves the problem of waiting for data to be displayed inside our GUI.

How to do it...

In order to create queues in Python, we have to import the Queue class from the queue module. Add the following statement towards the top of our GUI module:

```
from threading import Thread
from time import sleep
from queue import Queue
```

That gets us started.

Next, we create a queue instance.

```
def useQueues(self):
    guiQueue = Queue()      # create queue instance
```

In the preceding code we create a local `Queue` instance that is only accessible within this method. If we wish to access this queue from other places, we have to turn it into a member of our class by using the `self` keyword which binds the local variable to the entire class, making it available from any other method within our class. In Python, we often create class instance variables in the `__init__ (self)` method but Python is very pragmatic and enables us to create those member variables anywhere in the code.

Now we have an instance of a queue. We can prove that this works by printing it out.

In order to put data into the queue, we use the `put` command. In order to get data out of the queue, we use the `get` command.

```
# Create Queue instance
def useQueues(self):
    guiQueue = Queue()
    print(guiQueue)
    guiQueue.put('Message from a queue')
    print(guiQueue.get())
```

Running the modified code results in the message first being placed in the `Queue`, and then being taken out of the `Queue`, and then printed to the console.

```
    # Create Queue instance
    def useQueues(self):
        guiQueue = Queue()
        print(guiQueue)
        guiQueue.put('Message from a queue')
        print(guiQueue.get())
```

```
Console
<terminated> C:\EclipseWorkspace\Ch06\B04829_Ch06_Code\B04829_Ch06_GUI.py
<queue.Queue object at 0x0000000002C0C278>
Message from a queue
```

We can place many messages into the queue.

```
# Create Queue instance
def useQueues(self):
    guiQueue = Queue()
    print(guiQueue)
    for idx in range(10):
        guiQueue.put('Message from a queue: ' + str(idx))
    print(guiQueue.get())
```

We have placed 10 messages into the `Queue`, but we are only getting the first one out. The other messages are still inside of the `Queue`, waiting to be taken out in a FIFO fashion.

```
🖳 Console ⊠
<terminated> C:\EclipseWorkspace\Ch06\B04829_Ch06_Code\B04829_Ch06_GUI.py
<queue.Queue object at 0x0000000002BF4710>
Message from a queue: 0
```

In order to get all messages that have been placed into a `Queue` out, we can create an endless loop.

```
# Create Queue instance
def useQueues(self):
    guiQueue = Queue()
    print(guiQueue)
    for idx in range(10):
        guiQueue.put('Message from a queue: ' + str(idx))

    while True:
        print(guiQueue.get())
```

```
🖳 Console ⊠
<terminated> C:\EclipseWorkspace\Ch06\B04829_Ch06_Code\B04829_Ch06_GUI.py
<queue.Queue object at 0x0000000002BB47B8>
Message from a queue: 0
Message from a queue: 1
Message from a queue: 2
Message from a queue: 3
Message from a queue: 4
Message from a queue: 5
Message from a queue: 6
Message from a queue: 7
Message from a queue: 8
Message from a queue: 9
```

While this code works, unfortunately it freezes our GUI. In order to fix this, we have to call the method in its own thread, as we did in previous recipes.

Let's run our method in a thread and tie it to the button event:

```python
# Running methods in Threads
def createThread(self, num):
    self.runT = Thread(target=self.methodInAThread, args=[num])
    self.runT.setDaemon(True)
    self.runT.start()
    print(self.runT)
    print('createThread():', self.runT.isAlive())

    # textBoxes are the Consumers of Queue data
    writeT = Thread(target=self.useQueues, daemon=True)
    writeT.start()

# Create Queue instance
def useQueues(self):
    guiQueue = Queue()
    print(guiQueue)
    for idx in range(10):
        guiQueue.put('Message from a queue: ' + str(idx))
    while True:
        print(guiQueue.get())
```

When we now click the action `Button`, we no longer get an extraneous pop-up window and the code works.

```
Console ⌗
<terminated> C:\EclipseWorkspace\Ch06\B04829_Ch06_Code\B04829_Ch06_GUI.py
<__main__.OOP object at 0x0000000002B56400>
hi from Queue <__main__.OOP object at 0x0000000002B56400>
<Thread(Thread-1, started daemon 7088)>
createThread(): True
<queue.Queue object at 0x0000000002D10470>
Message from a queue: 0
Message from a queue: 1
Message from a queue: 2
Message from a queue: 3
Message from a queue: 4
Message from a queue: 5
Message from a queue: 6
Message from a queue: 7
Message from a queue: 8
Message from a queue: 9
```

How it works...

We have created a Queue, placed messages into one side of the Queue in a first-in-first-out (aka FIFO) fashion. We got the messages out of the Queue and then printed them to the console (stdout).

We realized that we have to call the method in its own Thread.

Passing queues among different modules

In this recipe, we will pass Queues around different modules. As our GUI code increases in complexity, we want to separate the GUI components from the business logic, separating them out into different modules.

Modularization gives us code reuse and also makes the code more readable.

Once the data to be displayed in our GUI comes from different data sources, we will face latency issues, which is what Queues solve. By passing instances of Queues among different Python modules, we are separating the different concerns of the modules' functionalities.

The GUI code ideally would only be concerned with creating and displaying widgets.
The business logic modules' job is to only do the business logic.

We have to combine the two elements, ideally using as few relations among the different modules, reducing code interdependence.

The coding principle of avoiding unnecessary dependencies is usually called "loose coupling".

In order to understand the significance of loose coupling, we can draw some boxes on a whiteboard or a piece of paper. One box represents our GUI class and code, while the other boxes represent business logic, databases, and so on.

Next, we draw lines between the boxes, graphing out the interdependencies between those boxes which are our Python modules.

The fewer lines we have between our Python boxes, the more loosely-coupled our design is.

Getting ready

In the previous recipe, we have started to use `Queues`. In this recipe we will pass instances of a `Queue` from our main GUI thread to other Python modules, which will enable us to write to the `ScrolledText` widget from another module while keeping our GUI responsive.

How to do it...

First, we create a new Python module in our project. Let's call it `Queues.py`. We'll place a function into it (no OOP necessary yet) and pass it an instance of the queue.

We also pass a self-reference of the class that creates the GUI form and widgets, which enables us to use all of the GUI methods from another Python module.

We do this in the button callback.

 This is the magic of OOP. In the middle of a class, we pass ourselves into a function we are calling from within the class, using the `self` keyword.

The code now looks like this.

```
import B04829_Queues as bq

class OOP():
    # Button callback
    def clickMe(self):
      # Passing in the current class instance (self)
        print(self)
        bq.writeToScrol(self)
```

The imported module contains the function we are calling,

```
def writeToScrol(inst):
    print('hi from Queue', inst)
    inst.createThread(6)
```

We have commented out the call to `createThread` in the button callback because we are now calling it from our new module.

```
# Threaded method does not freeze our GUI
# self.createThread()
```

By passing in a self-reference from the class instance to the function the class is calling in another module, we now have access to all of our GUI elements from other Python modules.

Running the code creates the following result.

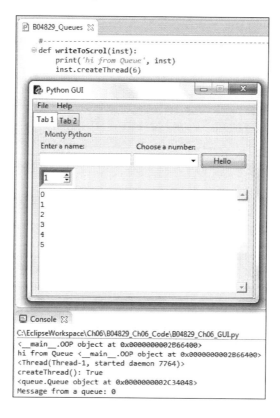

Next, we will create the `Queue` as a member of our class, placing a reference to it in the `__init__` method of the class.

```
class OOP():
    def __init__(self):
        # Create a Queue
        self.guiQueue = Queue()
```

Now we can put messages into the queue from our new module by simply using the passed-in class reference to our GUI.

```
def writeToScrol(inst):
    print('hi from Queue', inst)
    for idx in range(10):
```

```
        inst.guiQueue.put('Message from a queue: ' + str(idx))
    inst.createThread(6)
```

The `createThread` method in our GUI code now only reads from the queue, which got filled in by the business logic residing in our new module, which has separated the logic from our GUI module.

```
def useQueues(self):
    # Now using a class member Queue
    while True:
        print(self.guiQueue.get())
```

Running our modified code creates the same results. We have not broken anything (yet)!

How it works...

In order to separate the GUI widgets from the functionality that expresses the business logic, we created a class, made a queue a member of this class and, by passing an instance of the class into a function residing in a different Python module, we now have access to all of the GUI widgets as well as the `Queue`.

This recipe is an example of when it makes sense to program in OOP.

Using dialog widgets to copy files to your network

This recipe shows us how to copy files from your local hard drive to a network location.

We will do this by using one of Python's tkinter built-in dialogs, which enables us to browse our hard drive. We can then select a file to be copied.

This recipe also shows us how to make `Entry` widgets read-only and to default our `Entry` to a specified location, which speeds up the browsing of our hard drive.

Getting ready

We will extend **Tab 2** of the GUI we have been building in previous recipes.

How to do it...

Add the following code to our GUI in the `def createWidgets(self)` method towards the bottom where we created Tab Control 2.

The parent of the new widget frame is `tab2`, which we have created at the very beginning of the `createWidgets()` method. As long as you place the code shown as follows physically below the creation of `tab2`, it will work.

```
##############################################################
    def createWidgets(self):
        tabControl = ttk.Notebook(self.win)   # Create Tab
        tab2 = ttk.Frame(tabControl)          # Add a second tab
        tabControl.add(tab2, text='Tab 2')

# Create Manage Files Frame
mngFilesFrame = ttk.LabelFrame(tab2, text=' Manage Files: ')
mngFilesFrame.grid(column=0, row=1, sticky='WE', padx=10, pady=5)

# Button Callback
def getFileName():
    print('hello from getFileName')

# Add Widgets to Manage Files Frame
lb = ttk.Button(mngFilesFrame, text="Browse to File...",
command=getFileName)
lb.grid(column=0, row=0, sticky=tk.W)

file = tk.StringVar()
self.entryLen = scrolW
self.fileEntry = ttk.Entry(mngFilesFrame, width=self.entryLen,
textvariable=file)
self.fileEntry.grid(column=1, row=0, sticky=tk.W)

logDir = tk.StringVar()
self.netwEntry = ttk.Entry(mngFilesFrame, width=self.entryLen,
textvariable=logDir)
self.netwEntry.grid(column=1, row=1, sticky=tk.W)
        def copyFile():
        import shutil
        src  = self.fileEntry.get()
        file = src.split('/')[-1]
        dst  = self.netwEntry.get() + '\\'+ file
        try:
            shutil.copy(src, dst)
            mBox.showinfo('Copy File to Network',
                        'Success: File copied.')
```

```
        except FileNotFoundError as err:
            mBox.showerror('Copy File to Network',
                    '*** Failed to copy file! ***\n\n' + str(err))
        except Exception as ex:
            mBox.showerror('Copy File to Network',
                    '*** Failed to copy file! ***\n\n' + str(ex))

    cb = ttk.Button(mngFilesFrame, text="Copy File To :   ",
                    command=copyFile)
    cb.grid(column=0, row=1, sticky=tk.E)

    # Add some space around each label
    for child in mngFilesFrame.winfo_children():
        child.grid_configure(padx=6, pady=6)
```

This will add two buttons and two entries to **Tab 2** of our GUI.

We are not yet implementing the functionality of our button callback function.

Running the code creates the following GUI:

Clicking the **Browse to File...** button currently prints to the console.

We can use tkinter's built-in file dialogs so let's add the following `import` statements to the top of our Python GUI module.

```
from tkinter import filedialog as fd
from os import path
```

We can now use the dialogs in our code. Instead of hard-coding a path, we can use Python's os module to find the full path to where our GUI module resides.

```
def getFileName():
    print('hello from getFileName')
    fDir  = path.dirname(__file__)
    fName = fd.askopenfilename(parent=self.win, initialdir=fDir)
```

Clicking the browse button now opens up the `askopenfilename` dialog.

We can now open a file in this directory or browse to a different directory. After selecting a file and clicking the **Open** button in the dialog, we will save the full path to the file in the `fName` local variable.

It would be nice if, when we opened our Python `askopenfilename` dialog widget, we would automatically default to a directory so that we would not have to browse all the way to where we were looking for a particular file to be opened.

It is best to demonstrate how to do this by going back to our GUI **Tab 1**, which is what we will do next.

We can default values into Entry widgets. Back on our **Tab 1**, this is very easy. All we have to do is add the following two lines of code to the creation of the `Entry` widget.

```
# Adding a Textbox Entry widget
self.name = tk.StringVar()
nameEntered = ttk.Entry(self.monty, width=24, textvariable=self.name)
nameEntered.grid(column=0, row=1, sticky='W')
nameEntered.delete(0, tk.END)
nameEntered.insert(0, '< default name >')
```

When we now run the GUI, the `nameEntered` Entry has a default value.

We can get the full path to the module we are using with the following Python syntax and then we can create a new subfolder just below it. We can do this as a module level global, or we can create the subfolder within a method.

```
# Module level GLOBALS
GLOBAL_CONST = 42
fDir    = path.dirname(__file__)
netDir = fDir + '\\Backup'


def __init__(self):
    self.createWidgets()
    self.defaultFileEntries()
```

```
def defaultFileEntries(self):
    self.fileEntry.delete(0, tk.END)
    self.fileEntry.insert(0, fDir)
    if len(fDir) > self.entryLen:
        self.fileEntry.config(width=len(fDir) + 3)
        self.fileEntry.config(state='readonly')

    self.netwEntry.delete(0, tk.END)
    self.netwEntry.insert(0, netDir)
    if len(netDir) > self.entryLen:
        self.netwEntry.config(width=len(netDir) + 3)
```

We are setting defaults for both entry widgets and, after setting them, we make the local file entry widget read-only.

This order is important. We have to first populate the entry before we make it read-only.

We are also selecting **Tab 2** before calling the main event loop and no longer set the focus into the `Entry` of **Tab 1**. Calling `select` on our tkinter `notebook` is zero-based so by passing in the value of 1 we select **Tab 2**...

```
# Place cursor into name Entry
# nameEntered.focus()
tabControl.select(1)
```

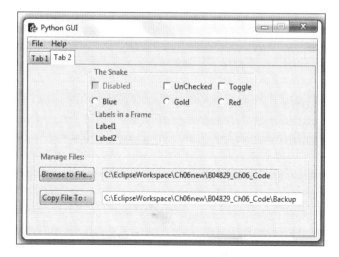

As we are not all on the same network, this recipe will use the local hard drive as an example for a network.

A UNC path is a Universal Naming Convention and what this means is that we can access a server on our network by using double backslashes to access a network server instead of the typical `C:\` when we access our local hard drive on a Windows PC.

 You just have to use the UNC and replace `C:\` with `\\<server name>\<folder>\`.

This example can be used to back up our code to a backup directory, which we can create if it does not exist by using `os.makedirs`.

```
# Module level GLOBALS
GLOBAL_CONST = 42

from os import makedirs
fDir    = path.dirname(__file__)
netDir = fDir + '\\Backup'
if not path.exists(netDir):
    makedirs(netDir, exist_ok = True)
```

After selecting a file to copy to somewhere else, we import the Python `shutil` module. We need the full path to the source of the file to be copied, a network or local directory path, and then we append the file name to the path where we are going to copy it, using `shutil.copy`.

 Shutil is short-hand notation for shell utility.

We also give feedback to the user via a message box to indicate whether the copying succeeded or failed. In order to do this, import `messagebox` and rename it `mBox`.

In the following code, we will mix two different approaches of where to place our import statements. In Python, we have some flexibility that other languages do not provide.

We typically place all of the import statements towards the very top of each of our Python modules so that it is clear which modules we are importing.

At the same time, a modern coding approach is to place the creation of variables close to the function or method where they are first being used.

In the following code, we import the message box at the top of our Python module, but then we also import the shutil Python module in a function.

Why would we wish to do this?

Does this even work?

The answer is, yes, it does work, and we are placing this import statement into a function because this is the only place in our code where we actually do need this module.

If we never call this method, then we will never import the module this method requires.

In a sense, you can view this technique as the lazy initialization design pattern.

If we don't need it, we don't import it until we really do require it in our Python code.

The idea here is that our entire code might require, let's say, twenty different modules. At runtime, which modules are really needed depends upon the user interaction. If we never call the `copyFile()` function then there is no need to import `shutil`.

Once we click the button that invokes the `copyFile()` function in this function, we import the required module.

```python
from tkinter import messagebox as mBox

def copyFile():
    import shutil
    src = self.fileEntry.get()
    file = src.split('/')[-1]
    dst = self.netwEntry.get() + '\\'+ file
    try:
      shutil.copy(src, dst)
      mBox.showinfo('Copy File to Network', 'Success: File copied.')
    except FileNotFoundError as err:
      mBox.showerror('Copy File to Network',
          '*** Failed to copy file! ***\n\n' + str(err))
    except Exception as ex:
      mBox.showerror('Copy File to Network',
          '*** Failed to copy file! ***\n\n' + str(ex))
```

When we now run our GUI and browse to a file and click copy, the file is copied to the location we specified in our `Entry` widget.

If the file does not exist or we forgot to browse to a file and are trying to copy the entire parent folder, the code will let us know this as well because we are using Python's built-in exception handling capabilities.

How it works...

We are copying files from our local hard drive to a network by using the Python shell utility. As most of us are not connected to the same local area network, we simulate the copying by backing up our code to a different local folder.

We are using one of tkinter's dialog controls and, by defaulting directory paths, we can increase our efficiency in copying files.

Using TCP/IP to communicate via networks

This recipe shows you how to use sockets to communicate via TCP/IP. In order to achieve this, we need both an IP address and a port number.

In order to keep things simple and independent of the ever-changing internet IP addresses, we will create our own local TCP/IP server and, as a client, learn how to connect to it and read data from a TCP/IP connection.

We will integrate this networking capability into our GUI by using the queues we created in previous recipes.

Getting ready

We will create a new Python module, which will be the TCP server.

How to do it...

One way to implement a TCP server in Python is to inherit from the `socketserver` module. We subclass `BaseRequestHandler` and then override the inherited `handle` method. In very few lines of Python code, we can implement a TCP server module.

```python
from socketserver import BaseRequestHandler, TCPServer

class RequestHandler(BaseRequestHandler):
    # override base class handle method
    def handle(self):
        print('Server connected to: ', self.client_address)
        while True:
            rsp = self.request.recv(512)
            if not rsp: break
            self.request.send(b'Server received: ' + rsp)

def startServer():
    serv = TCPServer(('', 24000), RequestHandler)
    serv.serve_forever()
```

We are passing in our `RequestHandler` class into a `TCPServer` initializer. The empty single quotes are a short cut for passing in localhost, which is our own PC. This is the IP address of 127.0.0.1. The second item in the tuple is the port number. We can choose any port number that is not in use on our local PC.

We just have to make sure that we are using the same port on the client side of the TCP connection, otherwise we would not be able to connect to the server. Of course, we have to start the server first before clients can connect to it.

We will modify our `Queues.py` module to become the TCP client.

```
from socket import socket, AF_INET, SOCK_STREAM

def writeToScrol(inst):
    print('hi from Queue', inst)
    sock = socket(AF_INET, SOCK_STREAM)
    sock.connect(('localhost', 24000))
    for idx in range(10):
        sock.send(b'Message from a queue: ' + bytes(str(idx).encode())
)
        recv = sock.recv(8192).decode()
        inst.guiQueue.put(recv)
    inst.createThread(6)
```

This is all the code we need to talk to the TCP server. In this example, we are simply sending some bytes to the server and the server sends them back, prepending some strings before returning the response.

This shows the principle of how TCP communications via networks work.

Once we know how to connect to a remote server via TCP/IP, we will use whatever commands are designed by the protocol of the program we are interested in communicating with. The first step is to connect before we can send commands to specific applications residing on a server.

In the `writeToScrol` function, we will use the same loop as before but now we will send the messages to the TCP server. The server modifies the received message and then sends it back to us. Next, we place it into the GUI member queue which, as in previous recipes, runs in its own `Thread`.

In Python 3, we have to send strings over sockets in binary format. Adding the integer index now becomes a little bit convoluted as we have to cast it to a string, encode it, and then cast the encoded string into bytes!

```
sock.send(b'Message from a queue: ' + bytes(str(idx).encode()) )
```

Note the b before the string and then, well, all the rest of the required casting...

We are starting the TCP server in its own thread in the initializer of the OOP class.

```
class OOP():
    def __init__(self):
    # Start TCP/IP server in its own thread
        svrT = Thread(target=startServer, daemon=True)
        svrT.start()
```

Clicking the **Click Me!** button on **Tab 1** now creates the following output in our `ScrolledText` widget, as well as on the console, and the response, due to using `Threads`, is very fast.

How it works...

We created a TCP server to simulate connecting to a server in our local area network or on the Internet. We turned our queues module into a TCP client. We are running both the queue and the server in their own background thread, which keeps our GUI very responsive.

Using URLOpen to read data from websites

This recipe shows how we can easily read entire webpages by using Python's built-in modules. We will display the webpage data first in its raw format and then decode it, and then we will display it in our GUI.

Getting ready

We will read the data from a webpage and then display it in the `ScrolledText` widget of our GUI.

How to do it...

First, we create a new Python module and name it `URL.py`.

We then import the required functionality to read webpages using Python.

We can do this in very few lines of code.

We are wrapping our code in a `try...except` block similar to Java and C#. This is a modern approach to coding which Python supports.

Whenever we have code that might not complete we can experiment with this code and, if it works, all is fine.

If the block of code in the `try...except` block does not work, the Python interpreter will throw one of several possible exceptions, which we then can catch. Once we have caught the exception we can decide what to do next.

There is a hierarchy of exceptions in Python and we can also create our own classes that inherit from and extend the Python exception classes.

In the code shown as follows, we are mainly concerned that the URL we are trying to open might not be available and so we wrap our code within a `try...except` code block.

If the code succeeds in opening the requested URL, all is fine.

If it fails, maybe because our internet connection is down, we fall into the exception part of the code and print out that an exception has occurred.

 You can read more about Python exception handling at `https://docs.python.org/3.4/library/exceptions.html`.

```
from urllib.request import urlopen
link = 'http://python.org/'
try:
    f = urlopen(link)
    print(f)
    html = f.read()
    print(html)
```

```
    htmldecoded = html.decode()
    print(htmldecoded)

except Exception as ex:
    print('*** Failed to get Html! ***\n\n' + str(ex))
```

By calling `urlopen` on the official Python website, we get the entire data as one long string.

The first print statement prints this long string out to the console.

We then call `decode` on the result and this time we get a little over 1,000 lines of web data, including some whitespace.

We are also printing out the type of calling `urlopen`, which is an `http.client.HTTPResponse` object. Actually, we are printing it out first.

Here is the official Python webpage we just read. If you are a web developer, you probably have some good ideas what to do with the parsed data.

We next display this data in our GUI inside the `ScrolledText` widget. In order to do so, we have to connect our new module to read the data from the webpage to our GUI.

In order to do this, we need a reference to our GUI, and one way to do this is by tying our new module to the **Tab 1** button callback.

We can return the decoded HTML data from the Python webpage to the `Button` widget, which we can then place in the `ScrolledText` control.

So, let's turn our code into a function and return the data to the calling code.

```
from urllib.request import urlopen
link = 'http://python.org/'
def getHtml():
    try:
        f = urlopen(link)
        #print(f)
        html = f.read()
        #print(html)
        htmldecoded = html.decode()
        #print(htmldecoded)
    except Exception as ex:
        print('*** Failed to get Html! ***\n\n' + str(ex))
    else:
        return htmldecoded
```

We can now write the data in our `button` callback method to the `ScrolledText` control by first importing the new module and then inserting the data into the widget. We also give it some sleep after the call to `writeToScrol`.

```
import B04829_Ch06_URL as url

# Button callback
def clickMe(self):
  bq.writeToScrol(self)
  sleep(2)
  htmlData = url.getHtml()
  print(htmlData)
  self.scr.insert(tk.INSERT, htmlData)
```

The HTML data is now displayed in our GUI widget.

How it works...

We create a new module to separate the code that gets the data from a webpage from our GUI code. This is always a good thing to do. We read in the webpage data and then return it to the calling code after decoding it. We then use the button callback function to place the returned data in the `ScrolledText` control.

This chapter introduced us to some advanced Python programming concepts, which we combined to produce a functional GUI program.

7

Storing Data in Our MySQL Database via Our GUI

In this chapter we will enhance our Python GUI by connecting to a MySQL database.

- ▸ Connecting to a MySQL database from Python
- ▸ Configuring the MySQL connection
- ▸ Designing the Python GUI database
- ▸ Using the SQL INSERT command
- ▸ Using the SQL UPDATE command
- ▸ Using the SQL DELETE command
- ▸ Storing and retrieving data from our MySQL database

Introduction

Before we can connect to a MySQL server, we have to have access to a MySQL server. The first recipe in this chapter will show you how to install the free MySQL Server Community Edition.

After successfully connecting to a running instance of our MySQL server, we will design and create a database that will accept a book title, which could be our own journal or a quote we found somewhere on the Internet. We will require a page number for the book, which could be blank, and then we will insert the quote we like from a book, journal, website or friend into our MySQL database using our GUI built in Python 3.

We will insert, modify, delete and display our favorite quotes using our Python GUI to issue these SQL commands and to display the data.

 CRUD is a database term you might come across that abbreviates the four basic SQL commands and stands for **Create**, **Read**, **Update**, and **Delete**.

Connecting to a MySQL database from Python

Before we can connect to a MySQL database, we have to connect to the MySQL server.

In order to do this, we need to know the IP address of the MySQL server as well as the port it is listening on.

We also have to be a registered user with a password in order to get authenticated by the MySQL server.

Getting ready

You will need to have access to a running MySQL server instance and you also need to have administrator privileges in order to create databases and tables.

There is a free MySQL Community Edition available from the official MySQL website. You can download and install it on your local PC from: `http://dev.mysql.com/downloads/`

 In this chapter, we are using MySQL Community Server (GPL) Release: 5.6.26.

How to do it...

In order to connect to MySQL, we first need to install a special Python connector driver. This driver will enable us to talk to the MySQL server from Python.

The driver is freely available on the MySQL website and comes with a very nice online tutorial. You can install it from:

`http://dev.mysql.com/doc/connector-python/en/index.html`

Make sure you choose the installer that matches the version of Python you have installed. In this chapter, we are using the installer for Python 3.4.

There is currently a little bit of a surprise at the end of the installation process. When we start the `.msi` installer we briefly see a MessageBox showing the progress of the installation, but then it disappears. We get no confirmation that the installation actually succeeded.

One way to verify that we installed the correct driver, that lets Python talk to MySQL, is by looking into the Python site-packages directory.

If your site-packages directory looks similar to the following screenshot and you see some new files that have `mysql_connector_python` in their name, well, then we did indeed install something...

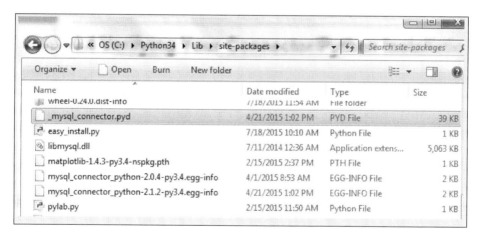

The official MySQL website mentioned above comes with a tutorial, at the following URL:

```
http://dev.mysql.com/doc/connector-python/en/connector-python-
tutorials.html
```

The online tutorial example on how to verify that installing the Connector/Python driver worked is a little bit misleading as it tries to connect to an employees' database that did not get created automatically, at least in my Community Edition.

The way to verify that our Connector/Python driver really did get installed is by just connecting to the MySQL server without specifying a particular database and then printing out the connection object.

> Replace the placeholder bracketed names `<adminUser>` and `<adminPwd>` with the real credentials you are using in your MySQL installation.
>
> If you installed the MySQL Community Edition, you are the administrator and will have chosen both a username and password during the MySQL installation.

```
import mysql.connector as mysql

conn = mysql.connect(user=<adminUser>, password=<adminPwd>,
                     host='127.0.0.1')
print(conn)

conn.close()
```

If running the preceding code results in the following output printed to the console, then we are good.

```
Console 
<terminated> C:\EclipseWorkspace\Ch07\B04829_Ch07_Code\B04829_Ch07_MySQL.py
<mysql.connector.connection.MySQLConnection object at 0x0000000000601978>
```

If you are not able to connect to the MySQL server, then something probably went wrong during the installation. If this is the case, try uninstalling MySQL, reboot your PC, and then run the MySQL installation again. Double-check that you downloaded the MySQL installer to match your version of Python. If you have more than one version of Python installed, that sometimes leads to confusion as the one you installed last gets prepended to the Windows path environmental variable and some installers just use the first Python version they can find in this location.

That happened to me when I installed a Python 32-bit version in addition to my 64-bit version and I was puzzled why some of my downloaded modules did not work.

The installers downloaded the 32-bit modules, which are incompatible with a 64-bit version of Python.

How it works...

In order to connect our GUI to a MySQL server, we need to be able to connect to the server with administrative privileges if we want to create our own database.

If the database already exists, then we just need the authorization rights to connect, insert, update, and delete data.

We will create a new database on a MySQL server in the next recipe.

Configuring the MySQL connection

In the previous recipe, we used the shortest way to connect to a MySQL server by hard-coding the credentials required for authentication into the `connection` method. While this is a fast approach for early development, we definitely do not want to expose our MySQL server credentials to anybody unless we *grant* permission to databases, tables, views, and related database commands to specific users.

A much safer way to get authenticated by a MySQL server is by storing the credentials in a configuration file, which is what we will do in this recipe.

We will use our configuration file to connect to the MySQL server and then create our own database on the MySQL server.

 We will use this database in all of the following recipes.

Getting ready

Access to a running MySQL server with administrator privileges is required to run the code shown in this recipe.

 The previous recipe shows how to install the free Community Edition of MySQL Server. The administrator privileges will enable you to implement this recipe.

How to do it...

First, we create a dictionary in the same module of the `MySQL.py` code.

```
# create dictionary to hold connection info
dbConfig = {
    'user': <adminName>,       # use your admin name
    'password': <adminPwd>,    # use your admin password
    'host': '127.0.0.1',       # IP address of localhost
    }
```

Next, in the connection method, we unpack the dictionary values. Instead of writing,

```
mysql.connect('user': <adminName>,  'password': <adminPwd>, 'host':
'127.0.0.1')
```

we use `(**dbConfig)`, which does the same as above but is much shorter.

```
import mysql.connector as mysql
# unpack dictionary credentials
conn = mysql.connect(**dbConfig)
print(conn)
```

This results in the same successful connection to the MySQL server, but the difference is that the connection method no longer exposes any mission-critical information.

 A database server is critical to your mission. You realize this once you have lost your valuable data...and can't find any recent backup!

```
Console ⊠
<terminated> C:\EclipseWorkspace\Ch07\B04829_Ch07_Code\B04829_Ch07_MySQL.py
<mysql.connector.connection.MySQLConnection object at 0x0000000000531978>
```

Now, placing the same username, password, database, and so on into a dictionary in the same Python module does not eliminate the risk of having the credentials seen by anyone perusing the code.

In order to increase database security, we first move the dictionary into its own Python module. Let's call the new Python module `GuiDBConfig.py`.

We then import this module and unpack the credentials, as we did before.

```
import GuiDBConfig as guiConf
# unpack dictionary credentials
conn = mysql.connect(**guiConf.dbConfig)
print(conn)
```

 Once we place this module into a secure place, separated from the rest of the code, we have achieved a better level of security for our MySQL data.

Now that we know how to connect to MySQL and have administrator privileges, we can create our own database by issuing the following commands:

```
GUIDB = 'GuiDB'

# unpack dictionary credentials
conn = mysql.connect(**guiConf.dbConfig)

cursor = conn.cursor()

try:
    cursor.execute("CREATE DATABASE {} DEFAULT CHARACTER SET 'utf8'".
format(GUIDB))

except mysql.Error as err:
    print("Failed to create DB: {}".format(err))

conn.close()
```

In order to execute commands to MySQL, we create a cursor object from the connection object.

A cursor is usually a place in a specific row in a database table, which we move up or down the table, but here we use it to create the database itself.

We wrap the Python code into a `try...except` block and use the built-in error codes of MySQL to tell us if anything went wrong.

We can verify that this block works by executing the database-creating code twice. The first time, it will create a new database in MySQL, and the second time it will print out an error message stating that this database already exists.

We can verify which databases exist by executing the following MySQL command using the very same cursor object syntax.

Instead of issuing the CREATE DATABASE command, we create a cursor and use it to execute the SHOW DATABASES command, the result of which we fetch and print to the console output.

```
import mysql.connector as mysql
import GuiDBConfig as guiConf

# unpack dictionary credentials
conn = mysql.connect(**guiConf.dbConfig)

cursor = conn.cursor()

cursor.execute("SHOW DATABASES")
print(cursor.fetchall())

conn.close()
```

 We retrieve the results by calling the fetchall method on the cursor object.

Running this code shows us which databases currently exist in our MySQL server instance. As we can see from the output, MySQL ships with several built-in databases, such as information_schema, and so on. We have successfully created our own guidb database, which is shown in the output. All other databases illustrated come shipped with MySQL.

```
Console ⌗                                                              ▣ ✖ ✖ ◐
<terminated> C:\EclipseWorkspace\Ch07\B04829_Ch07_Code\B04829_Ch07_MySQL.py
[('information_schema',), ('guidb',), ('mysql',), ('performance_schema',), ('sakila',), ('test',), ('world',)]
```

Note how, even though we specified the database when we created it in mixed-case letters as GuiDB, the SHOW DATABASES command shows all existing databases in MySQL in lower-case and displays our database as guidb.

How it works...

In order to connect our Python GUI to a MySQL database, we first have to know how to connect to the MySQL server. This requires establishing a connection and this connection will only be accepted by MySQL if we are able to provide the required credentials.

While it is easy to place strings into one line of Python code, when we deal with databases we have to be really thoughtful, because today's personal sandbox development environment, by tomorrow, could easily end up being accessible on the World Wide Web.

You do not want to compromise database security and the first part of this recipe showed ways to be more secure by placing the connection credentials to the MySQL server into a separate file, and by placing this file into a location where it is not accessible from the outside world, our database system will become more secure.

In a real-world production environment, both the MySQL server installation, connection credentials and this dbConfig file would be handled by IT system administrators who would enable you to import the dbConfig file to connect to the MySQL server without you knowing what the actual credentials are. Unpacking dbConfig would not expose the credentials as it does in our code.

The second part created our own database in a MySQL server instance and we will extend and use this database in the very next recipes, combining it with our Python GUI.

Designing the Python GUI database

Before we start creating tables and inserting data into them we have to design the database. Unlike changing local Python variable names, changing a database schema once it has been created and loaded with data is not that easy.

We would have to DROP the table, which means we would lose all the data that was in the table. So, before dropping a table, we would have to extract the data, then DROP the table, and recreate it under a different name and finally reimport the original data.

You get the picture...

Designing our GUI MySQL database means first thinking about what we want our Python application to do with it and then choose names for our tables that match the intended purpose.

Getting ready

We are working with the MySQL database we created in the previous recipe. A running instance of MySQL is necessary and the two previous recipes show how to install MySQL and all necessary additional drivers, as well as how to create the database we are using in this chapter.

How to do it...

First, we move widgets from our Python GUI around between the two tabs we created in the previous recipes, in order to organize our Python GUI better to connect to a MySQL database.

We rename several widgets and separate the code that accesses the MySQL data to what used to be named Tab 1, and we will move unrelated widgets to what we called in earlier recipes Tab 2.

We also adjust some internal Python variable names in order to understand our code better.

 Code readability is a coding virtue and not a waste of time.

Our refactored Python GUI now looks like the following screenshot. We have renamed the first tab as MySQL and created two tkinter LabelFrame widgets. We labeled the one on the top, Python Database, and it contains two labels and six tkinter entry widgets plus three buttons, which we aligned in four rows and three columns using the tkinter grid layout manager.

We will enter book titles and pages into the entry widgets and clicking the buttons will result in either inserting, retrieving, or modifying book quotations.

The LabelFrame at the bottom has a label of **Book Quotation** and the ScrolledText widget that is part of this frame will display our books and quotations.

We will create two SQL tables to hold our data. The first will hold the data for the book title and the book page. We will then join with the second table, which will hold the book quotation.

We will link the two tables together via primary to foreign key relations.

So, let's create the first database table now.

Before we do that, let's verify first that our database indeed has no tables. According to the online MySQL documentation, the command to view the tables that exist in a database is as follows.

13.7.5.38 SHOW TABLES syntax:

```
SHOW [FULL] TABLES [{FROM | IN} db_name]
        [LIKE 'pattern' | WHERE expr]
```

It is important to note that, in the preceding syntax, arguments in square brackets such as FULL are optional while arguments in curly braces such as FROM are required in the description for the SHOW TABLES command. The pipe symbol between FROM and IN means that the MySQL syntax requires one or the other.

```
# unpack dictionary credentials
conn = mysql.connect(**guiConf.dbConfig)
# create cursor
cursor = conn.cursor()
# execute command
cursor.execute("SHOW TABLES FROM guidb")
print(cursor.fetchall())

# close connection to MySQL
conn.close()
```

When we execute the SQL command in Python we get the expected result, which is an empty list, showing us that our database currently has no tables.

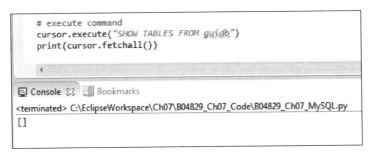

We can also first select the database by executing the USE <DB> command. Now, we don't have to pass it into the SHOW TABLES command because we already selected the database we want to talk to.

The following code creates the same true result as did the previous one:

```
cursor.execute("USE guidb")
cursor.execute("SHOW TABLES")
```

Now that we know how to verify that our database has no tables, let's create some. After we have created two tables, we will verify that they have truly made it into our database by using the same commands as before.

We create the first table, named `Books`, by executing the following code.

```
# connect by unpacking dictionary credentials
conn = mysql.connect(**guiConf.dbConfig)

# create cursor
cursor = conn.cursor()

# select DB
cursor.execute("USE guidb")

# create Table inside DB
cursor.execute("CREATE TABLE Books (            \
        Book_ID INT NOT NULL AUTO_INCREMENT,  \
        Book_Title VARCHAR(25) NOT NULL,      \
        Book_Page INT NOT NULL,               \
        PRIMARY KEY (Book_ID)                 \
    ) ENGINE=InnoDB")

# close connection to MySQL
conn.close()
```

We can verify that the table was created in our database by executing the following commands.

Now the result is no longer an empty list but a list that contains a tuple, showing the `books` table we just created.

We can use the MySQL command line client to see the columns in our table. In order to do this, we have to log in as the root user. We also have to append a semicolon to the end of the command.

On Windows, you simply double-click the MySQL command line client shortcut, which is automatically installed during the MySQL installation.

If you don't have a shortcut on your desktop, you can find the executable at the following path for a typical default installation:

`C:\Program Files\MySQL\MySQL Server 5.6\bin\mysql.exe`

Without a shortcut to run the MySQL client, you have to pass it some parameters:

- `C:\Program Files\MySQL\MySQL Server 5.6\bin\mysql.exe`
- `--defaults-file=C:\ProgramData\MySQL\MySQL Server 5.6\my.ini`
- `-uroot`
- `-p`

Either double-clicking the shortcut, or using the command line with the full path to the executable and passing in the required parameters, will bring up the MySQL command line client which prompts you to enter the password for the root user.

If you remember the password you assigned to the root user during the installation, you can then run the `SHOW COLUMNS FROM books;` command, as shown below. This will display the columns of our `books` table from our guidb.

 When executing commands in the MySQL client, the syntax is not Pythonic.

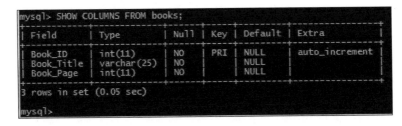

Next, we will create the second table that will store the book and journal quotations. We will create it by executing the following code:

```
# select DB
cursor.execute("USE guidb")

# create second Table inside DB
cursor.execute("CREATE TABLE Quotations ( \
        Quote_ID INT,                       \
        Quotation VARCHAR(250),             \
        Books_Book_ID INT,                  \
        FOREIGN KEY (Books_Book_ID)         \
            REFERENCES Books(Book_ID)       \
            ON DELETE CASCADE               \
    ) ENGINE=InnoDB")
```

Executing the SHOW TABLES command now shows that our database has two tables.

```
# execute command
cursor.execute("SHOW TABLES FROM guidb")
print(cursor.fetchall())
```

Console ⋈ Bookmarks
<terminated> C:\EclipseWorkspace\Ch07\B04829_Ch07_Code\B04829_Ch07_MySQL.py
[('books',), ('quotations',)]

We can see the columns by executing the SQL command using Python.

```
# execute command
cursor.execute("SHOW COLUMNS FROM quotations")
print(cursor.fetchall())

# close connection to MySQL
conn.close()
```

Console ⋈ Bookmarks
<terminated> C:\EclipseWorkspace\Ch07\B04829_Ch07_Code\B04829_Ch07_MySQL.py
[('Quote_ID', 'int(11)', 'YES', '', None, ''), ('Quotation', 'varchar(250)', 'YES', '', None, ''), ('Books_Book_ID', 'int(11)', 'YES', 'MUL', None, '')]

Using the MySQL client might present the data in a better format. We could also use Python's pretty print (pprint) feature.

```
from pprint import pprint

# execute command
cursor.execute("SHOW COLUMNS FROM quotations")
pprint(cursor.fetchall())

# close connection to MySQL
conn.close()
```

Console ⊠ Bookmarks
<terminated> C:\EclipseWorkspace\Ch07\B04829_Ch07_Code\B04829_Ch07_MySQL.py
```
[('Quote_ID', 'int(11)', 'YES', '', None, ''),
 ('Quotation', 'varchar(250)', 'YES', '', None, ''),
 ('Books_Book_ID', 'int(11)', 'YES', 'MUL', None, '')]
```

The MySQL client still shows our columns in a clearer format which can be seen when you run this client.

How it works...

We designed our Python GUI database and refactored our GUI in preparation to use our new database. We then created a MySQL database and created two tables within it.

We verified that the tables made it into our database by using both Python and the MySQL client that ships with the MySQL server.

In the next recipe, we will insert data into our tables.

Using the SQL INSERT command

This recipe presents the entire Python code that shows you how to create and drop MySQL databases and tables, as well as how to display the existing databases, tables, columns, and data of our MySQL instance.

After creating the database and tables, we will insert data into the two tables we are creating in this recipe.

We are using a primary to foreign key relationship to connect the data of the two tables.

We will go into the details of how this works in the following two recipes, where we modify and delete the data in our MySQL database.

Getting ready

This recipe builds on the MySQL database we created in the previous recipe and also shows you how to drop and recreate the GuiDB.

 Dropping the database of course deletes all data the database had in its tables, so we will also show you how to re-insert that data.

How to do it...

The entire code of our `MySQL.py` module is present in the code folder of this chapter, which is available for download from Packt Publishing's website. It creates the database, adds tables to it, and then inserts data into the two tables we created.

Here we will outline the code without showing all implementation details in order to preserve space, because it would take too many pages to show the entire code.

```python
import mysql.connector as mysql
import GuiDBConfig as guiConf

class MySQL():
    # class variable
    GUIDB  = 'GuiDB'

    #------------------------------------------------------------
    def connect(self):
        # connect by unpacking dictionary credentials
        conn = mysql.connector.connect(**guiConf.dbConfig)

        # create cursor
        cursor = conn.cursor()

        return conn, cursor

    #------------------------------------------------------------
```

```python
    def close(self, cursor, conn):
        # close cursor


#-------------------------------------------------------------
    def showDBs(self):
        # connect to MySQL


#-------------------------------------------------------------
    def createGuiDB(self):
        # connect to MySQL


#-------------------------------------------------------------
    def dropGuiDB(self):
        # connect to MySQL


#-------------------------------------------------------------
    def useGuiDB(self, cursor):
        '''Expects open connection.'''
        # select DB



#-------------------------------------------------------------
    def createTables(self):
        # connect to MySQL

        # create Table inside DB

#-------------------------------------------------------------
    def dropTables(self):
        # connect to MySQL


#-------------------------------------------------------------
    def showTables(self):
        # connect to MySQL


#-------------------------------------------------------------
    def insertBooks(self, title, page, bookQuote):
        # connect to MySQL

        # insert data
```

```
#---------------------------------------------------------
def insertBooksExample(self):
    # connect to MySQL

    # insert hard-coded data

#---------------------------------------------------------
def showBooks(self):
    # connect to MySQL

#---------------------------------------------------------
def showColumns(self):
    # connect to MySQL


#---------------------------------------------------------
def showData(self):
    # connect to MySQL

#---------------------------------------------------------
if __name__ == '__main__':

    # Create class instance
    mySQL = MySQL()
```

Running the preceding code creates the following tables and data in the database we created.

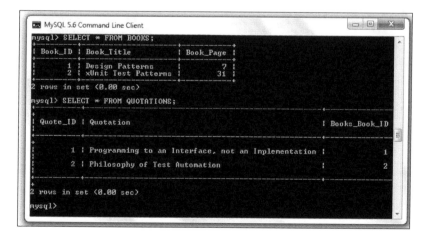

How it works...

We have created a MySQL database, established a connection to it, and then created two tables that hold the data for a favorite book or journal quotation.

We have distributed the data between two tables because the quotations tend to be rather large while the book titles and book page numbers are very short. By doing this, we can increase the efficiency of our database.

> In SQL database language, separating data into separate tables is called normalization.

Using the SQL UPDATE command

This recipe will use the code from the previous recipe, explain it in more detail, and then extend the code to update our data.

In order to update data we have previously inserted into our MySQL database tables, we use the SQL UPDATE command.

Getting ready

This recipe builds on the previous recipe, so read and study the previous recipe in order to follow the coding in this recipe where we modify existing data.

How to do it...

First, we will display the data to be modified by running the following Python to MySQL command:

```
import mysql.connector as mysql
import GuiDBConfig as guiConf

class MySQL():
    # class variable
    GUIDB   = 'GuiDB'
    #--------------------------------------------------------
    def showData(self):
        # connect to MySQL
```

```
        conn, cursor = self.connect()

        self.useGuiDB(cursor)

        # execute command
        cursor.execute("SELECT * FROM books")
        print(cursor.fetchall())

        cursor.execute("SELECT * FROM quotations")
        print(cursor.fetchall())

        # close cursor and connection
        self.close(cursor, conn)
#==========================================================
if __name__ == '__main__':
    # Create class instance
    mySQL = MySQL()
    mySQL.showData()
```

Running the code creates the following result:

```
 Console ☒   Bookmarks
<terminated> C:\EclipseWorkspace\Ch07\B04829_Ch07_Code\B04829_Ch07_MySQL.py
[(1, 'Design Patterns', 7), (2, 'xUnit Test Patterns', 31)]
[(1, 'Programming to an Interface, not an Implementation', 1), (2, 'Philosophy of Test Automation', 2)]
```

We might not agree with the "Gang of Four", so let's change their famous programming quote.

 The Gang of Four are the four authors who created the world famous book called *Design Patterns,* which strongly influenced our entire software industry to recognize, think, and code using software design patterns.

We will do this by updating our database of favorite quotes.

First, we retrieve the primary key value by searching for the book title and then we pass that value into our search for the quote.

```
        #----------------------------------------------------------
        def updateGOF(self):
            # connect to MySQL
            conn, cursor = self.connect()
```

```
            self.useGuiDB(cursor)

            # execute command
            cursor.execute("SELECT Book_ID FROM books WHERE Book_Title =
    'Design Patterns'")
            primKey = cursor.fetchall()[0][0]
            print(primKey)

            cursor.execute("SELECT * FROM quotations WHERE Books_Book_ID =
    (%s)", (primKey,))
            print(cursor.fetchall())

            # close cursor and connection
            self.close(cursor, conn)
    #===========================================================
    if __name__ == '__main__':
        # Create class instance
        mySQL = MySQL()
        mySQL.updateGOF()
```

This gives us the following result:

```
        #------------------------
        mySQL.updateGOF()
    ◀
```

```
🖳 Console ☒  📖 Bookmarks
<terminated> C:\EclipseWorkspace\Ch07\B04829_Ch07_Code\B04829_Ch07_MySQL.py
1
[(1, 'Programming to an Interface, not an Implementation', 1)]
```

Now that we know the primary key of the quote, we can update the quote by executing the following commands.

```
        #-------------------------------------------------------
    def updateGOF(self):
        # connect to MySQL
        conn, cursor = self.connect()

        self.useGuiDB(cursor)
```

```
        # execute command
        cursor.execute("SELECT Book_ID FROM books WHERE Book_Title =
'Design Patterns'")
        primKey = cursor.fetchall()[0][0]
        print(primKey)

        cursor.execute("SELECT * FROM quotations WHERE Books_Book_ID =
(%s)", (primKey,))
        print(cursor.fetchall())

        cursor.execute("UPDATE quotations SET Quotation = (%s) WHERE
Books_Book_ID = (%s)", \
                        ("Pythonic Duck Typing: If it walks like a duck
and talks like a duck it probably is a duck...", primKey))

        # commit transaction
        conn.commit ()

        cursor.execute("SELECT * FROM quotations WHERE Books_Book_ID =
(%s)", (primKey,))
        print(cursor.fetchall())

        # close cursor and connection
        self.close(cursor, conn)
#===========================================================
if __name__ == '__main__':
    # Create class instance
    mySQL = MySQL()
    #-----------------------
    mySQL.updateGOF()
    book, quote = mySQL.showData()
    print(book, quote)
```

By running the preceding code we make this programming classic more Pythonic.

As can be seen in the following screenshot, before we ran the preceding code, our title with Book_ID 1 was related via a primary to foreign key relationship to the quotation in the Books_Book_ID column of the quotation table.

This is the original quotation from the *Design Patterns* book.

We then updated the quotation related to this ID via the SQL UPDATE command.

None of the IDs have changed, but the quotation that is now associated with `Book_ID 1` has changed, as can be seen in the second MySQL client window, as follows.

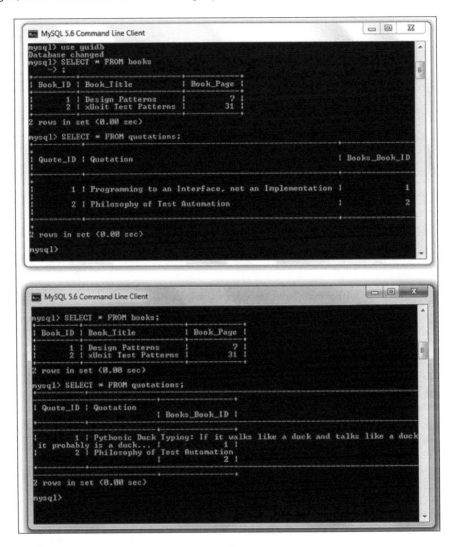

How it works...

In this recipe, we retrieved existing data from our database and database tables we created in earlier recipes. We inserted data into the tables and updated our data using the SQL `UPDATE` command.

Using the SQL DELETE command

In this recipe, we will use the SQL DELETE command to delete the data we created in the previous recipes.

While deleting data might at first sight sound trivial, once we get a rather large database design in production, things might not be that easy any more.

Because we have designed our GUI database by relating two tables via a primary to foreign key relation, when we delete certain data we do not end up with orphan records because this database design takes care of cascading deletes.

Getting ready

This recipe uses the MySQL database, tables, as well as the data inserted into those tables from the previous recipes in this chapter. In order to show how to create orphan records, we will have to change the design of one of our database tables.

How to do it...

We kept our database design simple by using only two database tables.

While this works when we delete data, there is always a chance of ending up with orphan records. What this means is that we delete data in one table but somehow do not delete the related data in another SQL table.

If we create our `quotations` table without a foreign key relationship to the `books` table, we can end up with orphan records.

```
# create second Table inside DB --
# No FOREIGN KEY relation to Books Table
cursor.execute("CREATE TABLE Quotations ( \
        Quote_ID INT AUTO_INCREMENT,          \
        Quotation VARCHAR(250),               \
        Books_Book_ID INT,                    \
        PRIMARY KEY (Quote_ID)                \
    ) ENGINE=InnoDB")
```

After inserting data into the `books` and `quotations` tables, if we execute the same `delete` statement as before we are only deleting the book with `Book_ID` 1, while the related quotation with the `Books_Book_ID` 1 is left behind.

This in an orphaned record. There no longer exists a book record that has a `Book_ID` of 1.

This situation can create a mess, which we can avoid by using cascading deletes.

We do this in the creation of the tables by adding certain database constraints. When we created the table that holds the quotations in a previous recipe, we created our `quotations` table with a foreign key constraint that explicitly references the primary key of the books table, linking the two.

```
# create second Table inside DB
cursor.execute("CREATE TABLE Quotations ( \
        Quote_ID INT AUTO_INCREMENT,          \
        Quotation VARCHAR(250),               \
        Books_Book_ID INT,                    \
        PRIMARY KEY (Quote_ID),               \
        FOREIGN KEY (Books_Book_ID)           \
            REFERENCES Books(Book_ID)         \
            ON DELETE CASCADE                 \
    ) ENGINE=InnoDB")
```

The `FOREIGN KEY` relation includes the `ON DELETE CASCADE` attribute, which basically tells our MySQL server to delete related records in this table when the records this foreign key relates to are deleted.

Without specifying the ON DELETE CASCADE attribute in the creation of our table we can neither delete nor update our data because an UPDATE is a DELETE followed by an INSERT.

Because of this design, no orphan records will be left behind, which is what we want.

 In MySQL, we have to specify ENGINE=InnoDB in order to use foreign keys.

Let's display the data in our database.

```
#===========================================================
if __name__ == '__main__':
    # Create class instance
    mySQL = MySQL()
    mySQL.showData()
```

This shows us the following data in our database tables:

```
Console ⨯   Bookmarks
<terminated> C:\EclipseWorkspace\Ch07\B04829_Ch07_Code\B04829_Ch07_MySQL.py
[(1, 'Design Patterns', 7), (2, 'xUnit Test Patterns', 31)]
[(1, 'Programming to an Interface, not an Implementation', 1), (2, 'Philosophy of Test Automation', 2)]
```

This shows us that we have two records that are related via primary to foreign key relationships.

When we now delete a record in the books table, we expect the related record in the quotations table to also be deleted by a cascading delete.

Let's try this by executing the following SQL commands in Python:

```python
import mysql.connector as mysql
import GuiDBConfig as guiConf

class MySQL():
    #------------------------------------------------------------
    def deleteRecord(self):
        # connect to MySQL
        conn, cursor = self.connect()
```

```
        self.useGuiDB(cursor)

        # execute command
        cursor.execute("SELECT Book_ID FROM books WHERE Book_Title =
'Design Patterns'")
        primKey = cursor.fetchall()[0][0]
        # print(primKey)

        cursor.execute("DELETE FROM books WHERE Book_ID = (%s)",
(primKey,))

        # commit transaction
        conn.commit ()

        # close cursor and connection
        self.close(cursor, conn)
#=============================================================
if __name__ == '__main__':
    # Create class instance
    mySQL = MySQL()
    #-----------------------
    mySQL.deleteRecord()
    mySQL.showData()
```

After executing the preceding commands to delete records, we get the following new results:

The famous `Design Patterns` are gone from our database of favorite quotations...

How it works...

We triggered cascading deletes in this recipe by designing our database in a solid fashion via primary to foreign key relationships with cascading deletes.

This keeps our data sane and integral.

In this recipe and the sample code we have referred to the same table names sometimes starting capitalized and at other times in all lower-case.

This works for a Windows default installation of MySQL but might not work on Linux unless we change a setting.

Here is a link to the official MySQL documentation: http://dev.mysql.com/doc/refman/5.0/en/identifier-case-sensitivity.html

In the next recipe, we will use the code of our `MySQL.py` module from our Python GUI.

Storing and retrieving data from our MySQL database

We will use our Python GUI to insert data into our MySQL database tables. We have already refactored the GUI we built in previous recipes in preparation for connecting and using a database.

We will use two textbox entry widgets into which we can type the book or journal title and the page number. We will also use a ScrolledText widget to type our favorite book quotations into, which we will then store in our MySQL database.

Getting ready

This recipe will build on the MySQL database and tables we created in previous recipes.

How to do it...

We will insert, retrieve, and modify our favorite quotations using our Python GUI. We have refactored the MySQL tab of our GUI in preparation for this.

In order to make the buttons do something, we will connect them to callback functions, as we did in previous recipes.

We will display the data in the ScrolledText widget below the buttons.

In order to do this, we will import the `MySQL.py` module, as we did before. All of the code that talks to our MySQL server instance and database resides in this module, which is a form of encapsulating code in the spirit of object-oriented programming.

We connect the **Insert Quote** button to the following callback function.

```
        # Adding a Button
        self.action = ttk.Button(self.mySQL, text="Insert Quote",
command=self.insertQuote)
        self.action.grid(column=2, row=1)
    # Button callback
    def insertQuote(self):
        title = self.bookTitle.get()
        page = self.pageNumber.get()
        quote = self.quote.get(1.0, tk.END)
        print(title)
        print(quote)
        self.mySQL.insertBooks(title, page, quote)
```

When we now run our code, we can insert data from our Python GUI into our MySQL database.

After entering a book title and book page plus a quotation from the book or movie, we insert the data into our database by clicking the **Insert Quote** button.

Our current design allows for titles, pages, and a quotation. We can also insert our favorite quotations from movies. While a movie does not have pages, we can use the page column to insert the approximate time when the quotation occurred within the movie.

Next, we can verify that all of this data made it into our database tables by issuing the same commands we used previously.

After inserting the data, we can verify that it made it into our two MySQL tables by clicking the **Get Quotes** button which then displays the data we inserted into our two MySQL database tables, as shown above.

Clicking the **Get Quotes** button invokes the callback method we associated with the button click event. This gives us the data that we display in our ScrolledText widget.

```
# Adding a Button
        self.action1 = ttk.Button(self.mySQL, text="Get Quotes",
command=self.getQuote)
        self.action1.grid(column=2, row=2)
    # Button callback
    def getQuote(self):
        allBooks = self.mySQL.showBooks()
        print(allBooks)
        self.quote.insert(tk.INSERT, allBooks)
```

We use the `self.mySQL` class instance variable to invoke the `showBooks()` method, which is part of the MySQL class we imported.

```
from B04829_Ch07_MySQL import MySQL
class OOP():
    def __init__(self):
        # create MySQL instance
        self.mySQL = MySQL()

class MySQL():
    #-----------------------------------------------------------
    def showBooks(self):
        # connect to MySQL
        conn, cursor = self.connect()

        self.useGuiDB(cursor)

        # print results
        cursor.execute("SELECT * FROM Books")
        allBooks = cursor.fetchall()
        print(allBooks)

        # close cursor and connection
        self.close(cursor, conn)

        return allBooks
```

How it works...

In this recipe, we imported the Python module that contains all of the coding logic to connect to our MySQL database and know how to insert, update, delete, and display the data.

We have now connected our Python GUI to this SQL logic.

8
Internationalization and Testing

In this chapter, we will internationalize and test our Python GUI covering the following recipes:

- ▶ Displaying widget text in different languages
- ▶ Changing the entire GUI language all at once
- ▶ Localizing the GUI
- ▶ Preparing the GUI for internationalization
- ▶ How to design a GUI in an agile fashion
- ▶ Do we need to test the GUI code?
- ▶ Setting debug watches
- ▶ Configuring different debug output levels
- ▶ Creating self-testing code using Python's __main__ section
- ▶ Creating robust GUIs using unit tests
- ▶ How to write unit tests using the Eclipse PyDev IDE

Introduction

In this chapter, we will internationalize our GUI by displaying text on labels, buttons, tabs, and other widgets, in different languages.

We will start simply and then explore how we can prepare our GUI for internationalization at the design level.

We will also localize the GUI, which is slightly different from internationalization.

 As these words are long, they have been abbreviated to use the first character of the word, followed by the total number of characters in between the first and last character, followed by the last character of the word.

So, internationalization becomes I18N and localization becomes L10N.

We will also test our GUI code and write unit tests and explore the value unit tests can provide in our development efforts which will lead us to the best practice of *refactoring* our code.

Displaying widget text in different languages

The easiest way to internationalize text strings in Python is by moving them into a separate Python module and then selecting the language to be displayed in our GUI by passing in a parameter to this module.

While this approach is not highly recommended, according to online search results, depending on the specific requirements of the application you are developing, this approach might still be the most pragmatic and fastest to implement.

Getting ready

We will reuse the Python GUI we created earlier. We have commented out one line of Python code that creates the MySQL tab because we do not talk to a MySQL database in this chapter.

How to do it...

In this recipe, we will start to I18N our GUI by changing the Windows title from English to another language.

As the name "GUI" is the same in other languages, we will first expand the name that enables us to see the visual effects of our changes.

Let's change our previous line of code:

```
self.win.title("Python GUI")
```

to:

```
self.win.title("Python Graphical User Interface")
```

The preceding code change results in the following title for our GUI program:

 In this chapter, we will use English and German to exemplify the principle of internationalizing our Python GUI.

Hard-coding strings into code is never too good an idea, so the first step we can do to improve our code is to separate all the strings that are visible in our GUI into a Python module of their own. This is the beginning of internationalizing the visible aspects of our GUI.

 While we are into I18N, we will do this very positive refactoring and the language translation all in one step.

Let's create a new Python module and name it `Resources.py`. Let's next move the English string of our GUI title into this module and then import this module into our GUI code.

 We are separating the GUI from the languages it displays, which is an OOP design principle.

Our new Python module, containing internationalized strings, now looks like this:

```
Class I18N():
'''Internationalization'''
    def __init__(self, language):
        if    language == 'en': self.resourceLanguageEnglish()
        elif  language == 'de': self.resourceLanguageGerman()
        else: raise NotImplementedError('Unsupported language.')

    def resourceLanguageEnglish(self):
        self.title = "Python Graphical User Interface"

    def resourceLanguageGerman(self):
        self.title = 'Python Grafische Benutzeroberflaeche'
```

We import this new Python module into our main Python GUI code, and then use it.

```
from B04829_Ch08_Resources import I18N
class OOP():
    def __init__(self):
        self.win = tk.Tk()                      # Create instance
        self.i18n = I18N('de')                  # Select language
        self.win.title(self.i18n.title)         # Add a title
```

Depending on which language we pass into the I18N class, our GUI will be displayed in that language.

Running the preceding code gives us the following internationalized result:

How it works...

We are breaking out the hard-coded strings that are part of our GUI into their own separate modules. We do this by creating a class, and within the class's __init__() method, we select which language our GUI will display, depending on the passed in language argument.

This works.

We can further modularize our code by separating the internationalized strings into separate files, potentially in XML or another format. We could also read them in from a MySQL database.

This is a "Separation of Concerns" coding approach, which is at the heart of OOP programming.

Changing the entire GUI language all at once

In this recipe, we will change the entire GUI display names all at once by refactoring all the previously hard-coded English strings into a separate Python module and then internationalizing those strings.

This recipe shows that it is a good design principle to avoid hard-coding any strings that our GUI displays but to separate the GUI code from the text that the GUI displays.

 Designing our GUI in a modular way makes internationalizing it much easier.

Getting ready

We will continue to use the GUI from the previous recipe. In that recipe, we had already internationalized the title of the GUI.

How to do it...

In order to internationalize the text being displayed in all of our GUI widgets, we have to move all hard-coded strings into a separate Python module, and this is what we do next.

Previously, strings of words that our GUI displayed were scattered all over our Python code.

Here is what our GUI looked like without I18N.

Every single string of every widget, including the title of our GUI, the tab control names, and so on, were all hard-coded and intermixed with the code that creates the GUI.

 It is a good idea to think about how we can best internationalize our GUI at the design phase of our GUI software development process.

The following is an excerpt of what our code looks like.

```
WIDGET_LABEL = ' Widgets Frame '
class OOP():
    def __init__(self):
        self.win = tk.Tk()                 # Create instance
        self.win.title("Python GUI")       # Add a title


    # Radiobutton callback function
    def radCall(self):
        radSel=self.radVar.get()
        if   radSel == 0: self.monty2.configure(text='Blue')
        elif radSel == 1: self.monty2.configure(text='Gold')
        elif radSel == 2: self.monty2.configure(text='Red')
```

In this recipe, we are internationalizing all strings displayed in our GUI widgets. We are not internationalizing the text *entered* into our GUI, because this depends on the local settings on your PC.

The following is the code for the English internationalized strings:

```
classI18N():
'''Internationalization'''

    def __init__(self, language):
        if   language == 'en': self.resourceLanguageEnglish()
        elif language == 'de': self.resourceLanguageGerman()
        else: raiseNotImplementedError('Unsupported language.')

    def resourceLanguageEnglish(self):
        self.title = "Python Graphical User Interface"

        self.file  = "File"
        self.new   = "New"
        self.exit  = "Exit"
        self.help  = "Help"
```

```
            self.about = "About"

            self.WIDGET_LABEL = ' Widgets Frame '

            self.disabled  = "Disabled"
            self.unChecked = "UnChecked"
            self.toggle    = "Toggle"

            # Radiobutton list
            self.colors   = ["Blue", "Gold", "Red"]
            self.colorsIn = ["in Blue", "in Gold", "in Red"]

            self.labelsFrame  = ' Labels within a Frame '
            self.chooseNumber = "Choose a number:"
            self.label2       = "Label 2"

            self.mgrFiles = ' Manage Files '

            self.browseTo = "Browse to File..."
            self.copyTo   = "Copy File To :    "
```

In our Python GUI module, all previously hard-coded strings are now replaced by an instance of our new I18N class, which resides in the `Resources.py` module.

Here is an example from our refactored `GUI.py` module:

```
    from B04829_Ch08_Resources import I18N

    class OOP():
        def __init__(self):
            self.win = tk.Tk()             # Create instance
            self.i18n = I18N('de')         # Select language
            self.win.title(self.i18n.title) # Add a title

        # Radiobutton callback function
        def radCall(self):
             radSel = self.radVar.get()
            if    radSel == 0: self.widgetFrame.configure(text=self.i18n.
    WIDGET_LABEL + self.i18n.colorsIn[0])
             elif radSel == 1: self.widgetFrame.configure(text=self.i18n.
    WIDGET_LABEL + self.i18n.colorsIn[1])
             elif radSel == 2: self.widgetFrame.configure(text=self.i18n.
    WIDGET_LABEL + self.i18n.colorsIn[2])
```

Note how all of the previously hard-coded English strings have been replaced by calls to the instance of our new I18N class.

An example is `self.win.title(self.i18n.title)`.

What this gives us is the ability to internationalize our GUI. We simply have to use the same variable names and combine them by passing in a parameter to select the language we wish to display.

We could change languages on the fly as part of the GUI as well, or we could read the local PC settings and decide which language our GUI text should display according to those settings.

We can now implement the translation to German by simply filling in the variable names with the corresponding words.

```python
class I18N():
    '''Internationalization'''
    def __init__(self, language):
        if   language == 'en': self.resourceLanguageEnglish()
        elif language == 'de': self.resourceLanguageGerman()
        else: raise NotImplementedError('Unsupported language.')

def resourceLanguageGerman(self):
        self.file  = "Datei"
        self.new   = "Neu"
        self.exit  = "Schliessen"
        self.help  = "Hilfe"
        self.about = "Ueber"

        self.WIDGET_LABEL = ' Widgets Rahmen '

        self.disabled  = "Deaktiviert"
        self.unChecked = "NichtMarkiert"
        self.toggle    = "Markieren"

        # Radiobutton list
        self.colors   = ["Blau", "Gold", "Rot"]
        self.colorsIn = ["in Blau", "in Gold", "in Rot"]

        self.labelsFrame  = ' EtikettenimRahmen '
        self.chooseNumber = "WaehleeineNummer:"
        self.label2       = "Etikette 2"
```

```
        self.mgrFiles = ' DateienOrganisieren '

        self.browseTo = "WaehleeineDatei... "
        self.copyTo   = "KopiereDateizu :       "
```

In our GUI code, we can now change the entire GUI display language in one line of Python code.

```
class OOP():
    def __init__(self):
        self.win = tk.Tk()          # Create instance
        self.i18n = I18N('de')      # Pass in language
```

Running the preceding code creates the following internationalized GUI:

How it works...

In order to internationalize our GUI, we refactored hard-coded strings into a separate module and then used the same class members to internationalize our GUI by passing in a string as the initializer of our I18N class, effectively controlling the language our GUI displays.

Localizing the GUI

After the first step of internationalizing our GUI, the next step is to localize it. Why would we wish to do this?

Well, here in the United States of America, we are all cowboys and we live in different time zones.

So while we are "internationalized" to the USA, our horses do wake up in different time zones (and do expect to be fed according to their own inner horse time zone schedule).

This is where localization comes in.

Getting ready

We are extending the GUI we developed in the previous recipe by localizing it.

How to do it...

We start by first installing the Python pytz time zone module, using pip. We type the following command in a command processor prompt:

```
pip install pytz
```

 In this book, we are using Python 3.4, which comes with the `pip` module built-in. If you are using an older version of Python, then you might have to install the `pip` module first.

When successful, we get the following result.

The screenshot shows that the command downloaded the `.whl` format. If you have not done so, you might have to install the Python `wheel` module first.

This installed the Python `pytz` module into the `site-packages` folder, so now we can import this module from our Python GUI code.

We can list all the existing time zones by running the following code, which will display the time zones in our `ScrolledText` widget. First we add a new `Button` widget to our GUI.

```
import pytz
class OOP():

    # TZ Button callback
    def allTimeZones(self):
        for tz in all_timezones:
            self.scr.insert(tk.INSERT, tz + '\n')


    def createWidgets(self):
        # Adding a TZ Button
        self.allTZs = ttk.Button(self.widgetFrame,
                                 text=self.i18n.timeZones,
                                 command=self.allTimeZones)
        self.allTZs.grid(column=0, row=9, sticky='WE')
```

Clicking our new `Button` widget results in the following output:

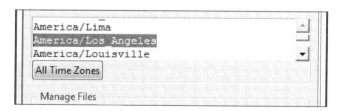

After we install the tzlocal Python module, we can print our current locale by running the following code:

```
    # TZ Local Button callback
    def localZone(self):
        from tzlocal import get_localzone
```

```
            self.scr.insert(tk.INSERT, get_localzone())

    def createWidgets(self):
        # Adding local TZ Button
        self.localTZ = ttk.Button(self.widgetFrame,
                                  text=self.i18n.localZone,
                                  command=self.localZone
        self.localTZ.grid(column=1, row=9, sticky='WE')
```

We have internationalized the strings of our two new action `Buttons` in `Resources.py`.

English version:

```
        self.timeZones = "All Time Zones"
        self.localZone = "Local Zone"
```

German version:

```
        self.timeZones = "Alle Zeitzonen"
        self.localZone = "Lokale Zone"
```

Clicking our new button now tells us which time zone we are in (hey, we didn't know that, didn't we...).

We can now translate our local time to a different time zone. Let's use USA Eastern Standard Time as an example.

We display our current local time in our unused Label 2 by improving our existing code.

```
import pytz
from datetime import datetime
class OOP():
    # Format local US time
    def getDateTime(self):
        fmtStrZone = ""%Y-%m-%d %H:%M:%S""
        self.lbl2.set(datetime.now().strftime(fmtStrZone))
```

```
        # Place labels into the container element
        ttk.Label(labelsFrame, text=self.i18n.chooseNumber).
grid(column=0, row=0)
        self.lbl2 = tk.StringVar()
        self.lbl2.set(self.i18n.label2)
        ttk.Label(labelsFrame, textvariable=self.lbl2).grid(column=0,
row=1)

        # Adding getTimeTZ Button
        self.dt = ttk.Button(self.widgetFrame, text=self.i18n.getTime,
command=self.getDateTime)
        self.dt.grid(column=2, row=9, sticky='WE')
```

When we run the code, our internationalized Label 2 (displayed as `Etikette 2` in German) will display the current local time.

We can now change our local time to US EST by first converting it to **Coordinated Universal Time** (**UTC**) and then applying the `timezone` function from the imported `pytz` module.

```
import pytz
class OOP():
    # Format local US time with TimeZone info
    def getDateTime(self):
        fmtStrZone = "%Y-%m-%d %H:%M:%S %Z%z"
        # Get Coordinated Universal Time
        utc = datetime.now(timezone('UTC'))
        print(utc.strftime(fmtStrZone))

        # Convert UTC datetime object to Los Angeles TimeZone
        la = utc.astimezone(timezone('America/Los_Angeles'))
        print(la.strftime(fmtStrZone))
```

```
# Convert UTC datetime object to New York TimeZone
ny = utc.astimezone(timezone('America/New_York'))
print(ny.strftime(fmtStrZone))

# update GUI label with NY Time and Zone
self.lbl2.set(ny.strftime(fmtStrZone))
```

Clicking the button now renamed as New York results in the following output:

Our Label 2 got updated with the current time in New York and we are printing the UTC times of the cities Los Angeles and New York with their respective time zone conversions, relative to UTC time to the Eclipse console, using a US date formatting string.

 UTC never observes Daylight Saving Time. During **Eastern Daylight Time (EDT)** UTC is four hours ahead and during **Standard Time (EST)** it is five hours ahead of the local time.

How it works...

In order to localize date and time information, we first need to convert our local time to UTC time. We then apply `timezone` information and use the `astimezone` function from the `pytz` Python time zone module to convert to any time zone in the entire world!

In this recipe, we have converted the local time of the USA west coast to UTC and then displayed the USA east coast time in Label 2 of our GUI.

Preparing the GUI for internationalization

In this recipe, we will prepare our GUI for internationalization by realizing that not all is as easy as could be expected when translating English into foreign languages.

We still have one problem to solve and that is how to properly display non-English Unicode characters from foreign languages.

One might expect that displaying the German ä, ö, and ü Unicode umlaut characters would be handled by Python 3 automatically, but this is not the case.

Getting ready

We will continue to use the Python GUI we developed in recent chapters. First, we will change the default language to German in the `GUI.py` initialization code.

We do this by uncommenting the line `self.i18n = I18N('de')`.

How to do it...

When we change the word `Ueber` to the correct German `Über` using the umlaut character, the Eclipse PyDev plugin is not too happy.

```
print("Über")
```

Save Problems

Save could not be completed. Try File > Save As... if the problem persists.

Reason:
Some characters cannot be mapped using "Cp1252" character encoding.
Either change the encoding or remove the characters which are not supported by the "Cp1252" character encoding.

OK   Save as UTF-8   Select First Character

We get an error message, which is a little bit confusing, because when we run the same line of code from within the Eclipse PyDev Console, we get the expected result.

```
C:\Python34\python.exe 3.4.3
>>> print("Über")
Über
>>> |
```

When we ask for the Python default encoding, we get the expected result, which is UTF-8.

 We can, of course, always resort to the direct representation of Unicode.

Using Windows' built-in character map, we can find the Unicode representation of the umlaut character, which is U+00DC for the capital U with an umlaut.

While this workaround is truly ugly, it does the trick. Instead of typing in the literal character Ü, we can pass in the Unicode of \u00DC to get this character correctly displayed in our GUI.

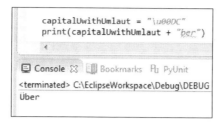

We can also just accept the change in the default encoding from Cp1252 to UTF-8 using PyDev with Eclipse, but we might not always get the prompt to do so.

Instead, we might see the following error message displayed:

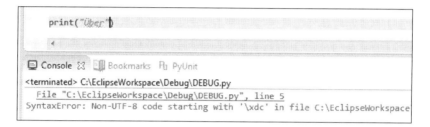

The way to solve this problem is to change the PyDev project's **Text file encoding** property to UTF-8.

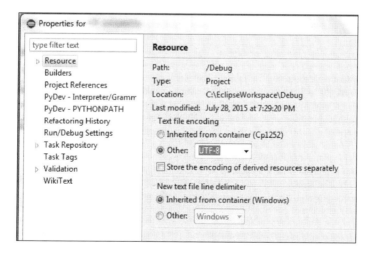

After changing the PyDev default encoding, we now can display those German umlaut characters. We also updated the title to use the correct German ä character.

How it works...

Internationalization and working with foreign language Unicode characters is often not as straightforward as we would wish. Sometimes, we have to find workarounds and expressing Unicode characters via Python by using the direct representation by prepending \u can do the trick.

At other times, we just have to find the settings of our development environment to adjust.

How to design a GUI in an agile fashion

The modern agile software development approach to design and coding came out of the lessons learned by software professionals. This method applies to a GUI as much as to any other code. One of the main keys of agile software development is the continuously applied process of refactoring.

One practical example of how refactoring our code can help us in our software development work is by first implementing some simple functionality using functions.

As our code grows in complexity, we might want to refactor our functions into methods of a class. This approach would enable us to remove global variables and also be more flexible about where inside the class we place methods.

While the functionality of our code has not changed, the structure has.

In this process, we code, test, refactor, and then test again. We do this in short cycles and often start with the minimum code required to get some functionality to work.

 Test-driven software development is one particular style of the agile development methodology.

While our GUI is working nicely, our main `GUI.py` code has been ever increasing in complexity and it has started to get a little bit harder to maintain an overview of our code.

This means we need to refactor our code.

Getting ready

We will refactor the GUI we created in previous chapters. We will use the English version of the GUI.

How to do it...

We have already broken out all names our GUI displays when we internationalized it in the previous recipe. That was an excellent start to refactoring our code.

 Refactoring is the process of improving the structure, readability, and maintainability of existing code. We are not adding new functionality.

In the previous chapters and recipes, we have been extending our GUI in a "Top-to-bottom" waterfall development approach, adding `import` to the top and code towards the bottom of the existing code.

While this was useful when looking at the code it now looks a little bit messy and we can improve this to help our future development.

Let us first clean up our `import` statement section, which currently looks like this:

```
#======================
# imports
#======================
import tkinter as tk
from tkinter import ttk
from tkinter import scrolledtext
from tkinter import Menu
from tkinter import Spinbox
import B04829_Ch08_ToolTip as tt
from threading import Thread
from time import sleep
from queue import Queue
from tkinter import filedialog as fd
from os import path
```

```
from tkinter import messagebox as mBox
from B04829_Ch08_MySQL import MySQL
from B04829_Ch08_Resources import I18N
from datetime import datetime
from pytz import all_timezones, timezone

# Module level GLOBALS
GLOBAL_CONST = 42
```

By simply grouping related imports, we can reduce the number of lines of code, which improves the readability of our imports, making them appear less overwhelming.

```
#=======================
# imports
#=======================
import tkinter as tk
from tkinter import ttk, scrolledtext, Menu, Spinbox, filedialog as
fd, messagebox as mBox
from queue import Queue
from os import path
import B04829_Ch08_ToolTip as tt
from B04829_Ch08_MySQL import MySQL
from B04829_Ch08_Resources import I18N
from B04829_Ch08_Callbacks_Refactored import Callbacks
from B04829_Ch08_Logger import Logger, LogLevel

# Module level GLOBALS
GLOBAL_CONST = 42
```

We can further refactor our code by breaking out the callback methods into their own modules. This improves readability by separating the different import statements into the modules they are required in.

Let us rename our GUI.py as GUI_Refactored.py and create a new module, which we name Callbacks_Refactored.py.

This gives us this new architecture.

```
#=======================
# imports
#=======================
import tkinter as tk
from tkinter import ttk, scrolledtext, Menu, Spinbox, \
                    filedialog as fd, messagebox as mBox
from queue import Queue
```

```
from os import path
import B04829_Ch08_ToolTip as tt
from B04829_Ch08_MySQL import MySQL
from B04829_Ch08_Resources import I18N
from B04829_Ch08_Callbacks_Refactored import Callbacks

# Module level GLOBALS
GLOBAL_CONST = 42

class OOP():
    def __init__(self):

        # Callback methods now in different module
        self.callBacks = Callbacks(self)
```

Note how we are passing in an instance of our own GUI class (`self`) when calling the `Callbacks` initializer.

Our new `Callbacks` class is as follows:

```
#=======================
# imports
#=======================
import tkinter as tk
from time import sleep
from threading import Thread
from pytz import all_timezones, timezone
from datetime import datetime

class Callbacks():
    def __init__(self, oop):
        self.oop = oop

    def defaultFileEntries(self):
        self.oop.fileEntry.delete(0, tk.END)
        self.oop.fileEntry.insert(0, 'Z:\\')          # bogus path
        self.oop.fileEntry.config(state='readonly')
        self.oop.netwEntry.delete(0, tk.END)
        self.oop.netwEntry.insert(0, 'Z:\\Backup')  # bogus path

    # Combobox callback
    def _combo(self, val=0):
        value = self.oop.combo.get()
        self.oop.scr.insert(tk.INSERT, value + '\n')
```

In the initializer of our new class, the passed-in GUI instance is saved under the name `self.oop` and used throughout this new Python class module.

Running the refactored GUI code still works. We have only increased readability and reduced the complexity of our code in preparation for further development work.

How it works...

We have first improved the readability of our code by grouping related import statements. We next broke out the callback methods into their own class and module in order to further reduce the complexity of our code.

We had already taken the same OOP approach by having the `ToolTip` class reside in its own module and by internationalizing all GUI strings in the previous recipes.

In this recipe, we went one step further in refactoring by passing our own instance into the callback method's class our GUI relies upon.

 Now that we better understand the value of a modular approach to software development, we will most likely start with this approach in our future software designs.

Do we need to test the GUI code?

Testing our software is an important activity during the coding phase, as well as when releasing service packs or bug fixes.

There are different levels of testing. The first level is developer testing, which often starts with the compiler or interpreter not letting us run our buggy code forcing us to test small parts of our code on the level of individual methods.

This is the first level of defense.

A second level of coding defensively is when our source code control system tells us about some conflicts to be resolved and does not let us check in our modified code.

This is very useful and absolutely necessary when we work professionally in a team of developers. The source code control system is our friend and points out changes that have been committed to a particular branch or top-of-tree either by ourselves or by our other developers, and tells us that our local version of the code is both outdated and has some conflicts that need to be resolved before we can submit our code into the repository.

This part assumes you use a source control system to manage and store your code. Examples include git, mercurial, svn, and several others. Git is a very popular source control and it is free for a single user.

A third level is the level of APIs where we encapsulate potential future changes to our code by only allowing interactions with our code via published interfaces.

 Please refer to "Program to an Interface, never an Implementation", *Design Patterns*, Page 17.

Another level of testing is integration testing, when half of the bridge we finally built meets the other half that the other development teams created and the two don't meet at the same height (say, one half ended up two meters or yards higher than the other half...).

Then, there is end user testing. While we built what they specified, it is not really what they wanted.

Oh well...I guess all of the preceding examples are valid reasons why we need to test our code both in the design and implementation stages.

Getting ready

We will test the GUI we have created in recent recipes and chapters. We will also show some simple examples of what can go wrong and why we need to keep testing our code and code we do call via APIs.

How to do it...

While many experienced developers grew up sprinkling `printf()` statements all over their code while debugging, many developers in the 21st century are accustomed to modern IDE development environments that efficiently speed up development time.

In this book, we are using the PyDev Python plug-in for the Eclipse IDE.

If you are just starting using an IDE like Eclipse with the PyDev plug-in, it might be a little bit overwhelming at first. The Python IDLE tool that ships with Python 3 also has a simpler debugger and you might wish to explore that first.

Whenever something goes wrong in our code, we have to debug it. The first step in doing this is to set break points and then step through our code, line by line, or method by method.

Stepping in and out of our code is a daily activity until the code runs smoothly.

In Python GUI programming, one of the first things that can go wrong is missing out on importing the required modules or importing existing modules.

Here is a simple example:

```
class OOP():
    def __init__(self):
        # Create instance
        self.win = tk.Tk()

Console 🔀   Bookmarks  🎵 PyUnit
<terminated> C:\EclipseWorkspace\Ch08\B04829_Ch08_Code\
Traceback (most recent call last):
  File "C:\EclipseWorkspace\Ch08\B04829_Ch08_Co
    oop = OOP()
  File "C:\EclipseWorkspace\Ch08\B04829_Ch08_Co
    self.win = tk.Tk()
NameError: name 'tk' is not defined
```

We are trying to create an instance of the tkinter class but things don't work as expected.

Well, we simply forgot to import the module and we can fix this by adding a line of Python code above our class creation, where the import statements live.

```
#=======================
# imports
#=======================
import tkinter as tk
```

This is an example in which our development environment does the testing for us. We just have to do the debugging and code fixing.

Another example more closely related to developer testing is when we code conditionals and, during our regular development, do not exercise all branches of logic.

Using an example from the previous chapter, let's say we click on the **Get Quotes** button and this works, but we never clicked on the **Mody Quote** button. The first button click creates the desired result, but the second throws an exception (because we had not yet implemented this code and probably forgot all about it).

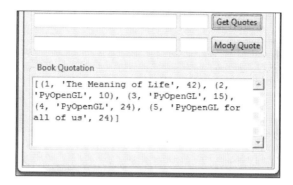

Clicking the **Mody Quote** button creates the following result:

Another potential area of bugs is when a function or method suddenly no longer returns the expected result. Let's say we are calling the following function, which returns the expected result.

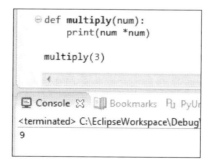

Then, someone makes a mistake, and we no longer get the previous results.

Instead of multiplying, we are raising by the power of the passed in number, and the result is no longer what it used to be.

 In software testing, this sort of bug is called regression.

How it works...

In this recipe, we emphasized the importance of software testing during several phases of the software development life cycle by showing several examples of where code can go wrong and introduce software defects (aka bugs).

Setting debug watches

In modern **Integrated Development Environments (IDEs)** like the PyDev plugin in Eclipse or another IDE such as NetBeans, we can set debug watches to monitor the state of our GUI during the execution of our code.

This is very similar to the Microsoft IDEs of Visual Studio and the more recent versions of Visual Studio.NET.

 Setting debug watches is a very convenient way to help our development efforts.

Getting ready

In this recipe, we will reuse the Python GUI we developed in earlier recipes. We are stepping through the code we previously developed and setting debug watches.

How to do it...

[While this recipe applies to the PyDev plugin in the Java-based Eclipse IDE, its principles also apply to many modern IDEs.]

The first position where we might wish to place a breakpoint is at the place where we make our GUI visible by calling the tkinter main event loop.

The green balloon symbol on the left is a breakpoint in PyDev/Eclipse. When we execute our code in debug mode, once the execution reaches the breakpoint, the execution of the code will be halted. At this point, we can see the values of all variables that are currently in scope. We can also type expressions into one of the debugger windows which will execute them, showing us the results. If the result is what we want, we might decide to change our code using what we have just learned.

We normally step through the code by either clicking an icon in the toolbar of our IDE or by using a keyboard shortcut (like pressing *F5* to step into code, *F6* to step over, and *F7* to step out of the current method).

```
#============================
# Start GUI
#============================
oop = OOP()
oop.win.mainloop()
```

Placing the breakpoint where we did and then stepping into this code turns out to be a problem because we end up in some low-level tkinter code we really do not wish to debug right now. We get out of the low-level tkinter code by clicking the Step-Out toolbar icon (which is the third yellow arrow on the right below the project menu) or by pressing *F7* (assuming we are using PyDev in Eclipse).

We started the debugging session by clicking the bug toolbar icon towards the right of the screenshot. If we execute without debugging, we click the green circle with the white triangle inside it, which is the icon to the right of the bug icon.

A better idea is to place our breakpoint closer to our own code in order to watch the values of some of our own Python variables.

In the event-driven world of modern GUIs, we have to place our breakpoints at code that gets invoked during events, for example button clicks.

Currently, one of our main functionalities resides in a button click event. When we click the button labeled **New York**, we create an event that then results in something happening in our GUI.

Let's place a breakpoint at the **New York** button callback method, which we named `getDateTime()`.

When we now run a debug session, we will stop at the breakpoint and then we can enable watches of variables that are in scope.

Using PyDev in Eclipse, we can right-click a variable and then select the watch command from the pop-up menu. The name of the variable, its type, and current value will be displayed in the expressions debug window shown in the next screenshot. We can also directly type into the expressions window.

The variables we are watching are not limited to simple data types. We can watch class instances, lists, dictionaries, and so on.

When watching these more complex objects, we can expand them in the expressions window and drill down into all of the values of the class instances, dictionaries, and so on.

We do this by clicking on the triangle to the left of our watched variable that appears left-most under the **Name** column next to each variable.

While we are printing out the values of the different time zone locations, in the long term, it is much more convenient and efficient to set debug watches. We do not have to clutter our code with old-fashioned C-style `printf()` statements.

If you are interested in learning how to install Eclipse with the PyDev plugin for Python, there is a great tutorial that will get you started installing all the necessary free software and then introduce you to PyDev within Eclipse by creating a simple, working Python program. `http://www.vogella.com/tutorials/Python/article.html`

How it works...

We use modern Integrated Development Environments (IDEs) in the 21st century that are freely available to help us to create solid code.

This recipe showed how to set debug watches, which is a fundamental tool in every developer's skill set. Stepping through our own code even when not hunting down bugs ensures that we understand our code and can lead to improving our code via refactoring.

The following is a quote from the first programming book I read, *Thinking in Java*, written by Bruce Eckel.

"Resist the urge to hurry, it will only slow you down."

– Bruce Eckel

Almost two decades later, this advice has passed the test of time.

Debug watches help us to create solid code and are not a waste of time.

Configuring different debug output levels

In this recipe, we will configure different debug levels that we can select and change at runtime. This allows us to control how much we want to drill down into our code when debugging our code.

We will create two new Python classes and place both of them into the same module.

We will use four different logging levels and we will write our debugging output to a log file we will create. If the log folder does not exist, we will create it automatically as well.

The name of the log file is the name of the executing script which is our refactored `GUI.py`. We can also choose other names for our log files by passing in the full path to the initializer of our logger class.

Getting ready

We will continue to use our refactored `GUI.py` code from the previous recipe.

How to do it...

First, we create a new Python module into which we place two new `classes`. The first `class` is very simple and defines the logging levels. This is basically an `enumeration`.

```
class LogLevel:
'''Define logging levels.'''
    OFF     = 0
    MINIMUM = 1
    NORMAL  = 2
    DEBUG   = 3
```

The second `class` creates a log file by using the passed in full path of the file name and places this into a `logs` folder. On first run, the `logs` folder might not exist so the code automatically creates the folder.

```
class Logger:
    ''' Create a test log and write to it. '''
    #------------------------------------------------------------
    def __init__(self, fullTestName, loglevel=LogLevel.DEBUG):
        testName = os.path.splitext(os.path.basename(fullTestName))[0]
        logName  = testName  + '.log'

        logsFolder = 'logs'
        if not os.path.exists(logsFolder):
            os.makedirs(logsFolder, exist_ok = True)

        self.log = os.path.join(logsFolder, logName)
        self.createLog()

        self.loggingLevel = loglevel
        self.startTime    = time.perf_counter()


    #------------------------------------------------------------
    def createLog(self):
        with open(self.log, mode='w', encoding='utf-8') as logFile:
            logFile.write(self.getDateTime() +
                          '\t\t*** Starting Test ***\n')
        logFile.close()
```

In order to write to our log file, we use the `writeToLog()` method. Inside the method, the first thing we do is check if the message has a logging level higher than the limit we set our desired logging output to. If the message has a lower level, we discard it and immediately return from the method.

If the message has a logging level that we want to display, we then check if it starts with a newline character, and if it does, we discard the newline by slicing the method starting at index 1, using Python's slice operator (`msg = msg[1:]`).

We then write one line to our log file consisting of the current date timestamp, two tab spaces, our message, and ending in a newline character.

```python
def writeToLog(self, msg='', loglevel=LogLevel.DEBUG):
    # control how much gets logged
    if loglevel > self.loggingLevel:
        return

    # open log file in append mode
    with open(self.log, mode='a', encoding='utf-8') as logFile:
        msg = str(msg)
        if msg.startswith('\n'):
            msg = msg[1:]
        logFile.write(self.getDateTime() + '\t\t' + msg + '\n')

    logFile.close()
```

We can now import our new Python module, and inside the __init__ section of our GUI code, we can create an instance of the `Logger` class.

```python
from os import path
from B04829_Ch08_Logger import Logger
class OOP():
    def __init__(self):
        # create Logger instance
        fullPath = path.realpath(__file__)
        self.log = Logger(fullPath)
        print(self.log)
```

We are retrieving the full path to our running GUI script via `path.realpath(__file__)` and passing this into the initializer of the `Logger` class. If the `logs` folder does not exist, it will automatically get created by our Python code.

This creates the following results:

```
# create Logger instance
fullPath = path.realpath(__file__)
self.log = Logger(fullPath)
print(self.log)
```

Console 23   Bookmarks PyUnit
<terminated> C:\EclipseWorkspace\Ch08\B04829_Ch08_Code\B04829_Ch08_GUI_Refactored.py
<B04829_Ch08_Logger.Logger object at 0x000000000034EE320>

The preceding screenshot shows that we created an instance of our new `Logger` class and the screenshot below shows that both the `logs` folder as well as the log were created.

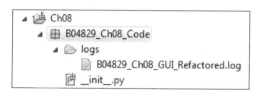

When we open up the log, we can see that the current date and time as well as a default string have been written into the log.

How it works...

In this recipe, we created our own logging class. While Python ships with a Logging module, it is very easy to create our own, which gives us absolute control over our logging format. This is very useful when we combine our own logging output with MS Excel or the Matplotlib we explored in previous recipes in a previous chapter.

In the next recipe, we will use Python's built-in `__main__` functionality to use the four different logging levels we have just created.

Creating self-testing code using Python's __main__ section

Python comes with a very nice feature that enables each module to self-test. Making use of this feature is a great way of making sure that changes to our code do not break existing code and, additionally, the __main__ self-testing section can serve as documentation for how each module works.

 After a few months or years, we sometimes forget what our code is doing, so having an explanation written in the code itself is indeed a great help.

It is a good idea to always add a self-testing section to every Python module, when possible. It is sometimes not possible, but, in most modules, it is possible to do so.

Getting ready

We will extend the previous recipe, so, in order to understand what the code in this recipe is doing, we have to first read and understand the code of the previous recipe.

How to do it...

First, we will explore the power of the Python __main__ self-testing section by adding this self-testing section to our `Resources.py` module. Whenever we run a module that has this self-testing section located at the bottom of the module, when the module is executed by itself, this code will run.

When the module is imported and used from other modules, the code in the __main__ self-testing section will not be executed.

This is the code that is also shown in the screenshot that follows:

```python
if __name__ == '__main__':
    language = 'en'
    inst = I18N(language)
    print(inst.title)

    language = 'de'
    inst = I18N(language)
    print(inst.title)
```

After adding the self-testing section, we now can run this module by itself and it creates useful output, while, at the same time, showing us that our code works as intended.

```
B04829_Ch08_Resources

    if __name__ == '__main__':
        language = 'en'
        inst = I18N(language)
        print(inst.title)

        language = 'de'
        inst = I18N(language)
        print(inst.title)


Console    Bookmarks    PyUnit
<terminated> C:\EclipseWorkspace\Ch08\B04829_Ch08_Code\B04829_Ch08_Resources.py
Python Graphical User Interface
Python Grafische Benutzeroberfläche
```

We are first passing in English as the language to be displayed in our GUI, and then we pass in German as the language that our GUI will display.

We are printing out the title of our GUI to show that our Python module works as we intended it to work.

 The next step is to use our logging capabilities which we created in the previous recipe.

We do this by first adding a __main__ self-testing section to our refactored GUI.py module and we then verify that we created an instance of our Logger class.

```
    if __name__ == '__main__':
        #=============================
        # Start GUI
        #=============================
        oop = OOP()
        print(oop.log)
        oop.win.mainloop()


Console    Bookmarks    PyUnit
<terminated> C:\EclipseWorkspace\Ch08\B04829_Ch08_Code\B04829_Ch08_GUI_Refactored.py
<B04829_Ch08_Logger.Logger object at 0x00000000034CD320>
```

We next write to our log file by using the command shown. We have designed our logging level to default to log every message, which is the DEBUG level and, because of this, we do not have to change anything. We just pass in the message to be logged to the `writeToLog` method.

```
if __name__ == '__main__':
#=======================
# Start GUI
#=======================
oop = OOP()
    print(oop.log)
    oop.log.writeToLog('Test message')
    oop.win.mainloop()
```

This gets written to our log file, as can be seen in the following screenshot of the log:

```
B04829_Ch08_GUI_Refactored.log  ⊠
2015-08-23 20:49:50        *** Starting Test ***
2015-08-23 20:49:50        Test message
```

Now we can control the logging by adding logging levels to our logging statements and set the level we wish to output. Let's add this capability to our New York button callback method in the `Callbacks.py` module which is the `getDateTime` method.

We change the previous `print` statements to `log` statements using different debug levels.

In the `GUI.py`, we import both new classes from our logger module.

```
from B04829_Ch08_Logger import Logger, LogLevel
```

Next, we create local instances of those classes.

```
# create Logger instance
fullPath = path.realpath(__file__)
self.log = Logger(fullPath)

# create Log Level instance
self.level = LogLevel()
```

As we are passing in an instance of the GUI class to the `Callbacks.py` initializer, we can use logging level constraints according to the `LogLevel` class we have created.

```
# Format local US time with TimeZone info
def getDateTime(self):
    fmtStrZone = "%Y-%m-%d %H:%M:%S %Z%z"
    # Get Coordinated Universal Time
    utc = datetime.now(timezone('UTC'))
    self.oop.log.writeToLog(utc.strftime(fmtStrZone),
                            self.oop.level.MINIMUM)

    # Convert UTC datetime object to Los Angeles TimeZone
    la = utc.astimezone(timezone('America/Los_Angeles'))
    self.oop.log.writeToLog(la.strftime(fmtStrZone),
                            self.oop.level.NORMAL)

    # Convert UTC datetime object to New York TimeZone
    ny = utc.astimezone(timezone('America/New_York'))
    self.oop.log.writeToLog(ny.strftime(fmtStrZone),
                            self.oop.level.DEBUG)

    # update GUI label with NY Time and Zone
    self.oop.lbl2.set(ny.strftime(fmtStrZone))
```

When we now click our New York button, depending upon the selected logging level, we get different output written to our log file. The default logging level is DEBUG, which means everything gets written to our log.

When we change the logging level, we control what gets written to our log. We do this by calling the `setLoggingLevel` method of the `Logger` class.

```
#------------------------------------------------------------
def setLoggingLevel(self, level):
    '''change logging level in the middle of a test.'''
    self.loggingLevel = level
```

In the `__main__` section of our GUI, we change the logging level to `MINIMUM`, which results in reduced output written to our log file.

```
if __name__ == '__main__':
#=======================
# Start GUI
#=======================
oop = OOP()
    oop.log.setLoggingLevel(oop.level.MINIMUM)
    oop.log.writeToLog('Test message')
    oop.win.mainloop()
```

Now, our log file no longer shows the `Test Message` and only shows messages that meet the set logging level.

```
B04829_Ch08_GUI_Refactored.log  ⊠
   2015-08-23 21:17:00      *** Starting Test ***
   2015-08-23 21:17:01      2015-08-24 04:17:01 UTC+0000
```

How it works...

In this recipe, we are making good use of Python's built-in `__main__` self-testing section. We introduced our own logging file and, at the same time, how to create different logging levels.

By doing this, we have full control over what gets written to our log files.

Creating robust GUIs using unit tests

Python comes with a built-in unit testing framework and, in this recipe, we will start to use this framework to test our Python GUI code.

Before we start to write unit tests, we want to design our testing strategy. We could easily intermix the unit tests with the code they are testing, but a better strategy is to separate the application code from the unit test code.

PyUnit has been designed according to the principles of all the other xUnit testing Frameworks.

Getting ready

We will test the internationalized GUI we created earlier in this chapter.

How to do it...

In order to use Python's built-in unit testing framework, we have to import the Python `unittest` module. Let's create a new module and name it `UnitTests.py`.

We first import the `unittest` module, then we create our own class and within this class we inherit and extend the `unittest.TestCase` class.

The simplest code to do it looks like this:

```python
import unittest


class GuiUnitTests(unittest.TestCase):
    pass


if __name__ == '__main__':
    unittest.main()
```

The code isn't doing much yet, but when we run it, we do not get any errors, which is a good sign.

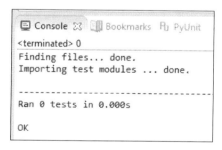

We actually do get an output written to the console stating that we successfully ran zero tests...

Hmm, that output is a bit misleading as all we have done so far is create a class that contains no actual testing methods.

We add testing methods that do the actual unit testing by following the default naming for all test methods to start with the word "test". This is an option that can be changed but it seems to be much easier and clearer to stick to this naming convention.

Let's add a test method that will test the title of our GUI. This will verify that, by passing in the expected arguments, we get the expected result.

```python
import unittest
from B04829_Ch08_Resources import I18N

class GuiUnitTests(unittest.TestCase):

    def test_TitleIsEnglish(self):
        i18n = I18N('en')
        self.assertEqual(i18n.title,
                        "Python Graphical User Interface")
```

We are importing our `I18N` class from our `Resources.py` module, passing in English as the language to be displayed in our GUI. As this is our first unit test, we are printing out the Title result as well, just to make sure we know what we are getting back. We next use the `unittest assertEqual` method to verify that our title is correct.

Running this code gives us an **OK**, which means that the unit test passed.

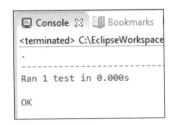

The unit test runs and succeeds, which is indicated by one dot and the word "OK". If it had failed or gotten an error we would not have got the dot but an "F" or "E" as the output.

We can now do the same automated unit testing check by verifying the title for the German version of our GUI.

We simply copy, paste, and modify our code.

```
import unittest
from B04829_Ch08_Resources import I18N

class GuiUnitTests(unittest.TestCase):

    def test_TitleIsEnglish(self):
        i18n = I18N('en')
        self.assertEqual(i18n.title,
                         "Python Graphical User Interface")

    def test_TitleIsGerman(self):
        i18n = I18N('en')
        self.assertEqual(i18n.title,
                         'Python Grafische Benutzeroberfl'
                + "\u00E4" + 'che')
```

Now we are testing our internationalized GUI title in two languages and getting the following result when running the code:

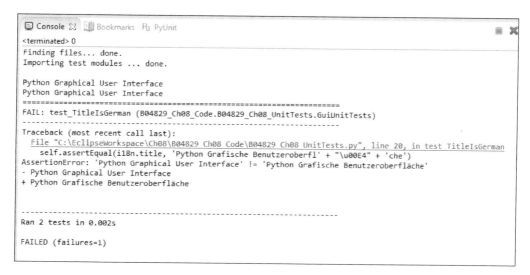

We ran two unit tests but, instead of an OK, we got a failure. What happened?

Our `assertion` failed for the German version of our GUI...

While debugging our code, it turns out that in the copy, paste, and modify approach of our unit test code, we forgot to pass in German as the language. We can easily fix this.

```
def test_TitleIsGerman(self):
    # i18n = I18N('en')            # <= Bug in Unit Test
    i18n = I18N('de')
    self.assertEqual(i18n.title,
                'Python Grafische Benutzeroberfl'
                + "\u00E4" + 'che')
```

When we rerun our unit tests, we again get the expected result of all tests passing.

 Unit testing code is code and can have bugs too.

While the purpose of writing unit tests is really to test our application code, we have to make sure that our tests are written correctly. One approach from the **Test-Driven-Development** (**TDD**) methodology might help us.

 In TDD, we develop the unit tests before we actually write the application code. Now, if a test passes for a method that does not even exist, something is wrong. The next step is to create the non-existing method and make sure it will fail. After that, we can write the minimum amount of code necessary to make the unit test pass.

How it works...

In this recipe, we have begun to test our Python GUI, writing unit tests in Python. We have seen that Python unit test code is just code and can contain mistakes that need to be corrected. In the next recipe, we will extend this recipe's code and use the graphical unit test runner that comes with the PyDev plugin for the Eclipse IDE.

How to write unit tests using the Eclipse PyDev IDE

In the previous recipe, we started to use Python's unit testing capabilities, and in this recipe, we will ensure the quality of our GUI code by further using this capability.

We will unit test our GUI in order to make sure that the internationalized strings our GUI displays are as expected.

In the previous recipe, we encountered some bugs in our unit testing code but, typically, our unit tests will find regression bugs that are caused by modifying existing application code, not the unit test code. Once we have verified that our unit testing code is correct, we do not usually change it.

 Our unit tests also serve as documentation of what we expect our code to do.

By default, Python's unit tests are executed with a textural unit test runner and we can run this in the PyDev plug-in from within the Eclipse IDE. We can also run the very same unit tests from a console window.

In addition to the text runner in this recipe, we will explore PyDev's graphical unit test feature that can be used from within the Eclipse IDE.

Getting ready

We are extending the previous recipe, in which we began to use Python unit tests.

How to do it...

The Python unit testing framework comes with what are called fixtures.

Refer to the following URLs for a description of what a test fixture is:

- `https://docs.python.org/3.4/library/unittest.html`
- `https://en.wikipedia.org/wiki/Test_fixture`
- `http://www.boost.org/doc/libs/1_51_0/libs/test/doc/html/utf/user-guide/fixture.html`

What this means is that we can create `setup()` and `teardown()` unit testing methods so that the `setup()` method is called at the beginning before any single test is executed, and at the end of every single unit test, the `teardown()` method is called.

This fixture capability provides us with a very controlled environment in which we can run our unit tests. It is similar to using pre- and post-conditions.

Let's set up our unit testing environment. We will create a new testing class which focuses on the previously mentioned correctness of code.

 `unittest.main()` runs any method that starts with the prefix "test", no matter how many classes we create within a given Python module.

```python
import unittest
from B04829_Ch08_Resources import I18N
from B04829_Ch08_GUI_Refactored import OOP as GUI

class GuiUnitTests(unittest.TestCase):

    def test_TitleIsEnglish(self):
        i18n = I18N('en')
        self.assertEqual(i18n.title,
                         "Python Graphical User Interface")

    def test_TitleIsGerman(self):
        # i18n = I18N('en')              # <= Bug in Unit Test
        i18n = I18N('de')
        self.assertEqual(i18n.title,
                         'Python Grafische Benutzeroberfl'
                         + "\u00E4" + 'che')

class WidgetsTestsEnglish(unittest.TestCase):

    def setUp(self):
        self.gui = GUI('en')

    def tearDown(self):
        self.gui = None

    def test_WidgetLabels(self):
        self.assertEqual(self.gui.i18n.file, "File")
        self.assertEqual(self.gui.i18n.mgrFiles, ' Manage Files ')
        self.assertEqual(self.gui.i18n.browseTo,
                         "Browse to File...")
if __name__ == '__main__':
    unittest.main()
```

This creates the following output:

```
Console  ⊠   Bookmarks   PyUnit
<terminated> 0
Finding files... done.
Importing test modules ... done.

---------------------------------------
Ran 3 tests in 0.001s

OK
```

The preceding unit testing code shows that we can create several unit testing classes and they can all be run in the same module by calling `unittest.main`.

It also shows that the `setup()` method does not count as a test in the output of the unit test report (the count of tests is 3) while, at the same time, it did its intended job as we can now access our class instance variable `self.gui` from within the unit test method.

We are interested in testing the correctness of all of our labels and especially catching bugs when we make changes to our code.

If we have copied and pasted strings from our application code to the testing code, it will catch any unintended changes with the click of a unit testing framework button.

We also want to test that invoking any of our `Radiobutton` widgets in any language results in the `labelframe` widget `text` being updated. In order to automatically test this, we have to do two things.

First, we have to retrieve the value of the `labelframe text` widget and assign the value to a variable we name `labelFrameText`. We have to use the following syntax because the properties of this widget are being passed in and retrieved via a dictionary data type:

```python
self.gui.widgetFrame['text']
```

We can now verify the default text and then the internationalized versions after clicking one of the Radiobutton widgets programmatically.

```python
class WidgetsTestsGerman(unittest.TestCase):

    def setUp(self):
        self.gui = GUI('de')

    def test_WidgetLabels(self):
        self.assertEqual(self.gui.i18n.file, "Datei")
        self.assertEqual(self.gui.i18n.mgrFiles,
```

```
                                           ' Dateien Organisieren ')
            self.assertEqual(self.gui.i18n.browseTo,
                                            "Waehle eine Datei... ")


    def test_LabelFrameText(self):
        labelFrameText = self.gui.widgetFrame['text']
        self.assertEqual(labelFrameText, " Widgets Rahmen ")
        self.gui.radVar.set(1)
        self.gui.callBacks.radCall()
        labelFrameText = self.gui.widgetFrame['text']
        self.assertEqual(labelFrameText,
                                " Widgets Rahmen in Gold")
```

After verifying the default `labelFrameText` we programmatically set the radio button to index 1 and then programmatically invoke the radio button's callback method.

```
            self.gui.radVar.set(1)
            self.gui.callBacks.radCall()
```

 This is basically the same action as clicking the radio button in the GUI but we do this button click event via code in the unit tests.

Then we verify that our text in the `labelframe` widget has changed as intended.

When we run the unit tests from within Eclipse with the Python PyDev plugin, we get the following output written to the Eclipse console.

Run from a command prompt, we get similar output once we navigate to the folder where our code currently resides.

Using Eclipse, we can also choose to run our unit tests, not as a simple Python script, but as a Python unit test script, which gives us some colorful output instead of the black and white world of the old DOS prompt.

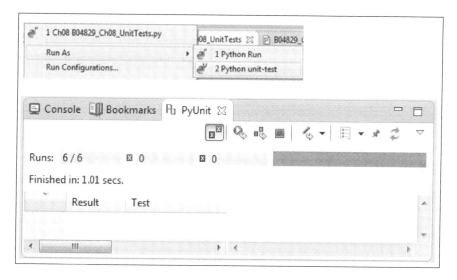

The unit testing result bar is green, which means that all our unit tests have passed. The preceding screenshot also shows that the GUI test runner is much slower than the textual test runner: 1.01 seconds compared to 0.466 seconds in Eclipse.

How it works...

We have extended our unit testing code by testing `labels`, programmatically invoking a `Radiobutton` and then verifying in our unit tests that the corresponding `text` property of the `labelframe` widget has changed as expected. We have tested two different languages.

We then moved on to use the built-in Eclipse/PyDev graphical unit test runner.

9

Extending Our GUI with the wxPython Library

In this chapter, we will enhance our Python GUI by using the wxPython library.

- How to install the wxPython library
- How to create our GUI in wxPython
- Quickly adding controls using wxPython
- Trying to embed a main wxPython app in a main tkinter app
- Trying to embed our tkinter GUI code into wxPython
- How to use Python to control two different GUI frameworks
- How to communicate between the two connected GUIs

Introduction

In this chapter, we will introduce another Python GUI toolkit that currently does not ship with Python. It is called wxPython.

There are two versions of this library. The original is called Classic while the newest is called by its development project code name, Phoenix.

In this book, we are solely programming using Python 3, and because the new Phoenix project is aimed at supporting Python 3, this is the version of wxPython we are using in this chapter.

First, we will create a simple wxPython GUI, and then we will try to connect both the tkinter-based GUIs we developed in this book with the new wxPython library.

wxPython is a Python binding to wxWidgets.

The w in wxPython stands for the Windows OS and the x stands for Unix-based operating systems such as Linux and OS X.

If things don't work out using these two GUI toolkits in unison, we will attempt to use Python to solve any problems and then we will use **Inter Process Communication (IPC)** within Python to make sure that our Python code works as we want it to work.

How to install the wxPython library

The wxPython library does not ship with Python, so, in order to use it, we first have to install it.

This recipe will show us where and how to find the right version to install to match both the installed version of Python and the operating system we are running.

The wxPython third-party library has been around for more than 17 years, which indicates that it is a robust library.

Getting ready

In order to use wxPython with Python 3, we have to install the wxPython Phoenix version.

How to do it...

When searching online for wxPython, we will probably find the official website at www. wxpython.org.

If we click on the download link for MS Windows, we can see several Windows installers, all of which are for Python 2.x only.

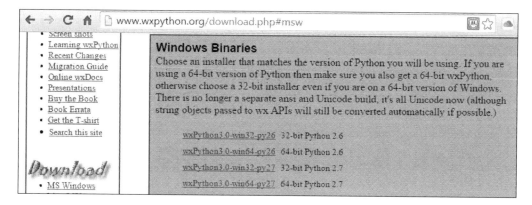

To use wxPython with Python 3, we have to install the wxPython/Phoenix library. We can find the installer at the snapshot-builds link:

```
http://wxpython.org/Phoenix/snapshot-builds/
```

From here, we can select the wxPython/Phoenix version that matches both our versions of Python and our OS. I am using Python 3.4 running on a 64-bit Windows 7 OS.

The Python wheel (.whl) installer package has a numbering scheme.

For us, the most important part of this scheme is that we are installing the wxPython/Phoenix build that is for Python 3.4 (the cp34 in the installer name) and for the Windows 64-bit OS (the win_amd64 part of the installer name).

After successfully downloading the wxPython/Phoenix package, we can now navigate to the directory where it resides and install this package using pip.

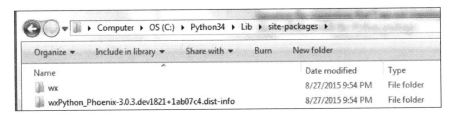

We have a new folder called wx in our Python `site-packages` folder.

 wx is the folder name the wxPython/Phoenix library installed into. We will import this module into our Python code.

We can verify that our installation worked by executing this simple demo script from the official wxPython/Phoenix website. The link to the official website is http://wxpython. org/Phoenix/docs/html/.

```
import wx
app = wx.App()
frame = wx.Frame(None, -1, "Hello World")
frame.Show()
app.MainLoop()
```

Running the preceding Python 3 script creates the following GUI using wxPython/Phoenix.

How it works...

In this recipe, we successfully installed the correct version of the wxPython toolkit, which we can use with Python 3. We found the Phoenix project for this GUI toolkit, which is the current and active development line. Phoenix will replace the Classic wxPython toolkit in time and is especially aimed at working well with Python 3.

After successfully installing the wxPython/Phoenix toolkit, we then created a GUI using this toolkit in only five lines of code.

 We previously achieved the same results by using tkinter.

How to create our GUI in wxPython

In this recipe, we will start to create our Python GUIs using the wxPython GUI toolkit.

We will first recreate several of the widgets we previously created using tkinter, which ships with Python.

Then, we will explore some of the widgets the wxPython GUI toolkit offers, which are harder to create using tkinter.

Getting ready

The previous recipe showed you how to install the correct version of wxPython that matches both your version of Python and the OS you are running.

How to do it...

A good place to start exploring the wxPython GUI toolkit is by going to the following URL: http://wxpython.org/Phoenix/docs/html/gallery.html

This webpage displays many wxPython widgets. By clicking on any of them, we are taken to their documentation, which is a very nice and helpful feature to quickly learn about a wxPython control.

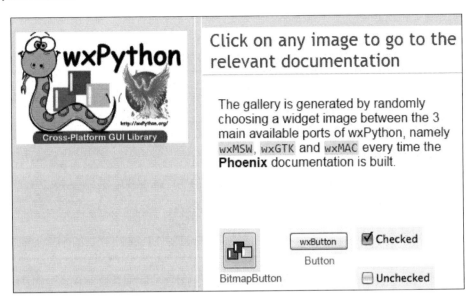

The following screenshot shows the documentation for a wxPython button widget.

We can very quickly create a working window that comes with a title, a menu bar, and also a status bar. This status bar displays the text of a menu item when hovering the mouse over it. This can be achieved by writing the following code:

```
# Import wxPython GUI toolkit
import wx
```

```python
# Subclass wxPython frame
class GUI(wx.Frame):
    def __init__(self, parent, title, size=(200,100)):
        # Initialize super class
        wx.Frame.__init__(self, parent, title=title, size=size)

        # Change the frame background color
        self.SetBackgroundColour('white')

        # Create Status Bar
        self.CreateStatusBar()

        # Create the Menu
        menu= wx.Menu()

        # Add Menu Items to the Menu
        menu.Append(wx.ID_ABOUT, "About", "wxPython GUI")
        menu.AppendSeparator()
        menu.Append(wx.ID_EXIT,"Exit"," Exit the GUI")

        # Create the MenuBar
        menuBar = wx.MenuBar()

        # Give the MenuBar a Title
        menuBar.Append(menu,"File")

        # Connect the MenuBar to the frame
        self.SetMenuBar(menuBar)

        # Display the frame
        self.Show()

# Create instance of wxPython application
app = wx.App()

# Call sub-classed wxPython GUI increasing default Window size
GUI(None, "Python GUI using wxPython", (300,150))

# Run the main GUI event loop
app.MainLoop()
```

This creates the following GUI, which is written in Python using the wxPython library.

In the previous code, we inherited from wx.Frame. In the following code, we inherit from wx.Panel and we pass in wx.Frame to the __init__() method of our class.

> In wxPython, the top-level GUI window is called a frame. There cannot be a wxPython GUI without a frame and the frame has to be created as part of a wxPython application.
>
> We create both the application and the frame at the bottom of our code.

In order to add widgets to our GUI, we have to attach them to a panel. The parent of the panel is the frame (our top-level window) and the parent of the widgets we place into the panel is the panel.

The following code adds a multiline textbox widget to a panel whose parent is a frame. We also add a button widget to the panel widget, which, when clicked, prints out some text to the textbox.

Here is the complete code:

```
import wx                    # Import wxPython GUI toolkit
class GUI(wx.Panel):          # Subclass wxPython Panel
    def __init__(self, parent):

        # Initialize super class
        wx.Panel.__init__(self, parent)

        # Create Status Bar
        parent.CreateStatusBar()

        # Create the Menu
        menu= wx.Menu()
```

```python
        # Add Menu Items to the Menu
        menu.Append(wx.ID_ABOUT, "About", "wxPython GUI")
        menu.AppendSeparator()
        menu.Append(wx.ID_EXIT,"Exit"," Exit the GUI")

        # Create the MenuBar
        menuBar = wx.MenuBar()

        # Give the Menu a Title
        menuBar.Append(menu,"File")

        # Connect the MenuBar to the frame
        parent.SetMenuBar(menuBar)

        # Create a Print Button
        button = wx.Button(self, label="Print", pos=(0,60))

        # Connect Button to Click Event method
        self.Bind(wx.EVT_BUTTON, self.printButton, button)

        # Create a Text Control widget
        self.textBox = wx.TextCtrl(
self, size=(280,50), style=wx.TE_MULTILINE)

    def printButton(self, event):
        self.textBox.AppendText(
"The Print Button has been clicked!")


app = wx.App()         # Create instance of wxPython application
frame = wx.Frame(None, title="Python GUI using wxPython",
size=(300,180))        # Create frame
GUI(frame)             # Pass frame into GUI
frame.Show()           # Display the frame
app.MainLoop()         # Run the main GUI event loop
```

Running the preceding code and clicking our wxPython button widget results in the following GUI output:

How it works...

We have created our own GUI in this recipe using the mature wxPython GUI toolkit. In only a few lines of Python code, we were able to create a fully functional GUI that comes with `Minimize`, `Maximize`, and `Exit` buttons. We added a menu bar, a multi-line text-control, and a button. We also created a status bar that displays text when we select a menu item. We placed all these widgets into a Panel container widget.

We hooked up the button to print to the text control.

When hovering over a menu item, some text gets displayed in the status bar.

Quickly adding controls using wxPython

In this recipe, we will recreate the GUI we originally created earlier in this book with tkinter , but this time, we will be using the wxPython library. We will see how easy and quick it is to use the wxPython GUI toolkit to create our own Python GUIs.

We will not recreate the entire functionality we created in previous chapters. For example, we will not internationalize our wxPython GUI nor connect it to a MySQL database. We will recreate the visual aspects of the GUI and add some functionality.

 Comparing different libraries gives us the choice of which toolkits to use for our own Python GUI development and we can combine several of those toolkits in our own Python code.

Getting ready

Ensure you have the wxPython module installed to follow this recipe.

How to do it...

First, we create our Python OOP class as we did before using tkinter, but this time we inherit from and extend the wx.Frame class. For clarity reasons, we no longer call our class OOP but instead rename it as MainFrame.

 In wxPython, the main GUI window is called a Frame.

We also create a callback method that closes the GUI when we click the Exit Menu Item and declare a light-gray tuple as the background color for our GUI.

```python
import wx
BACKGROUNDCOLOR = (240, 240, 240, 255)

class MainFrame(wx.Frame):
    def __init__(self, *args, **kwargs):
        wx.Frame.__init__(self, *args, **kwargs)

        self.createWidgets()
        self.Show()

    def exitGUI(self, event):      # callback
        self.Destroy()

    def createWidgets(self):
        self.CreateStatusBar()        # wxPython built-in method
        self.createMenu()
        self.createNotebook()
```

Next, we add a tabbed control to our GUI by creating an instance of the wxPython Notebook class and assign it as the parent to our own custom class named Widgets.

The `notebook` class instance variable has `wx.Panel` as its parent.

```
def createNotebook(self):
    panel = wx.Panel(self)
    notebook = wx.Notebook(panel)
    widgets = Widgets(notebook) # Custom class explained below
    notebook.AddPage(widgets, "Widgets")
    notebook.SetBackgroundColour(BACKGROUNDCOLOR)
    # layout
    boxSizer = wx.BoxSizer()
    boxSizer.Add(notebook, 1, wx.EXPAND)
    panel.SetSizerAndFit(boxSizer)
```

 In wxPython, the tabbed widget is named `Notebook`, just as in tkinter.

Every `Notebook` widget needs to have a parent and, in order to lay out widgets in the `Notebook` in wxPython, we use different kinds of sizers.

 wxPython sizers are layout managers similar to tkinter's grid layout manager.

Next, we add controls to our Notebook page. We do this by creating a separate class that inherits from `wx.Panel`.

```
class Widgets(wx.Panel):
    def __init__(self, parent):
        wx.Panel.__init__(self, parent)
        self.createWidgetsFrame()
        self.addWidgets()
        self.layoutWidgets()
```

We modularize our GUI code by breaking it into small methods, following Python OOP programming best practices, which keeps our code manageable and understandable.

```
#------------------------------------------------------------
def createWidgetsFrame(self):
    self.panel = wx.Panel(self)
    staticBox = wx.StaticBox( self.panel, -1, "Widgets Frame" )
    self.statBoxSizerV = wx.StaticBoxSizer(staticBox,
                                            wx.VERTICAL)
```

```
#----------------------------------------------------------
def layoutWidgets(self):
    boxSizerV = wx.BoxSizer( wx.VERTICAL )
    boxSizerV.Add( self.statBoxSizerV, 1, wx.ALL )
    self.panel.SetSizer( boxSizerV )
    boxSizerV.SetSizeHints( self.panel )


#----------------------------------------------------------
def addWidgets(self):
    self.addCheckBoxes()
    self.addRadioButtons()
    self.addStaticBoxWithLabels()
```

 When using wxPython StaticBox widgets, in order to successfully lay them out, we use a combination of a `StaticBoxSizer` and a regular `BoxSizer`. The wxPython StaticBox is very similar to the tkinter LabelFrame widget.

Embedding a `StaticBox` within another `StaticBox` is straightforward in tkinter, but using wxPython is a little non-intuitive. One way to make it work is shown as follows:

```
def addStaticBoxWithLabels(self):
    boxSizerH = wx.BoxSizer(wx.HORIZONTAL)
    staticBox = wx.StaticBox( self.panel, -1,
"Labels within a Frame" )
    staticBoxSizerV = wx.StaticBoxSizer( staticBox, wx.VERTICAL )
    boxSizerV = wx.BoxSizer( wx.VERTICAL )
    staticText1 = wx.StaticText( self.panel, -1,
"Choose a number:" )
    boxSizerV.Add( staticText1, 0, wx.ALL)
    staticText2 = wx.StaticText( self.panel, -1,"Label 2")
    boxSizerV.Add( staticText2, 0, wx.ALL )
    #----------------------------------------------------------
    staticBoxSizerV.Add( boxSizerV, 0, wx.ALL )
    boxSizerH.Add(staticBoxSizerV)
    #----------------------------------------------------------
    boxSizerH.Add(wx.TextCtrl(self.panel))
    # Add local boxSizer to main frame
    self.statBoxSizerV.Add( boxSizerH, 1, wx.ALL )
```

First, we create a horizontal `BoxSizer`. Next, we create a vertical `StaticBoxSizer` because we want to arrange two labels in a vertical layout in this frame.

In order to arrange another widget to the right of the embedded `StaticBox`, we have to assign both the embedded `StaticBox` with its children controls and the next widget to the horizontal `BoxSizer` and then assign this `BoxSizer`, which now contains both our embedded `StaticBox` and our other widgets, to the main `StaticBox`.

Does this sound confusing?

You have to just experiment with these sizers to get a feel for how to use them. Start with the code for this recipe and comment out some code, or modify some x and y coordinates to see the effects.

It is also good to read the official wxPython documentation to learn more.

 The important thing is knowing where in the code to add to the different sizers in order to achieve the layout we wish.

In order to create the second `StaticBox` below the first, we create separate `StaticBoxSizers` and assign them to the same panel.

```
class Widgets(wx.Panel):
    def __init__(self, parent):
        wx.Panel.__init__(self, parent)
        self.panel = wx.Panel(self)
        self.createWidgetsFrame()
        self.createManageFilesFrame()
        self.addWidgets()
        self.addFileWidgets()
        self.layoutWidgets()


    #------------------------------------------------------------
    def createWidgetsFrame(self):
        staticBox = wx.StaticBox(
self.panel, -1, "Widgets Frame", size=(285, -1) )
        self.statBoxSizerV = wx.StaticBoxSizer(
staticBox, wx.VERTICAL)


    #------------------------------------------------------------
    def createManageFilesFrame(self):
        staticBox = wx.StaticBox(
```

```
        self.panel, -1, "Manage Files", size=(285, -1) )
            self.statBoxSizerMgrV = wx.StaticBoxSizer(
    staticBox, wx.VERTICAL)


        #-----------------------------------------------------------
        def layoutWidgets(self):
            boxSizerV = wx.BoxSizer( wx.VERTICAL )
            boxSizerV.Add( self.statBoxSizerV, 1, wx.ALL )
            boxSizerV.Add( self.statBoxSizerMgrV, 1, wx.ALL )

            self.panel.SetSizer( boxSizerV )
            boxSizerV.SetSizeHints( self.panel )


        #-----------------------------------------------------------
        def addFileWidgets(self):
            boxSizerH = wx.BoxSizer(wx.HORIZONTAL)
            boxSizerH.Add(wx.Button(
    self.panel, label='Browse to File...'))
            boxSizerH.Add(wx.TextCtrl(
    self.panel, size=(174, -1), value= "Z:\\" ))

            boxSizerH1 = wx.BoxSizer(wx.HORIZONTAL)
            boxSizerH1.Add(wx.Button(
    self.panel, label='Copy File To:    '))
            boxSizerH1.Add(wx.TextCtrl(
    self.panel, size=(174, -1), value= "Z:\\Backup" ))

            boxSizerV = wx.BoxSizer(wx.VERTICAL)
            boxSizerV.Add(boxSizerH)
            boxSizerV.Add(boxSizerH1)

            self.statBoxSizerMgrV.Add( boxSizerV, 1, wx.ALL )
```

The following code instantiates the main event loop which runs our wxPython GUI program.

```
    #=====================
    # Start GUI
    #=====================
    app = wx.App()
    MainFrame(None, title="Python GUI using wxPython", size=(350,450))
    app.MainLoop()
```

The final result of our wxPython GUI looks like this:

How it works...

We design and lay out our wxPython GUI in several classes.

Once we have done this in the bottom section of our Python module, we create an instance of the wxPython application. Next, we instantiate our wxPython GUI code.

After that, we call the main GUI event loop that executes all of our Python code running within this application process. This displays our wxPython GUI.

Whatever code we place between the creation of the app and calling its main event loop becomes our wxPython GUI.

It might take some time to really get used to the wxPython library and its API, but once we understand how to use it, this library is really fun and a powerful tool to build our own Python GUIs. There also is a visual designer tool that can be used with wxPython: http://www.cae.tntech.edu/help/programming/wxdesigner-getting-started/view

This recipe used OOP to learn how to use the wxPython GUI toolkit.

Trying to embed a main wxPython app in a main tkinter app

Now that we have created the same GUI using both the Python's built-in tkinter library as well as the wxPython wrapper of the wxWidgets library, we really do need to combine the GUIs we created using these technologies.

 Both the wxPython and the tkinter libraries have their own advantages. In online forums such as `http://stackoverflow.com/`, we often see questions such as, which one is better? Which GUI toolkit should I use? This suggests that we have to make an "either-or" decision. We do not have to make such a decision.

One of the main challenges in doing so is that each GUI toolkit has to have its own event loop.

In this recipe, we will try to embed a simple wxPython GUI by calling it from our tkinter GUI.

Getting ready

We will reuse the tkinter GUI we built in a previous recipe in *Chapter 1, Creating the GUI Form and Adding Widgets*.

How to do it...

We are starting from a simple tkinter GUI that looks like this:

Next, we will try to invoke a simple wxPython GUI, which we created in a previous recipe in this chapter.

This is the entire code to do this in a simple, non-OOP way:

```
#============================================================
import tkinter as tk
from tkinter import ttk
from tkinter import scrolledtext

win = tk.Tk()

win.title("Python GUI")
aLabel = ttk.Label(win, text="A Label")
aLabel.grid(column=0, row=0)
ttk.Label(win, text="Enter a name:").grid(column=0, row=0)
name = tk.StringVar()
nameEntered = ttk.Entry(win, width=12, textvariable=name)
nameEntered.grid(column=0, row=1)
ttk.Label(win, text="Choose a number:").grid(column=1, row=0)
number = tk.StringVar()
numberChosen = ttk.Combobox(win, width=12, textvariable=number)
numberChosen['values'] = (1, 2, 4, 42, 100)
numberChosen.grid(column=1, row=1)
numberChosen.current(0)
scrolW  = 30
scrolH  = 3
scr = scrolledtext.ScrolledText(win, width=scrolW, height=scrolH,
wrap=tk.WORD)
scr.grid(column=0, sticky='WE', columnspan=3)
nameEntered.focus()


#============================================================
def wxPythonApp():
    import wx
    app = wx.App()
    frame = wx.Frame(None, -1, "wxPython GUI", size=(200,150))
    frame.SetBackgroundColour('white')
    frame.CreateStatusBar()
    menu= wx.Menu()
    menu.Append(wx.ID_ABOUT, "About", "wxPython GUI")
    menuBar = wx.MenuBar()
    menuBar.Append(menu,"File")
    frame.SetMenuBar(menuBar)
    frame.Show()
```

```
    app.MainLoop()

action = ttk.Button(win, text="Call wxPython GUI", command=
wxPythonApp )
action.grid(column=2, row=1)


#======================
# Start GUI
#======================
win.mainloop()
```

Running the preceding code starts a wxPython GUI from our tkinter GUI after clicking the tkinter `Button` control.

How it works...

The important part is that we placed the entire wxPython code into its own function, which we named `def wxPythonApp()`.

In the callback function for the button click-event, we simply call this code.

 One thing to note is that we have to close the wxPython GUI before we can continue using the tkinter GUI.

Trying to embed our tkinter GUI code into wxPython

In this recipe, we will go in the opposite direction to the previous recipe and try to call our tkinter GUI code from within a wxPython GUI.

Getting ready

We will reuse some of the wxPython GUI code we created in a previous recipe in this chapter.

How to do it...

We will start from a simple wxPython GUI, which looks like this:

Next, we will try to invoke a simple tkinter GUI.

This is the entire code to do this in a simple, non-OOP way:

```
#================================================================
def tkinterApp():
    import tkinter as tk
    from tkinter import ttk
    win = tk.Tk()
    win.title("Python GUI")
    aLabel = ttk.Label(win, text="A Label")
    aLabel.grid(column=0, row=0)
    ttk.Label(win, text="Enter a name:").grid(column=0, row=0)
    name = tk.StringVar()
    nameEntered = ttk.Entry(win, width=12, textvariable=name)
    nameEntered.grid(column=0, row=1)
    nameEntered.focus()
    def buttonCallback():
        action.configure(text='Hello ' + name.get())
    action = ttk.Button(win, text="Print", command=buttonCallback)
    action.grid(column=2, row=1)
    win.mainloop()
```

```
#================================================================
import wx
app = wx.App()
frame = wx.Frame(None, -1, "wxPython GUI", size=(200,180))
frame.SetBackgroundColour('white')
frame.CreateStatusBar()
menu= wx.Menu()
menu.Append(wx.ID_ABOUT, "About", "wxPython GUI")
menuBar = wx.MenuBar()
menuBar.Append(menu,"File")
frame.SetMenuBar(menuBar)
textBox = wx.TextCtrl(frame, size=(180,50), style=wx.TE_MULTILINE)

def tkinterEmbed(event):
    tkinterApp()


button = wx.Button(frame, label="Call tkinter GUI", pos=(0,60))
frame.Bind(wx.EVT_BUTTON, tkinterEmbed, button)
frame.Show()

#======================
# Start wxPython GUI
#======================
app.MainLoop()
```

Running the preceding code starts a tkinter GUI from our wxPython GUI after clicking the wxPython `Button` widget. We can then enter text into the tkinter textbox. By clicking its button, the button text gets updated with the name.

After starting the tkinter event loop, the wxPython GUI is still responsive because we can type into the `TextCtrl` widget while the tkinter GUI is up and running.

 In the previous recipe, we could not use our tkinter GUI until we had closed the wxPython GUI. Being aware of this difference can help our design decisions if we want to combine the two Python GUI technologies.

We can also create several tkinter GUI instances by clicking the wxPython GUI button several times. We cannot, however, close the wxPython GUI while any tkinter GUIs are still running. We have to close them first.

How it works...

In this recipe we went in the opposite direction to the previous recipe by first creating a GUI using wxPython and then, from wit-hin it, creating several GUI instances built using tkinter.

The wxPython GUI remained responsive while one or more tkinter GUIs were running. However, clicking the tkinter button only updated its button text in the first instance.

How to use Python to control two different GUI frameworks

In this recipe, we will explore ways to control the tkinter and wxPython GUI frameworks from Python. We have already used the Python threading module to keep our GUI responsive in the previous chapter, so here we will attempt to use the same approach.

We will see that things don't always work in a way that would be intuitive.

However, we will improve our tkinter GUI from being unresponsive while we invoke an instance of the wxPython GUI from within it.

Getting ready

This recipe will extend a previous recipe from this chapter in which we tried to embed a main wxPython GUI into our tkinter GUI.

How to do it...

When we created an instance of a wxPython GUI from our tkinter GUI, we could no longer use the tkinter GUI controls until we closed the one instance of the wxPython GUI. Let's improve on this now.

Our first attempt might be to use threading from the tkinter button callback function.

For example, our code might look like this:

```
def wxPythonApp():
    import wx
    app = wx.App()
    frame = wx.Frame(None, -1, "wxPython GUI", size=(200,150))
    frame.SetBackgroundColour('white')
    frame.CreateStatusBar()
    menu= wx.Menu()
    menu.Append(wx.ID_ABOUT, "About", "wxPython GUI")
    menuBar = wx.MenuBar()
    menuBar.Append(menu,"File")
    frame.SetMenuBar(menuBar)
    frame.Show()
    app.MainLoop()

def tryRunInThread():
    runT = Thread(target=wxPythonApp)
    runT.setDaemon(True)
    runT.start()
    print(runT)
    print('createThread():', runT.isAlive())

action = ttk.Button(win, text="Call wxPython GUI",
command=tryRunInThread)
```

At first, this seems to be working, which would be intuitive as the tkinter controls are no longer disabled and we can create several instances of the wxPython GUI by clicking the button. We can also type into and select the other tkinter widgets.

However, once we try to close the GUIs, we get an error from wxWidgets, and our Python executable crashes.

In order to avoid this, instead of trying to run the entire wxPython application in a thread, we can change the code to make only the wxPython `app.MainLoop` run in a thread.

```
def wxPythonApp():
    import wx
    app = wx.App()
    frame = wx.Frame(None, -1, "wxPython GUI", size=(200,150))
    frame.SetBackgroundColour('white')
    frame.CreateStatusBar()
    menu= wx.Menu()
    menu.Append(wx.ID_ABOUT, "About", "wxPython GUI")
    menuBar = wx.MenuBar()
    menuBar.Append(menu,"File")
    frame.SetMenuBar(menuBar)
    frame.Show()

    runT = Thread(target=app.MainLoop)
    runT.setDaemon(True)
    runT.start()
    print(runT)
    print('createThread():', runT.isAlive())

action = ttk.Button(win, text="Call wxPython GUI",
command=wxPythonApp)
action.grid(column=2, row=1)
```

How it works...

We first tried to run the entire wxPython GUI application in a thread, but this did not work as the wxPython main event loop expects to be the main thread of the application.

We found a workaround for this by only running the wxPython `app.MainLoop` in a thread, which tricks it into believing it is the main thread.

One side-effect of this approach is that we can no longer individually close all of the wxPython GUI instances. At least one of them only closes when we close the wxPython GUI which created the threads as daemons.

I am not quite sure why this is. Intuitively, one might expect to be able to close all daemon threads without having to wait for the main thread that created them to close first.

It possibly has to do with a reference counter not having been set to zero while our main thread is still running.

On a pragmatic level, this is how it currently works.

How to communicate between the two connected GUIs

In the previous recipes, we found ways to connect a wxPython GUI with a tkinter GUI, invoking one from the other and vice versa.

While both GUIs were successfully running at the same time, they did not really communicate with each other as they were only launching one another.

In this recipe, we will explore ways to make the two GUIs talk to each other.

Getting ready

Reading one of the previous recipes might be a good preparation for this recipe.

In this recipe, we will use a slightly modified GUI code compared to the previous recipe, but most of the basic GUI-building code is the same.

How to do it...

In the previous recipes, one of our main challenges was how to combine two GUI technologies that were designed to be the one-and-only GUI toolkit for an application. We found various simple ways to combine them.

We will again launch the wxPython GUI from a tkinter GUI main event loop and start the wxPython GUI in its own thread that runs within the tkinter process.

In order to do this, we will use a shared global multiprocessing Python queue.

 While it is often best to avoid global data in this recipe, they are a practical solution and Python globals are really only global in the module they have been declared in.

Here is the Python code that makes the two GUIs communicate with each other to a certain degree. In order to save space, this is not pure OOP code.

We are also not showing the creation code for all of the widgets. That code is the same as in previous recipes.

```
# Ch09_Communicate.py
import tkinter as tk
from tkinter import ttk
```

```
from threading import Thread

win = tk.Tk()
win.title("Python GUI")


from multiprocessing import Queue
sharedQueue = Queue()
dataInQueue = False

def putDataIntoQueue(data):
    global dataInQueue
    dataInQueue =  True
    sharedQueue.put(data)

def readDataFromQueue():
    global dataInQueue
    dataInQueue = False
    return sharedQueue.get()
#===========================================================
import wx
class GUI(wx.Panel):
    def __init__(self, parent):
        wx.Panel.__init__(self, parent)
        parent.CreateStatusBar()
        button = wx.Button(self, label="Print", pos=(0,60))
        self.Bind(wx.EVT_BUTTON, self.writeToSharedQueue, button)


    #-----------------------------------------------------
    def writeToSharedQueue(self, event):
        self.textBox.AppendText(
                      "The Print Button has been clicked!\n")
        putDataIntoQueue('Hi from wxPython via Shared Queue.\n')
        if dataInQueue:
            data = readDataFromQueue()
            self.textBox.AppendText(data)

            text.insert('0.0', data) # insert data into GUI


#===========================================================
def wxPythonApp():
        app = wx.App()
```

```
      frame = wx.Frame(
          None, title="Python GUI using wxPython", size=(300,180))
      GUI(frame)
      frame.Show()
      runT = Thread(target=app.MainLoop)
      runT.setDaemon(True)
      runT.start()
      print(runT)
      print('createThread():', runT.isAlive())
#================================================================
action = ttk.Button(win, text="Call wxPython GUI",
command=wxPythonApp)
action.grid(column=2, row=1)

#=====================
# Start GUI
#=====================
win.mainloop()
```

Running the preceding code first creates the tkinter part of the program and, when we click the button in this GUI, it runs the wxPython GUI. Both are running at the same time as before, but this time, there is an extra level of communication between the two GUIs.

The tkinter GUI is shown on the left-hand side of the preceding screenshot and, by clicking the **Call wxPython GUI** button, we invoke an instance of the wxPython GUI. We can create several instances by clicking the button several times.

 All of the created GUIs remain responsive. They do not crash nor freeze.

Clicking the **Print** button on any of the wxPython GUI instances writes one sentence to its own `TextCtrl` widget and then writes another line to itself as well as to the tkinter GUI. You will have to scroll up to see the first sentence in the wxPython GUI.

 The way this works is by using a module-level queue and a tkinter `Text` widget

One important element to note is that we create a thread to run the wxPython `app.MainLoop`, as we did in the previous recipe.

```
def wxPythonApp():
        app = wx.App()
        frame = wx.Frame(
None, title="Python GUI using wxPython", size=(300,180))
        GUI(frame)
        frame.Show()
        runT = Thread(target=app.MainLoop)
        runT.setDaemon(True)
        runT.start()
```

We create a class that inherits from `wx.Panel` and name it `GUI`. We then instantiate an instance of this class in the preceding code.

We create a button click-event callback method in this class, which then calls the procedural code that was written above it. Because of this, the class has access to the functions and can write to the shared queue.

```
        #---------------------------------------------------------
        def writeToSharedQueue(self, event):
            self.textBox.AppendText(
    "The Print Button has been clicked!\n")
            putDataIntoQueue('Hi from wxPython via Shared Queue.\n')
            if dataInQueue:
                data = readDataFromQueue()
                self.textBox.AppendText(data)
                text.insert('0.0', data) # insert data into tkinter
```

We first check if the data has been placed in the shared queue in the preceding method and, if that is the case, we then print the common data to both GUIs.

> The putDataIntoQueue() line places data into the queue and readDataFromQueue() reads it back out saving it in the data variable.
>
> text.insert('0.0', data) is the line that writes this data into the tkinter GUI from the **Print** button's wxPython callback method.

Following are the procedural functions (not methods, for they are not bound) that are being called in the code and that make it work.

```
from multiprocessing import Queue
sharedQueue = Queue()
dataInQueue = False

def putDataIntoQueue(data):
    global dataInQueue
    dataInQueue =  True
    sharedQueue.put(data)

def readDataFromQueue():
    global dataInQueue
    dataInQueue = False
    return sharedQueue.get()
```

We are using a simple Boolean flag named dataInQueue to communicate when the data is available in the queue.

How it works...

In this recipe, we have successfully combined the two GUIs we created in a similar fashion, but previously standalone and not talking to each other. However, in this recipe, we connected them further by making one GUI launch another and, via a simple multiprocessing Python queue mechanism, we were able to make them communicate with each other, writing data from a shared queue into both GUIs.

There are many very advanced and complicated technologies available to connect different processes, threads, pools, locks, pipes, TCP/IP connections, and so on.

In the Pythonic spirit, we found a simple solution that works for us. Once our code becomes more complicated, we might have to refactor it, but this is a good beginning.

10

Creating Amazing 3D GUIs with PyOpenGL and PyGLet

In this chapter we will create amazing Python GUIs that display true 3-Dimensional images that can be rotated around themselves so that we can look at them from all sides.

- ▸ PyOpenGL transforms our GUI
- ▸ Our GUI in 3D!
- ▸ Using bitmaps to make our GUI pretty
- ▸ PyGLet transforms our GUI more easily than PyOpenGL
- ▸ Our GUI in amazing colors
- ▸ Creating a slide show using tkinter

Introduction

In this chapter, we will transform our GUI by giving it true 3-dimensional capabilities. We will use two Python third-party packages. PyOpenGL is a Python binding to the OpenGL standard, which is a graphics library that comes built-in with all major operating systems. This gives the resulting widgets a native look and feel.

Pyglet is another Python binding to the OpenGL library, but it can also create GUI applications, which can make coding using Pyglet easier than using PyOpenGL.

PyOpenGL transforms our GUI

In this recipe, we will successfully create a Python GUI that imports PyOpenGL modules and does actually work!

In order to do so, we need to overcome some initial challenges.

This recipe will show one proven way that does work. If you experiment on your own and get stuck, remember the famous words from Thomas A. Edison.

 Thomas Edison, inventor of the light bulb, answered a question from a reporter who talked about Edison's failures. Edison replied:

"I have not failed. I've just found 10,000 ways that won't work."

First, we have to install the PyOpenGL extension module.

After successfully installing the PyOpenGL modules that match our OS architecture, we will create some example code.

Getting ready

We will install the PyOpenGL package. In this book, we are using Windows 7 64-bit OS and Python 3.4. The screenshot of downloads that follows is for this configuration.

We will also be using wxPython. If you do not have wxPython installed, you can read some recipes from the previous chapter about how to install wxPython and how to use this GUI framework.

 We are using the wxPython Phoenix release, which is the newest release and is intended to replace the original Classic wxPython release in the future.

How to do it...

In order to use PyOpenGL, we have to first install it. The following URL is the official Python package installer website:

```
https://pypi.python.org/pypi/PyOpenGL/3.0.2#downloads
```

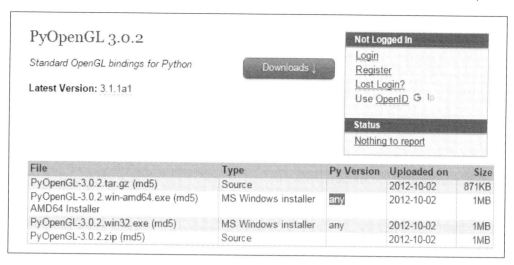

This seems to be the correct installation but, as it turns out, it doesn't work with Windows 7 64-bit OS with Python 3.4.3 64-bit.

A better place to look for Python installation packages was mentioned in a recipe in a previous chapter. You are probably already familiar with it. We download the package that matches both our OS and our Python version. It comes with the new `.whl` format, so we have to install the Python wheel package first.

 How to install the Python wheel package is described in a previous recipe.

Installing PyOpenGL via the `PyOpenGL-3.1.1a1-cp34-none-win_amd64.whl` file using the `pip` command is both successful and installs all of the 64-bit modules we require.

Replace `<your full path>` with the full path you downloaded the wheel installer to.

```
pip install <your full path> PyOpenGL-3.1.1a1-cp34-none-win_amd64.whl
```

When we now try to import some PyOpenGL modules, it works, as can be seen in this code example:

```
# Ch10_import_OpenGL.py
import wx
from wx import glcanvas
from OpenGL.GL import *
from OpenGL.GLUT import *
```

All this code is doing is importing several of the OpenGL Python modules. It does not do anything else but, when we run our Python module, we do not get any errors.

This proves that we have successfully installed the OpenGL bindings to Python.

Now our development environment has been successfully set up and we can try it out using wxPython.

 Many online examples are restricted to using Python 2.x, as well as using the Classic version of wxPython. We are using Python 3 and Phoenix.

Using the code based on the wxPython demo examples creates a working 3D cube. In comparison, running the cone example did not work, but this example got us started on the right track.

Here is the URL:

```
http://wiki.wxpython.org/GLCanvas%20update
```

Here are some modifications to the code:

```
import wx
from wx import glcanvas
from OpenGL.GL import *
from OpenGL.GLUT import *

class MyCanvasBase(glcanvas.GLCanvas):
    def __init__(self, parent):
        glcanvas.GLCanvas.__init__(self, parent, -1)

# This context was missing from the code
        self.context = glcanvas.GLContext(self)   # <- added

    def OnPaint(self, event):
        dc = wx.PaintDC(self)
# We have to pass in a context ------
#           self.SetCurrent()                     # commented out
            self.SetCurrent(self.context)         # <- changed
```

We now can create the following GUI:

In the Classic version of wxPython `SetCurrent()` did not require a context. Here is some code we might find when searching online.

```python
def OnPaint(self, event):

    dc = wx.PaintDC(self)
    self.SetCurrent()
    if not self.init:
        self.InitGL()
        self.init = True
    self.OnDraw()
```

The preceding code does not work when using wxPython Phoenix. We can look up the correct syntax for Phoenix online.

How it works...

In this recipe, we had our first experiences of OpenGL with PyOpenGL Python bindings. While OpenGL can create truly amazing images in true 3D, we ran into some challenges along the way and then found solutions to these challenges that made it work.

 We are coding in Python, creating 3D images!

Our GUI in 3D!

In this recipe we will create our own GUI using wxPython. We are reusing some code from the wxPython demo examples, which we have reduced to the minimum code required to display OpenGL in 3D.

 OpenGL is a very large library. We will not go into detailed explanations of this library. There are a lot of books and online documentation available if you want to study OpenGL further. It has its own shading language.

Getting ready

Reading the previous recipe is probably good preparation for this recipe.

How to do it...

As the entire Python code is a little bit long here, we will show just a little bit of the code.

The entire code is available online and this Python module is called:

```
# Ch10_wxPython_OpenGL_GUI
import wx
from wx import glcanvas
from OpenGL.GL import *
from OpenGL.GLUT import *

#-----------------------------------------------------
class CanvasBase(glcanvas.GLCanvas):
    def __init__(self, parent):
```

```
glcanvas.GLCanvas.__init__(self, parent, -1)
self.context = glcanvas.GLContext(self)
self.init = False

# Cube 3D start rotation
self.last_X = self.x = 30
self.last_Y = self.y = 30

self.Bind(wx.EVT_SIZE, self.sizeCallback)
self.Bind(wx.EVT_PAINT, self.paintCallback)
self.Bind(wx.EVT_LEFT_DOWN, self.mouseDownCallback)
self.Bind(wx.EVT_LEFT_UP, self.mouseUpCallback)
self.Bind(wx.EVT_MOTION, self.mouseMotionCallback)

def sizeCallback(self, event):
    wx.CallAfter(self.setViewport)
    event.Skip()

def setViewport(self):
    self.size = self.GetClientSize()
    self.SetCurrent(self.context)
    glViewport(0, 0, self.size.width, self.size.height)

def paintCallback(self, event):
    wx.PaintDC(self)
    self.SetCurrent(self.context)
    if not self.init:
        self.initGL()
        self.init = True
    self.onDraw()

def mouseDownCallback(self, event):
    self.CaptureMouse()
    self.x, self.y = self.last_X, self.last_Y = event.GetPosition()

def mouseUpCallback(self, evt):
    self.ReleaseMouse()

def mouseMotionCallback(self, evt):
    if evt.Dragging() and evt.LeftIsDown():
        self.last_X, self.last_Y = self.x, self.y
```

```
            self.x, self.y = evt.GetPosition()
            self.Refresh(False)


#--------------------------------------------------------
class CubeCanvas(CanvasBase):
    def initGL(self):
        # set viewing projection
        glMatrixMode(GL_PROJECTION)
        glFrustum(-0.5, 0.5, -0.5, 0.5, 1.0, 3.0)

        # position viewer
        glMatrixMode(GL_MODELVIEW)
        glTranslatef(0.0, 0.0, -2.0)

        # position object
        glRotatef(self.y, 1.0, 0.0, 0.0)
        glRotatef(self.x, 0.0, 1.0, 0.0)

        glEnable(GL_DEPTH_TEST)
        glEnable(GL_LIGHTING)
        glEnable(GL_LIGHT0)

    def onDraw(self):
        # clear color and depth buffers
        glClear(GL_COLOR_BUFFER_BIT | GL_DEPTH_BUFFER_BIT)

        # draw six faces of a cube
        glBegin(GL_QUADS)
        glNormal3f( 0.0, 0.0, 1.0)
        glVertex3f( 0.5, 0.5, 0.5)
        glVertex3f(-0.5, 0.5, 0.5)
        glVertex3f(-0.5,-0.5, 0.5)
        glVertex3f( 0.5,-0.5, 0.5)

        glNormal3f( 0.0, 0.0,-1.0)
        glVertex3f(-0.5,-0.5,-0.5)


#============================================================
app = wx.App()
```

```
frame = wx.Frame(None, title="Python GUI using wxPython",
size=(300,230))
GUI(frame)
frame.Show()
app.MainLoop()
```

The preceding screenshot shows our wxPython GUI. When we click the button widget, the following second window appears.

We can now use the mouse to turn the cube around to see all of its six sides.

We can also maximize this window and the coordinates will scale and we can spin this cube around in this much larger window!

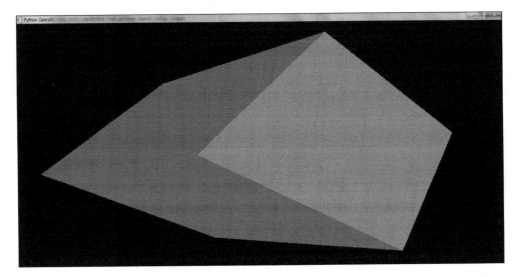

The cube could also be a Star Trek space ship!

We just have to become an advanced programmer in this technology if this is what we want to develop.

 Many video games are being developed using OpenGL.

How it works...

We first created a regular wxPython GUI and placed a button widget onto it. Clicking this button invokes the imported OpenGL 3D libraries. The code used is part of the wxPython demo examples, which we slightly modified to make it work with Phoenix.

 This recipe glued our own GUI to this library.

OpenGL is such a huge and impressive library. This recipe gave a taste of how to create a working example in Python.

 Often a working example is all we need to get started on our journey.

Using bitmaps to make our GUI pretty

This recipe was inspired by a wxPython IDE builder framework that, at some point in time, used to work.

It does not work with Python 3 and wxPython Phoenix, but the code is very cool.

We will reuse a bitmap image from the large amount of code this project supplies.

Before time runs out, you can fork the Google code on GitHub.

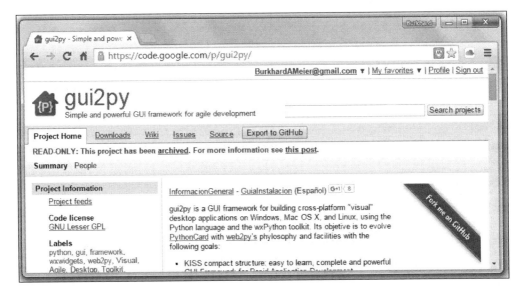

Getting ready

We will continue to use wxPython in this recipe, so reading at least parts of the previous chapter might be useful as a preparation for this recipe.

How to do it...

After reverse-engineering the gui2py code and making other changes to this code, we might achieve the following window widget, which displays a nice, tiled background.

Of course, we lost a lot of widgets refactoring the code from the website mentioned previously, yet it does give us a cool background, and clicking the **Quit** button still works.

The next step is to figure out how to integrate the interesting part of the code into our own GUI.

We do this by adding the following code to the GUI of the previous recipe.

```
#------------------------------------------------------------
class GUI(wx.Panel):                    # Subclass wxPython Panel
    def __init__(self, parent):
        wx.Panel.__init__(self, parent)

        imageFile = 'Tile.bmp'
        self.bmp = wx.Bitmap(imageFile)
        # react to a resize event and redraw image
        parent.Bind(wx.EVT_SIZE, self.canvasCallback)
```

```
def canvasCallback(self, event=None):
    # create the device context
    dc = wx.ClientDC(self)
    brushBMP = wx.Brush(self.bmp)
    dc.SetBrush(brushBMP)
    width, height = self.GetClientSize()
    dc.DrawRectangle(0, 0, width, height)
```

 We have to bind to parent, not self, otherwise our bitmap will not show up.

Running our improved code now tiles a bitmap as the background of our GUI.

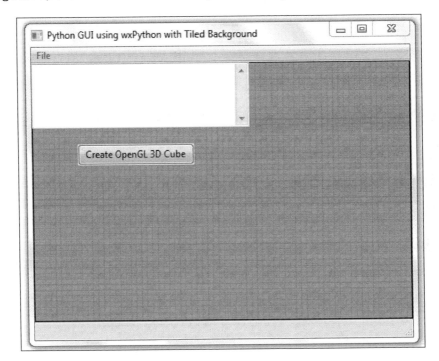

Clicking the button still invokes our OpenGL 3D drawing, so we did not lose any functionality.

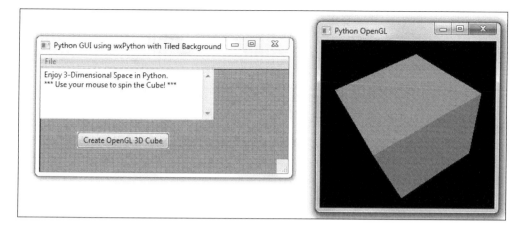

How it works...

In this recipe, we enhanced our GUI by using a bitmap as a background. We tiled the bitmap image and when we resized the GUI window, the bitmap automatically adjusted itself to fill in the entire area of the Canvas we were painting on using the device context.

   The preceding wxPython code can load different image file formats.

PyGLet transforms our GUI more easily than PyOpenGL

In this recipe, we will use the PyGLet GUI development framework to create our GUIs.

PyGLet is easier to use than PyOpenGL as it comes with its own GUI event loop, so we do not need to use tkinter or wxPython to create our GUI.

How to do it...

In order to use Pyglet, we first have to install this third-party Python plugin.

Using the `pip` command, we can easily install the library and a successful installation looks like this in our `site-packages` Python folder:

The online documentation is located at this website for the current release:

```
https://pyglet.readthedocs.org/en/pyglet-1.2-maintenance/
```

A first experience using the Pyglet library may look like this:

```python
import pyglet

window = pyglet.window.Window()
label = pyglet.text.Label('PyGLet GUI',
                          font_size=42,
                          x=window.width//2, y=window.height//2,
                          anchor_x='center', anchor_y='center')

@window.event
def on_draw():
    window.clear()
    label.draw()

pyglet.app.run()
```

The preceding code is from the official pyglet.org website and results in the following fully functional GUI:

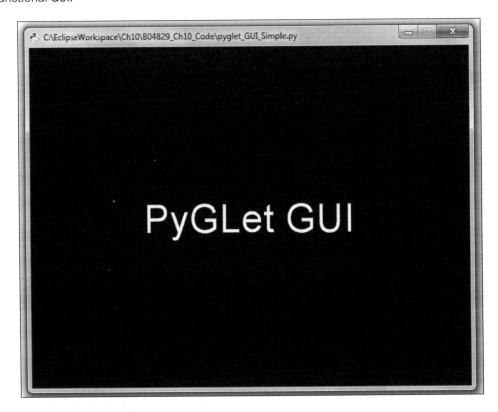

How it works...

In this recipe, we used another third-party Python module that wraps the OpenGL library.

This library comes with its own event loop processing power, which enables us to avoid having to rely on yet another library to create a running Python GUI.

We have explored the official website that shows us how to install and use this fantastic GUI library.

Our GUI in amazing colors

In this recipe, we will extend our GUI written using Pyglet from the previous recipe, by turning it into true 3D.

We will also add some fancy colors to it. This recipe was inspired by some sample code from the *OpenGL SuperBible* book series. It creates a very colorful cube, which we can turn around in 3-dimensional space using the keyboard up, down, left, and right buttons.

We have slightly improved the sample code by making the image turn when holding down one of the keys instead of having to press and release the key.

Getting ready

The previous recipe explains how to install PyGLet and gives you an introduction to this library. If you have not done so, it is probably a good idea to browse through that chapter.

In the online documentation, PyGLet is usually spelled in all lower-case. While this might be a Pythonic way, we capitalize the first letter of a class and we use lower case for variable, method, and function names to start each name.

We do not use underscores in this book unless necessary to clarify code.

How to do it...

The following code creates the 3-dimensional colored cube shown below it. This time, we will use the keyboard arrow keys to rotate the image, instead of the mouse.

```
import pyglet
from pyglet.gl import *
from pyglet.window import key
from OpenGL.GLUT import *

WINDOW    = 400
INCREMENT = 5

class Window(pyglet.window.Window):

    # Cube 3D start rotation
    xRotation = yRotation = 30
```

```
    def __init__(self, width, height, title=''):
        super(Window, self).__init__(width, height, title)
        glClearColor(0, 0, 0, 1)
        glEnable(GL_DEPTH_TEST)

    def on_draw(self):
        # Clear the current GL Window
        self.clear()

        # Push Matrix onto stack
        glPushMatrix()

        glRotatef(self.xRotation, 1, 0, 0)
        glRotatef(self.yRotation, 0, 1, 0)

        # Draw the six sides of the cube
        glBegin(GL_QUADS)

        # White
        glColor3ub(255, 255, 255)
        glVertex3f(50,50,50)

        # Yellow
        glColor3ub(255, 255, 0)
        glVertex3f(50,-50,50)

        # Red
        glColor3ub(255, 0, 0)
        glVertex3f(-50,-50,50)
        glVertex3f(-50,50,50)

        # Blue
        glColor3f(0, 0, 1)
        glVertex3f(-50,50,-50)

        # <… more color defines for cube faces>

        glEnd()

        # Pop Matrix off stack
        glPopMatrix()

    def on_resize(self, width, height):
        # set the Viewport
        glViewport(0, 0, width, height)

        # using Projection mode
        glMatrixMode(GL_PROJECTION)
```

```
        glLoadIdentity()

        aspectRatio = width / height
        gluPerspective(35, aspectRatio, 1, 1000)

        glMatrixMode(GL_MODELVIEW)
        glLoadIdentity()
        glTranslatef(0, 0, -400)


    def on_text_motion(self, motion):
        if motion == key.UP:
            self.xRotation -= INCREMENT
        elif motion == key.DOWN:
            self.xRotation += INCREMENT
        elif motion == key.LEFT:
            self.yRotation -= INCREMENT
        elif motion == key.RIGHT:
            self.yRotation += INCREMENT


if __name__ == '__main__':
    Window(WINDOW, WINDOW, 'Pyglet Colored Cube')
    pyglet.app.run()
```

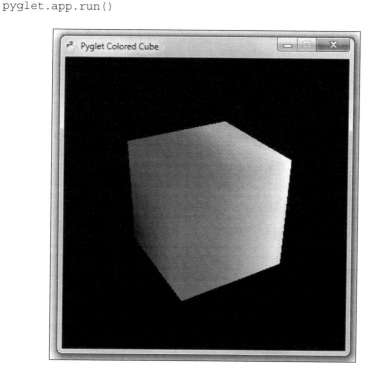

Using the keyboard arrow keys, we can spin the 3D cube around.

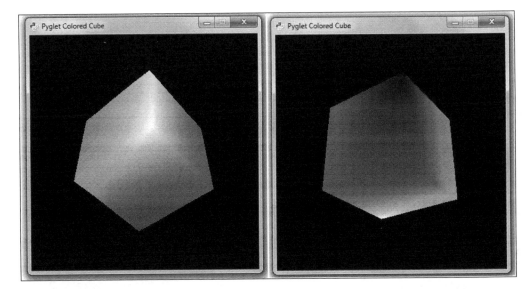

How it works...

In this recipe, we have used pyglet to create a colorful cube, which we can rotate in 3-dimensional space using the keyboard arrow keys.

We have defined several colors for the six faces of our cube and we have used pyglet to create our main window frame.

The code is similar to a previous recipe in this chapter, in which we used the wxPython library to create a cube. The reason for this is that underneath the hood, both wxPython and pyglet use the OpenGL library.

Creating a slideshow using tkinter

In this recipe, we will create a nice working slideshow GUI using pure Python.

We will see the limitations the core Python built-ins have, and then we will explore another third-party module available called Pillow, which extends tkinter's built-in functionality in regards to image processing.

While the name Pillow might sound a little bit strange at first, it actually comes with a lot of history behind it.

We are only using Python 3.4 and above in this book.

We are not going back to Python 2.

Guido has expressed his decision to intentionally break backwards compatibility and has decided that Python 3 is the future of Python programming.

For GUIs and images, the older line of Python 2 has this very powerful module named PIL, which stands for Python Image Library. This library comes with a very large amount of functionality, which several years after the very successful creation of Python 3 has not been translated for Python 3.

Many developers still choose to use Python 2 instead of the future, as designed by the Benevolent Dictator of Python, because Python 2 still has more libraries available.

That is a little bit sad.

Fortunately, another imaging library has been created to work with Python 3 and it is named PIL plus something.

Pillow is not compatible with the Python 2 PIL library.

Getting ready

In the first part of this recipe, we will use pure Python. In order to improve the code, we will install another Python module using pip functionality. So, while you are most likely familiar with pip, a little knowledge of how to use it might be useful.

How to do it...

First, we will create a working GUI that shuffles slides within a window frame using pure Python.

Here is the working code and following it are some screenshots of the results of running this code:

```python
from tkinter import Tk, PhotoImage, Label
from itertools import cycle
from os import listdir
```

```
class SlideShow(Tk):
    # inherit GUI framework extending tkinter
    def __init__(self, msShowTimeBetweenSlides=1500):
        # initialize tkinter super class
        Tk.__init__(self)

        # time each slide will be shown
        self.showTime = msShowTimeBetweenSlides

        # look for images in current working directory
        listOfSlides = [slide for slide in listdir() if slide.
endswith('gif')]

        # cycle slides to show on the tkinter Label
        self.iterableCycle = cycle((PhotoImage(file=slide), slide) for
slide in listOfSlides)

        # create tkinter Label widget which can display images
        self.slidesLabel = Label(self)

        # create the Frame widget
        self.slidesLabel.pack()


    def slidesCallback(self):
        # get next slide from iterable cycle
        currentInstance, nameOfSlide = next(self.iterableCycle)

        # assign next slide to Label widget
        self.slidesLabel.config(image=currentInstance)

        # update Window title with current slide
        self.title(nameOfSlide)

        # recursively repeat the Show
        self.after(self.showTime, self.slidesCallback)


#=================================
# Start GUI
#=================================
win = SlideShow()
```

```
win.after(0, win.slidesCallback())
win.mainloop()
```

Here is another moment in time in the unfolding slideshow.

While the slides sliding are truly impressive, the built-in capabilities of pure Python tkinter GUIs do not support the very popular `.jpg` format, so we have to reach out to another Python library.

In order to use Pillow, we first have to install it using the `pip` command.

A successful installation looks like this:

Pillow supports .jpg formats and, in order to use it, we to have to slightly change our syntax.

Using Pillow is an advanced topic that will not be covered in this edition of the book.

How it works...

Python is a very wonderful tool, and in this recipe, we have explored several ways to use and extend it.

[When a finger points at the moon, it is not the moon itself, just a pointer.]

11
Best Practices

In this chapter, we will explore best practices related to our Python GUI.

- ▸ Avoiding spaghetti code
- ▸ Using __init__ to connect modules
- ▸ Mixing fall-down and OOP coding
- ▸ Using a code naming convention
- ▸ When not to use OOP
- ▸ How to use design patterns successfully
- ▸ Avoiding complexity

Introduction

In this chapter, we will explore different best practices that can help us to build our GUI in an efficient way and keep it both maintainable and extendible.

These best practices will also help us to debug our GUI to get it just the way we want it to be.

Avoiding spaghetti code

In this recipe, we will explore a typical way to create spaghetti code and then we will see a much better way of how to avoid such code.

 Spaghetti code is code in which a lot of functionality is intertangled.

Getting ready

We will create a new, simple GUI written in Python using the tkinter built-in Python library.

How to do it...

Having searched online and read the documentation, we might start by writing the following code to create our GUI:

```
# Spaghetti Code ###########################
def PRINTME(me):print(me)
import tkinter
x=y=z=1
PRINTME(z)
from tkinter import *
scrolW=30;scrolH=6
win=tkinter.Tk()
if x:chVarUn=tkinter.IntVar()
from tkinter import ttk
WE='WE'
import tkinter.scrolledtext
outputFrame=tkinter.ttk.LabelFrame(win,text=' Type into the scrolled
text control: ')
scr=tkinter.scrolledtext.
ScrolledText(outputFrame,width=scrolW,height=scrolH,wrap=tkinter.WORD)
e='E'
scr.grid(column=1,row=1,sticky=WE)
outputFrame.grid(column=0,row=2,sticky=e,padx=8)
lFrame=None
if y:chck2=tkinter.Checkbutton(lFrame,text="Enabled",variable=chVarUn)
wE='WE'
if y==x:PRINTME(x)
lFrame=tkinter.ttk.LabelFrame(win,text="Spaghetti")
chck2.grid(column=1,row=4,sticky=tkinter.W,columnspan=3)
PRINTME(z)
lFrame.grid(column=0,row=0,sticky=wE,padx=10,pady=10)
chck2.select()
try: win.mainloop()
except:PRINTME(x)
chck2.deselect()
if y==x:PRINTME(x)
# End Pasta ###########################
```

Running the preceding code results in the following GUI:

This is not quite the GUI we intended. We wanted it to look something more like this:

While the spaghetti code created a GUI, the code is very hard to debug because there is so much confusion in the code.

The following is the code that produces the desired GUI:

```
#======================
# imports
#======================
import tkinter as tk
from tkinter import ttk
from tkinter import scrolledtext


#======================
# Create instance
```

```
#======================
win = tk.Tk()


#======================
# Add a title
#======================
win.title("Python GUI")


#========================
# Disable resizing the GUI
#========================
win.resizable(0,0)


#==============================================================
# Adding a LabelFrame, Textbox (Entry) and Combobox
#==============================================================
lFrame = ttk.LabelFrame(win, text="Python GUI Programming Cookbook")
lFrame.grid(column=0, row=0, sticky='WE', padx=10, pady=10)


#==============================================================
# Using a scrolled Text control
#==============================================================
outputFrame = ttk.LabelFrame(win, text=' Type into the scrolled text
control: ')
outputFrame.grid(column=0, row=2, sticky='E', padx=8)
scrolW  = 30
scrolH  =  6
scr = scrolledtext.ScrolledText(outputFrame, width=scrolW,
height=scrolH, wrap=tk.WORD)
scr.grid(column=1, row=0, sticky='WE')


#==============================================================
# Creating a checkbutton
#==============================================================
chVarUn = tk.IntVar()
check2 = tk.Checkbutton(lFrame, text="Enabled", variable=chVarUn)
check2.deselect()
check2.grid(column=1, row=4, sticky=tk.W, columnspan=3)


#======================
# Start GUI
#======================
win.mainloop()
```

How it works...

In this recipe, we compared spaghetti code to good code. Good code has many advantages over the spaghetti code.

It has clearly commented sections.

Spaghetti code:

```
def PRINTME(me):print(me)
import tkinter
x=y=z=1
PRINTME(z)
from tkinter import *
```

Good code:

```
#=======================
# imports
#=======================
import tkinter as tk
from tkinter import ttk
```

It has a natural flow that follows how the widgets get laid out in the GUI main form.

In the spaghetti code, the bottom LabelFrame gets created before the top LabelFrame and it is intermixed with an import statement and some widget creation.

Spaghetti code:

```
import tkinter.scrolledtext
outputFrame=tkinter.ttk.LabelFrame(win,text=' Type into the scrolled
text control: ')
scr=tkinter.scrolledtext.
ScrolledText(outputFrame,width=scrolW,height=scrolH,wrap=tkinter.WORD)
e='E'
scr.grid(column=1,row=1,sticky=WE)
outputFrame.grid(column=0,row=2,sticky=e,padx=8)
lFrame=None
if y:chck2=tkinter.Checkbutton(lFrame,text="Enabled",variable=chVarUn)
wE='WE'
if y==x:PRINTME(x)
lFrame=tkinter.ttk.LabelFrame(win,text="Spaghetti")
```

Good code:

```
#=================================================================
# Adding a LabelFrame, Textbox (Entry) and Combobox
#=================================================================
lFrame = ttk.LabelFrame(win, text="Python GUI Programming Cookbook")
lFrame.grid(column=0, row=0, sticky='WE', padx=10, pady=10)


#=================================================================
# Using a scrolled Text control
#=================================================================
outputFrame = ttk.LabelFrame(win, text=' Type into the scrolled text
control: ')
outputFrame.grid(column=0, row=2, sticky='E', padx=8)
```

It does not contain unnecessary variable assignments and neither does it have a `print` function that does not do the debugging one might expect it to do when reading the code.

Spaghetti code:

```
def PRINTME(me):print(me)
x=y=z=1
e='E'
WE='WE'
scr.grid(column=1,row=1,sticky=WE)
wE='WE'
if y==x:PRINTME(x)
lFrame.grid(column=0,row=0,sticky=wE,padx=10,pady=10)
PRINTME(z)
try: win.mainloop()
except:PRINTME(x)
chck2.deselect()
if y==x:PRINTME(x)
```

Good code:

Has none of the above.

The `import` statements only import the required modules. They are not cluttered throughout the code. There are no duplicate `import` statements. There is no `import *` statement.

Spaghetti code:

```
import tkinter 1
x=y=z=1
```

```
PRINTME(z)
from tkinter import *
scrolW=30;scrolH=6
win=tkinter.Tk()
if x:chVarUn=tkinter.IntVar()
from tkinter import ttk
WE='WE'
import tkinter.scrolledtext
```

Good code:

```
import tkinter as tk
from tkinter import ttk
from tkinter import scrolledtext
```

The chosen variable names are quite meaningful. There are no unnecessary `if` statements that use the number 1 instead of `True`.

Spaghetti code:

```
x=y=z=1
if x:chVarUn=tkinter.IntVar()
wE='WE'
```

Good code:

```
#=============================================================
# Using a scrolled Text control
#=============================================================
outputFrame = ttk.LabelFrame(win, text=' Type into the scrolled text
control: ')
outputFrame.grid(column=0, row=2, sticky='E', padx=8)
scrolW  = 30
scrolH  =  6
scr = scrolledtext.ScrolledText(outputFrame, width=scrolW,
height=scrolH, wrap=tk.WORD)
scr.grid(column=1, row=0, sticky='WE')
```

We did not lose the intended window title and our check button ended up in the correct position. We also made the `LabelFrame` surrounding the check button visible.

Spaghetti code:

We lost both the window title and did not display the top `LabelFrame`. The check button ended up in the wrong place.

Good code:

```
#=====================
# Create instance
#=====================
win = tk.Tk()


#=====================
# Add a title
#=====================
win.title("Python GUI")


#============================================================
# Adding a LabelFrame, Textbox (Entry) and Combobox
#============================================================
lFrame = ttk.LabelFrame(win, text="Python GUI Programming Cookbook")
lFrame.grid(column=0, row=0, sticky='WE', padx=10, pady=10)


#============================================================
# Creating a checkbutton
#============================================================
chVarUn = tk.IntVar()
check2 = tk.Checkbutton(lFrame, text="Enabled", variable=chVarUn)
check2.deselect()
check2.grid(column=1, row=4, sticky=tk.W, columnspan=3)


#=====================
# Start GUI
#=====================
win.mainloop()
```

Using __init__ to connect modules

When we create a new Python project using the PyDev plugin for the Eclipse IDE, it automatically creates a __init__.py module. We can also create it ourselves manually when not using Eclipse.

 The __init__.py module is usually empty and then has a size of 0 kilobytes.

We can use this usually empty module to connect different Python modules by entering code into it. This recipe will show how to do this.

Getting ready

We will create a new GUI similar to the one we created in the previous recipe.

How to do it...

As our project becomes larger and larger, we naturally break it out into several Python modules. Using a modern IDE such as Eclipse, it is surprisingly complicated to find modules that are located in different subfolders either above or below the code that needs to import it.

One practical way to get around this limitation is to use the __init__.py module.

 In Eclipse, we can set the Eclipse internal project environment to certain folders and our Python code will find it. But outside of Eclipse, for example when running from a command window, there is sometimes a mismatch in the Python module import mechanism and the code will not run.

Here is a screenshot of the empty __init__.py module, which appears not with the name __init__ but with the name of the PyDev package it belongs to when opened in the Eclipse code editor. The "1" on the left side of the code editor is the line number and not any code written in this module. There is absolutely no code in this empty __init__.py module.

This file is empty, but it does exist.

When we run the following code and click the clickMe Button, we get the result shown following the code. This is a regular Python module that does not yet use the __init__.py module.

The __init__.py module is not the same as the __init__(self) method of a Python class.

```python
#   Ch11_GUI__init.py
#======================
# imports
#======================
import tkinter as tk
from tkinter import ttk


#======================
# Create instance
#======================
win = tk.Tk()


#======================
# Add a title
#======================
win.title("Python GUI")


#================================================================
# Adding a LabelFrame and a Button
#================================================================
lFrame = ttk.LabelFrame(win, text="Python GUI Programming Cookbook")
lFrame.grid(column=0, row=0, sticky='WE', padx=10, pady=10)

def clickMe():
    from tkinter import messagebox
    messagebox.showinfo('Message Box', 'Hi from same Level.')

button = ttk.Button(lFrame, text="Click Me ", command=clickMe)
button.grid(column=1, row=0, sticky=tk.S)


#======================
# Start GUI
#======================
win.mainloop()
```

In the preceding code, we created the following function, which imports Python's message box and then uses it to display the message box window:

```
def clickMe():
    from tkinter import messagebox
    messagebox.showinfo('Message Box', 'Hi from same Level.')
```

When we move the `clickMe()` message box code into a nested directory folder and try to `import` it into our GUI module, we run into some problems.

We have created three sub-folders below where our Python module lives. We then placed the `clickMe()` message box code into a new Python module, which we named `MessageBox.py`. This module lives in `Folder3`, three levels below where our Python module lives.

We need to import this `MessageBox.py` module in order to use the `clickMe()` function that this module contains.

At first, it appears to work because it seems we can import the new nested module as we are not getting any errors or warnings from the Eclipse IDE.

We are using Python's relative import syntax:

```
from .Folder1.Folder2.Folder3.MessageBox import clickme
```

This can be seen in the following screenshot:

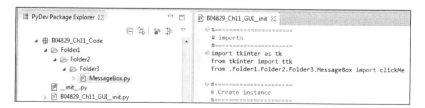

We have deleted the local `clickMe()` function and now our callback should use the imported `clickMe()` function, but it is not working as expected. Instead of the expected popup window, we get an import system error when we run the code:

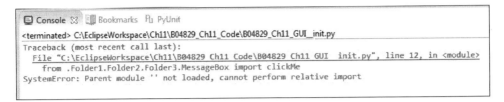

```
Console 🖫  Bookmarks  🗗 PyUnit
<terminated> C:\EclipseWorkspace\Ch11\B04829_Ch11_Code\B04829_Ch11_GUI__init.py
Traceback (most recent call last):
  File "C:\EclipseWorkspace\Ch11\B04829 Ch11 Code\B04829 Ch11 GUI  init.py", line 12, in <module>
    from .Folder1.Folder2.Folder3.MessageBox import clickMe
SystemError: Parent module '' not loaded, cannot perform relative import
```

We can add the subfolder where our new function lives as an external library in Eclipse by going to the PyDev Project properties and adding ourselves as an external library. This does not seem very intuitive, but it does work.

When we now comment out the folder structure and, instead, directly import the function from the module which is nested to three levels, the code works as expected.

```
#======================
# imports
#======================
import tkinter as tk
from tkinter import ttk
# from .Folder1.Folder2.Folder3.MessageBox import clickMe
from MessageBox import clickMe
```

This function displays a different text in a message box:

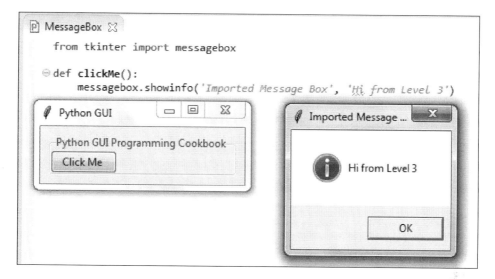

A better way to achieve the same result is to use Python's built-in __init__.py module.

After deleting the previously Eclipse-specific external library dependency, we can now use this module directly.

The code we place into this module runs before all of our other code if we import the __init__.py module into our program, as of Python 3.4.3.

Ignore the PyDev Unresolved Import (red circle with a cross) error. This import is necessary; it makes our code run and the entire Python importing mechanism work.

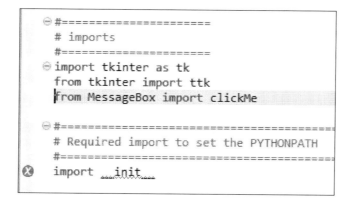

After importing the __init__.py module into our program, we can use it. The first test to check if it works is to code a print statement into this module.

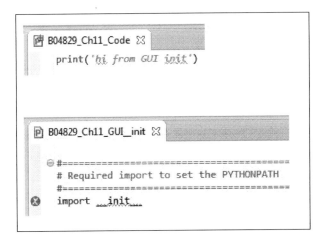

By adding the following code, we can find out programmatically where we are located:

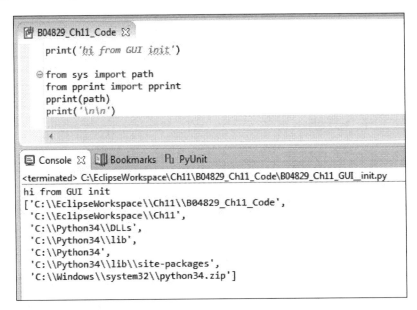

Now, we can initialize our Python search path from within this __init__.py module by adding the following code to the same __init__.py module:

```
print('hi from GUI init\n')
from sys import path
```

```
from pprint import pprint
#==========================================================
# Required setup for the PYTONPATH in order to find
# all package folders
#==========================================================
from site import addsitedir
from os import getcwd, chdir, pardir
for _ in range(10):
    curFull = getcwd()
    curDir = curFull.split('\\')[-1]
    if 'B04829_Ch11_Code' == curDir:
        addsitedir(curFull)
        addsitedir(curFull + '\\Folder1\\Folder2\\Folder3\\')
        break
    chdir(pardir)
pprint(path)
```

When we now run our GUI code, we get the same expected windows, but we have removed our dependency on the Eclipse PYTHONPATH variable.

Now we can successfully run the same code outside of the Eclipse PyDev plugin.

 Our code has become more Pythonic.

How it works...

In this recipe, we discovered a limitation of using the PyDev plugin, which comes free with the wonderful and free Eclipse IDE.

We first found a workaround in the Eclipse IDE, and next, we became independent from this IDE by becoming Pythonic.

 Using pure Python is usually the best way to go.

Mixing fall-down and OOP coding

Python is an object-oriented programming language yet it does not always make sense to use OOP. For simple scripting tasks, the legacy waterfall coding style is still appropriate.

In this recipe, we will create a new GUI that mixes both the fall-down coding style with the more modern OOP coding style.

We will create an OOP-style class that will display a tooltip when we hover the mouse over a widget in a Python GUI that we will create using a waterfall style.

 Fall-down and waterfall coding styles are the same. It means that we have to physically place code above code before we can call it from the code below. In this paradigm, the code literally falls down from the top of our program to the bottom of our program when we execute the code.

Getting ready

In this recipe, we will create a GUI using tkinter, which is similar to the GUI we created in the first chapter of this book.

How to do it...

In Python, we can bind functions to classes by turning them into methods using the `self` keyword. This is a truly wonderful capability of Python and it allows us to create large systems that are understandable and maintainable.

Sometimes, when we only write short scripts, OOP does not make sense because we find ourselves prepending a lot of variables with the `self` keyword and the code gets unnecessarily large when it does not need to be.

Let's first create a Python GUI using tkinter and code it in the waterfall style.

The following code creates the GUI:

```
#=======================
# imports
#=======================
import tkinter as tk
from tkinter import ttk
from tkinter import messagebox


#=======================
# Create instance
#=======================
win = tk.Tk()


#=======================
```

```
# Add a title
#=====================
win.title("Python GUI")


#=========================
# Disable resizing the GUI
#=========================
win.resizable(0,0)


#===============================================================
# Adding a LabelFrame, Textbox (Entry) and Combobox
#===============================================================
lFrame = ttk.LabelFrame(win, text="Python GUI Programming Cookbook")
lFrame.grid(column=0, row=0, sticky='WE', padx=10, pady=10)


#===============================================================
# Labels
#===============================================================
ttk.Label(lFrame, text="Enter a name:").grid(column=0, row=0)
ttk.Label(lFrame, text="Choose a number:").grid(column=1, row=0,
sticky=tk.W)


#===============================================================
# Buttons click command
#===============================================================
def clickMe(name, number):
    messagebox.showinfo('Information Message Box', 'Hello '+name+
                    ', your number is: ' + number)


#===============================================================
# Creating several controls in a loop
#===============================================================
names        = ['name0', 'name1', 'name2']
nameEntries  = ['nameEntry0', 'nameEntry1', 'nameEntry2']

numbers        = ['number0', 'number1', 'number2']
numberEntries = ['numberEntry0', 'numberEntry1', 'numberEntry2']

buttons = []

for idx in range(3):
    names[idx] = tk.StringVar()
```

```
        nameEntries[idx] = ttk.Entry(lFrame, width=12,
textvariable=names[idx])
        nameEntries[idx].grid(column=0, row=idx+1)
        nameEntries[idx].delete(0, tk.END)
        nameEntries[idx].insert(0, '<name>')

        numbers[idx] = tk.StringVar()
        numberEntries[idx] = ttk.Combobox(lFrame, width=14,
textvariable=numbers[idx])
        numberEntries[idx]['values'] = (1+idx, 2+idx, 4+idx, 42+idx,
100+idx)
        numberEntries[idx].grid(column=1, row=idx+1)
        numberEntries[idx].current(0)

        button = ttk.Button(lFrame, text="Click Me "+str(idx+1),
command=lambda idx=idx: clickMe(names[idx].get(), numbers[idx].get()))
        button.grid(column=2, row=idx+1, sticky=tk.W)
        buttons.append(button)
#======================
# Start GUI
#======================
win.mainloop()
```

When we run the code, we get the GUI and it looks like this:

We can improve our Python GUI by adding tooltips. The best way to do this is to isolate the code that creates the tooltip functionality from our GUI.

We do this by creating a separate class that has the tooltip functionality, and then we create an instance of this class in the same Python module that creates our GUI.

Using Python, there is no need to place our ToolTip class into a separate module. We can place it just above the procedural code and then call it from below this code.

The code now looks like this:

```
#=====================
# imports
#=====================
import tkinter as tk
from tkinter import ttk
from tkinter import messagebox


#------------------------------------------------
class ToolTip(object):
    def __init__(self, widget):
        self.widget = widget
        self.tipwindow = None
        self.id = None
        self.x = self.y = 0


#------------------------------------------------
def createToolTip(widget, text):
    toolTip = ToolTip(widget)
    def enter(event): toolTip.showtip(text)
    def leave(event): toolTip.hidetip()
    widget.bind('<Enter>', enter)
    widget.bind('<Leave>', leave)


#------------------------------------------------
# further down the module we call the createToolTip function
#------------------------------------------------


for idx in range(3):
    names[idx] = tk.StringVar()
    nameEntries[idx] = ttk.Entry(
lFrame, width=12, textvariable=names[idx])
    nameEntries[idx].grid(column=0, row=idx+1)
    nameEntries[idx].delete(0, tk.END)
    nameEntries[idx].insert(0, '<name>')

    numbers[idx] = tk.StringVar()
    numberEntries[idx] = ttk.Combobox(
lFrame, width=14, textvariable=numbers[idx])
    numberEntries[idx]['values'] = (
1+idx, 2+idx, 4+idx, 42+idx, 100+idx)
    numberEntries[idx].grid(column=1, row=idx+1)
```

```
        numberEntries[idx].current(0)

        button = ttk.Button(
    lFrame, text="Click Me "+str(idx+1), command=lambda idx=idx:
    clickMe(names[idx].get(), numbers[idx].get()))
        button.grid(column=2, row=idx+1, sticky=tk.W)
        buttons.append(button)


    #-------------------------------------------------
        # Add Tooltips to more widgets
        createToolTip(nameEntries[idx], 'This is an Entry widget.')
        createToolTip(
    numberEntries[idx], 'This is a DropDown widget.')
        createToolTip(buttons[idx], 'This is a Button widget.')
    #-------------------------------------------------
```

Running the code creates tooltips for our widgets when we hover the mouse over them.

How it works...

In this recipe, we created a Python GUI in a procedural way, and later, we added a class to the top of the module.

We can very easily mix and match both procedural and OOP programming in the same Python module.

Using a code naming convention

The previous recipes in this book have not used a structured code naming convention. This recipe will show you the value of adhering to a code naming scheme because it helps us to find the code we want to extend, as well as reminds us of the design of our program.

Getting ready

In this recipe, we will look at the Python module names from the first chapter of this book and compare them to better naming conventions.

How to do it...

In the first chapter of this book, we created our first Python GUI. We improved our GUI by incrementing the different code module names via sequential numbers.

It looked like this:

While this is a typical way to code, it does not provide much meaning. When we write our Python code during development, it is very easy to increment numbers.

Later, coming back to this code, we don't have much of an idea which Python module provides which functionality, and sometimes, our last incremented modules are not as good as earlier versions.

 A clear naming convention does help.

We can compare the module names from *Chapter 1, Creating the GUI Form and Adding Widgets*, to the names from *Chapter 8, Internationalization and Testing*, which are much more meaningful.

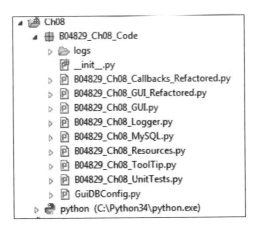

While not perfect, the names chosen for the different Python modules, indicate what each module's responsibility is. When we want to add more unit tests, it is clear in which module they reside.

The following is another example of how to use a code naming convention to create a GUI in Python:

Replace the word PRODUCT with the product you are currently working on.

The entire application is a GUI. All parts are connected. The DEBUG.py module is only used for debugging our code. The main function to invoke the GUI has its name reversed when compared to all of the other modules. It starts with Gui and ends in a .pyw extension.

It is the only Python module that has this extension name.

From this naming convention, if you are familiar enough with Python, it will be obvious that, in order to run this GUI, you double-click the Gui_PRODUCT.pyw module.

All other Python modules contain functionality to supply to the GUI as well as execute the underlying business logic to fulfil the purpose this GUI addresses.

How it works...

Naming conventions for Python code modules are a great help in keeping us efficient and remembering our original design. When we need to debug and fix a defect or add new functionality, they are the first resource to look at.

 Incrementing module names by numbers is not very meaningful and eventually wastes development time.

On the other hand, naming Python variables is more of a free form. Python infers types, so we do not have to specify that a variable will be of type <list> (it might not be or actually, later in the code, it might become a different type).

A good idea for naming variables is to make them descriptive and it is also a good idea not to abbreviate too much.

If we wish to point out that a certain variable is designed to be of type <list>, then it is much more intuitive to use the full word list instead of lst.

It is similar for number instead of num.

While it is a good idea to have very descriptive names for variables, sometimes that can get too long. In Apple's Objective-C language, some variable and function names are extreme:
thisIsAMethodThatDoesThisAndThatAndAlsoThatIfYouPassInNIntegers:1:2:3

 Use common sense when naming variables, methods, and functions.

When not to use OOP

Python comes built-in with object-oriented programming capabilities, but at the same time, we can write scripts that do not need to use OOP.

For some tasks, OOP does not make sense.

This recipe will show when not to use OOP.

Getting ready

In this recipe, we will create a Python GUI similar to previous recipes. We will compare the OOP code to the non-OOP alternative way of programming.

How to do it...

Let's first create a new GUI using **OOP** methodology. The following code will create the GUI displayed below the code:

```
import tkinter as tk
from tkinter import ttk
from tkinter import scrolledtext
from tkinter import Menu

class OOP():
    def __init__(self):
        self.win = tk.Tk()
        self.win.title("Python GUI")
        self.createWidgets()

    def createWidgets(self):
        tabControl = ttk.Notebook(self.win)
        tab1 = ttk.Frame(tabControl)
        tabControl.add(tab1, text='Tab 1')
        tabControl.pack(expand=1, fill="both")
        self.monty = ttk.LabelFrame(tab1, text=' Monty Python ')
        self.monty.grid(column=0, row=0, padx=8, pady=4)

        ttk.Label(self.monty, text="Enter a name:").grid(
column=0, row=0, sticky='W')
        self.name = tk.StringVar()
        nameEntered = ttk.Entry(
```

```
self.monty, width=12, textvariable=self.name)
        nameEntered.grid(column=0, row=1, sticky='W')

        self.action = ttk.Button(self.monty, text="Click Me!")
        self.action.grid(column=2, row=1)

        ttk.Label(self.monty,
text="Choose a number:").grid(column=1, row=0)
        number = tk.StringVar()
        numberChosen = ttk.Combobox(self.monty,
width=12, textvariable=number)
        numberChosen['values'] = (42)
        numberChosen.grid(column=1, row=1)
        numberChosen.current(0)

        scrolW = 30; scrolH = 3
        self.scr = scrolledtext.ScrolledText(
self.monty, width=scrolW, height=scrolH, wrap=tk.WORD)
        self.scr.grid(column=0, row=3, sticky='WE', columnspan=3)

        menuBar = Menu(tab1)
        self.win.config(menu=menuBar)
        fileMenu = Menu(menuBar, tearoff=0)
        menuBar.add_cascade(label="File", menu=fileMenu)
        helpMenu = Menu(menuBar, tearoff=0)
        menuBar.add_cascade(label="Help", menu=helpMenu)

        nameEntered.focus()
#==========================
oop = OOP()
oop.win.mainloop()
```

We can achieve the same GUI without using an OOP approach by restructuring our code slightly. First, we remove the OOP class and its __init__ method.

Next, we move all methods to the left and remove the self class reference which turns them into unbound functions.

We also remove any other self references our previous code had. Then, we move the createWidgets function call below the point of the function's declaration. We place it just above the mainloop call.

In the end, we achieve the same GUI but without using OOP.

The refactored code is shown as follows:

```python
import tkinter as tk
from tkinter import ttk
from tkinter import scrolledtext
from tkinter import Menu


def createWidgets():
    tabControl = ttk.Notebook(win)
    tab1 = ttk.Frame(tabControl)
    tabControl.add(tab1, text='Tab 1')
    tabControl.pack(expand=1, fill="both")
    monty = ttk.LabelFrame(tab1, text=' Monty Python ')
    monty.grid(column=0, row=0, padx=8, pady=4)

    ttk.Label(monty, text="Enter a name:").grid(
column=0, row=0, sticky='W')
    name = tk.StringVar()
    nameEntered = ttk.Entry(monty, width=12, textvariable=name)
    nameEntered.grid(column=0, row=1, sticky='W')

    action = ttk.Button(monty, text="Click Me!")
    action.grid(column=2, row=1)

    ttk.Label(monty, text="Choose a number:").grid(
column=1, row=0)
    number = tk.StringVar()
    numberChosen = ttk.Combobox(
monty, width=12, textvariable=number)
    numberChosen['values'] = (42)
    numberChosen.grid(column=1, row=1)
    numberChosen.current(0)
```

```
        scrolW = 30; scrolH = 3
        scr = scrolledtext.ScrolledText(
    monty, width=scrolW, height=scrolH, wrap=tk.WORD)
        scr.grid(column=0, row=3, sticky='WE', columnspan=3)

        menuBar = Menu(tab1)
        win.config(menu=menuBar)
        fileMenu = Menu(menuBar, tearoff=0)
        menuBar.add_cascade(label="File", menu=fileMenu)
        helpMenu = Menu(menuBar, tearoff=0)
        menuBar.add_cascade(label="Help", menu=helpMenu)

        nameEntered.focus()
#======================
win = tk.Tk()
win.title("Python GUI")
createWidgets()
win.mainloop()
```

How it works...

Python enables us to use OOP when it makes sense. Other languages such as Java and C# force us to always use the OOP approach to coding. In this recipe, we explored a situation when it did not make sense to use OOP.

 The OOP approach will be more extendible if the codebase grows but, if it's certain that it is the only code that's needed then there's no need to go through OOP.

How to use design patterns successfully

In this recipe, we will create widgets for our Python GUI by using the factory design pattern.

In previous recipes, we created our widgets either manually one at a time or dynamically in a loop.

Using the factory design pattern, we will use the factory to create our widgets.

Getting ready

We will create a Python GUI which has three buttons each having different styles.

How to do it...

Towards the top of our Python GUI module, just below the import statements, we create several classes:

```python
import tkinter as tk
from tkinter import ttk
from tkinter import scrolledtext
from tkinter import Menu

class ButtonFactory():
    def createButton(self, type_):
        return buttonTypes[type_]()

class ButtonBase():
    relief     ='flat'
    foreground ='white'
    def getButtonConfig(self):
        return self.relief, self.foreground

class ButtonRidge(ButtonBase):
    relief     ='ridge'
    foreground ='red'

class ButtonSunken(ButtonBase):
    relief     ='sunken'
    foreground ='blue'

class ButtonGroove(ButtonBase):
    relief     ='groove'
    foreground ='green'

buttonTypes = [ButtonRidge, ButtonSunken, ButtonGroove]

class OOP():
    def __init__(self):
        self.win = tk.Tk()
        self.win.title("Python GUI")
        self.createWidgets()
```

We create a base class which our different button style classes inherit from and in which each of them overrides the `relief` and `foreground` configuration properties. All subclasses inherit the `getButtonConfig` method from this base class. This method returns a tuple.

We also create a button factory class and a list that holds the names of our button subclasses. We name the list `buttonTypes` as our factory will create different types of buttons.

Further down in the module we create the button widgets, using the same `buttonTypes` list.

```
def createButtons(self):

    factory = ButtonFactory()

    # Button 1
    rel = factory.createButton(0).getButtonConfig()[0]
    fg  = factory.createButton(0).getButtonConfig()[1]
    action = tk.Button(self.monty,
text="Button "+str(0+1), relief=rel, foreground=fg)
    action.grid(column=0, row=1)

    # Button 2
    rel = factory.createButton(1).getButtonConfig()[0]
    fg  = factory.createButton(1).getButtonConfig()[1]
    action = tk.Button(self.monty,
text="Button "+str(1+1), relief=rel, foreground=fg)
    action.grid(column=1, row=1)

    # Button 3
    rel = factory.createButton(2).getButtonConfig()[0]
    fg  = factory.createButton(2).getButtonConfig()[1]
    action = tk.Button(self.monty,
text="Button "+str(2+1), relief=rel, foreground=fg)
    action.grid(column=2, row=1)
```

First, we create an instance of the button factory and then we use our factory to create our buttons.

 The items in the `buttonTypes` list are the names of our subclasses.

We invoke the `createButton` method and then immediately call the `getButtonConfig` method of the base class and retrieve the configuration properties using dot notation.

When we run the entire code, we get the following Python tkinter GUI:

We can see that our Python GUI factory did indeed create different buttons, each having a different style. They differ in the color of their text and in their relief property.

How it works...

In this recipe, we used the factory design pattern to create several widgets that have different styles. We can easily use this design pattern to create entire GUIs.

Design patterns are a very exciting tool in our software development toolbox.

Avoiding complexity

In this recipe, we will extend our Python GUI and learn ways to handle the ever-increasing complexity of our software development efforts.

Our co-workers and clients love the GUIs we create in Python and ask for more and more features to add to our GUI.

This increases complexity and can easily ruin our original nice design.

Getting ready

We will create a new Python GUI similar to those in previous recipes and will add many features to it in the form of widgets.

How to do it...

We will start with a Python GUI that has two tabs and looks like this:

The first new feature request we receive is to add functionality to **Tab 1**, which clears the `scrolledtext` widget.

Easy enough. We just add another button to **Tab 1**.

```
# Adding another Button
self.action = ttk.Button(.
self.monty, text="Clear Text", command=self.clearScrol)
self.action.grid(column=2, row=2)
```

We also have to create the callback method to add the desired functionality, which we define towards the top of our class and outside the method that creates our widgets.

```
# Button callback
def clickMe(self):
    self.action.configure(text='Hello ' + self.name.get())


# Button callback Clear Text
def clearScrol(self):
    self.scr.delete('1.0', tk.END)
```

Now our GUI has a new button and, when we click it, we clear the text of the `ScrolledText` widget.

In order to add this functionality, we had to add code in two places in the same Python module.

We inserted the new button in the `createWidgets` method (not shown) and then we created a new callback method, which our new button calls when it is clicked. We placed this code just below the callback of our first button.

Our next feature request is to add more functionality. The business logic is encapsulated in another Python module. We invoke this new functionality by adding three more buttons to **Tab 1**. We use a loop to do this.

```python
# Adding more Feature Buttons
for idx in range(3):
    b = ttk.Button(
        self.monty, text="Feature" + str(idx+1))
    b.grid(column=idx, row=4)
```

Our GUI now looks like this:

Next, our customers ask for more features and we use the same approach. Our GUI now looks as follows:

 This is not too bad. When we get new feature requests for another 50 new features, we start to wonder if our approach is still the best approach to use...

One way to handle the ever-increasing complexity our GUI has to handle is by adding tabs. By adding more tabs and placing related features into their own tab, we get control of the complexity and make our GUI more intuitive.

Here is the code that creates our new **Tab 3** and, below it, is our new Python GUI:

```
# Tab Control 3  -----------------------------------------
        tab3 = ttk.Frame(tabControl)          # Add a tab
        tabControl.add(tab3, text='Tab 3')    # Make tab visible

        monty3 = ttk.LabelFrame(tab3, text=' New Features ')
        monty3.grid(column=0, row=0, padx=8, pady=4)

        # Adding more Feature Buttons
        startRow = 4
        for idx in range(24):
            if idx < 2:
                colIdx = idx
                col = colIdx
            else:
                col += 1
            if not idx % 3:
                startRow += 1
                col = 0

            b = ttk.Button(monty3, text="Feature " + str(idx+1))
            b.grid(column=col, row=startRow)

        # Add some space around each label
        for child in monty3.winfo_children():
            child.grid_configure(padx=8)
```

How it works...

In this recipe, we added several new widgets to our GUI in order to add more functionality to our Python GUI. We saw how more and more new feature requests easily got our nice GUI design into a state where it became less clear how to use the GUI.

 Suddenly, widgets took over the world...

We saw how to handle complexity by modularizing our GUI by breaking large features into smaller pieces and arranging them in functionally-related areas using tabs.

While complexity has many aspects, modularizing and refactoring code is usually a very good approach to handling software code complexity.

In programming, at certain times, we run into a wall and get stuck. We keep banging our head against this wall but nothing happens.

Sometimes we feel like we want to give up.

However, miracles do happen...

If we keep on banging against this wall, at a certain moment in time, the wall will collapse and the road will be open.

At that point in time, we can make a positive dent in the software universe.

Index

Symbols

__init__
used, for connecting modules 298-305
__main__ section
used, for creating self-testing code 220-224

A

appearance, of widgets
defining 61-63

B

bitmaps
using 275-279
buttons
creating 7, 8
text property, changing 7, 8

C

callback functions
writing 85, 86
canvas widget
using 67
chart
creating 100, 101
creating, Matplotlib used 92-94
labels, placing on 102-106
legend, adding to 106-109
scaling 109-111
check button
creating, with different initial states 14, 15
code naming convention
using 310-313
code readability 162

combo box widgets
defining 12, 13
complexity
avoiding 320-325
controls
adding, wxPython used 244-250
Coordinated Universal Time (UTC) 199
CRUD (Create, Read, Update, and Delete)
defining 154

D

data
obtaining, from widget 73-75
retrieving, from MySQL database 181-184
storing, from MySQL database 181-184
debug output levels
configuring 216-219
debug watches
setting 212-216
design patterns
using 317-320
dialog widgets
used, for copying files to network 136-144
DRY principle 17

E

Eastern Daylight Time (EDT) 200
Eclipse PyDev IDE
used, for writing unit tests 229-233

F

fall-down
mixing, with OOP coding 306-310
fixtures

Thank you for buying
Python GUI Programming Cookbook

About Packt Publishing

Packt, pronounced 'packed', published its first book, *Mastering phpMyAdmin for Effective MySQL Management*, in April 2004, and subsequently continued to specialize in publishing highly focused books on specific technologies and solutions.

Our books and publications share the experiences of your fellow IT professionals in adapting and customizing today's systems, applications, and frameworks. Our solution-based books give you the knowledge and power to customize the software and technologies you're using to get the job done. Packt books are more specific and less general than the IT books you have seen in the past. Our unique business model allows us to bring you more focused information, giving you more of what you need to know, and less of what you don't.

Packt is a modern yet unique publishing company that focuses on producing quality, cutting-edge books for communities of developers, administrators, and newbies alike. For more information, please visit our website at www.packtpub.com.

About Packt Open Source

In 2010, Packt launched two new brands, Packt Open Source and Packt Enterprise, in order to continue its focus on specialization. This book is part of the Packt open source brand, home to books published on software built around open source licenses, and offering information to anybody from advanced developers to budding web designers. The Open Source brand also runs Packt's open source Royalty Scheme, by which Packt gives a royalty to each open source project about whose software a book is sold.

Writing for Packt

We welcome all inquiries from people who are interested in authoring. Book proposals should be sent to author@packtpub.com. If your book idea is still at an early stage and you would like to discuss it first before writing a formal book proposal, then please contact us; one of our commissioning editors will get in touch with you.

We're not just looking for published authors; if you have strong technical skills but no writing experience, our experienced editors can help you develop a writing career, or simply get some additional reward for your expertise.

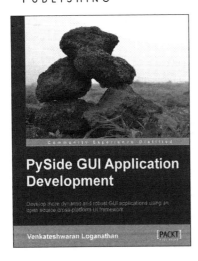

PySide GUI Application Development

ISBN: 978-1-84969-959-4   Paperback: 140 pages

Develop more dynamic and robust GUI applications using and open source cross-platform UI framework

1. Designed for beginners to help them get started with GUI application development.

2. Develop your own applications by creating customized widgets and dialogs.

3. Written in a simple and elegant structure to help you easily understand how to program various GUI components.

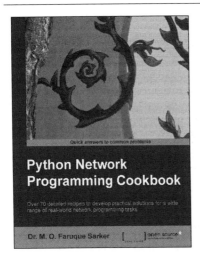

Python Network Programming Cookbook

ISBN: 978-1-84951-346-3   Paperback: 234 pages

Over 70 detailed recipes to develop practical solutions for a wide range of real-world network programming tasks

1. Demonstrates how to write various besopke client/server networking applications using standard and popular third-party Python libraries.

2. Learn how to develop client programs for networking protocols such as HTTP/HTTPS, SMTP, POP3, FTP, CGI, XML-RPC, SOAP and REST.

3. Provides practical, hands-on recipes combined with short and concise explanations on code snippets.

Please check **www.PacktPub.com** for information on our titles

wxPython 2.8 Application Development Cookbook

ISBN: 978-1-84951-178-0   Paperback: 308 pages

Over 80 practical recipes for developing feature-rich applications using wxPython

1. Develop flexible applications in wxPython.

2. Create interface translatable applications that will run on Windows, Macintosh OSX, Linux, and other UNIX like environments.

3. Learn basic and advanced user interface controls.

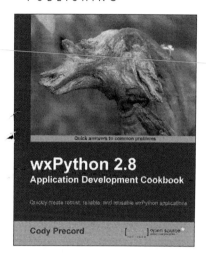

Expert Python Programming

ISBN: 978-1-84719-494-7   Paperback: 372 pages

Best practices for designing, coding, and distributing your Python software

1. Learn Python development best practices from an expert, with detailed coverage of naming and coding conventions.

2. Apply object-oriented principles, design patterns, and advanced syntax tricks.

3. Manage your code with distributed version control.

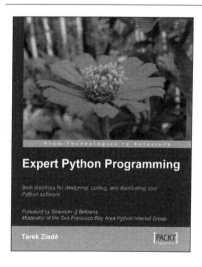

Please check **www.PacktPub.com** for information on our titles

Made in the USA
Middletown, DE
21 August 2016